THE TIMES
OF MY LIFE

SIR
JOHN GORMAN

THE TIMES
OF MY LIFE

AN AUTOBIOGRAPHY

LEO COOPER

First Published in Great Britain 2002 by
LEO COOPER
an imprint of Pen & Sword Books
47 Church Street
Barnsley, S. Yorkshire, S70 2AS

Copyright © 2002 John Gorman

ISBN 0 0 85052 906 9

A CIP record for this book is available from the British Library

Typeset in 10/12.5pt Plantin by
Phoenix Typesetting, Burley-in-Wharfedale, West Yorkshire.

CONTENTS

INTRODUCTION

In another century John Gorman might have been the model for Franz Hals' *Laughing Cavalier*; in this one he is something of a survival for the qualities of honour and honesty, loyalty to the church and the regiment, and old-world charm and courtliness.

His story, told with a simple innocence, captures the spirit of the man, his humanity and kindliness, and recounts the major events of a incident-packed life with a disarming air of modesty and self-deprecation.

Sir John was a hero at twenty-one, awarded the Military Cross for disabling a German Super-Tiger tank on the battlefield of Normandy by the simple, if courageous, expedient of ramming it broadside with a smaller tank. When we think of men in armour and "the casques which did affright the air at Agincourt", we forget that in these and other wars, arms were borne heroically by boys, forced by circumstances to become men before their time. Some, through death, never became men. Some who survived remained as boys, the experience of war their greatest hour.

John Gorman was one of those who took the war in his stride, learned from it a painful rite of passage and went on to live out a full and varied life – but still a life of service. The qualities which had made him a good officer – a clear view of what he was fighting for, a belief in its rightness, respect for the terrain, loyalty to the corps and an enduring respect for and care of his men, – remained with him for life and made him the good manager that he is.

This book, however, is about more than management, it is about family and friendship. In a way, though, one theme suffuses and illuminates the other. The influence of a father, spartan perhaps but committed to police service, and a mother with deep religious conviction with a medical background, shine through, and John manages to combine the two. In son, as in father, there is the sense of public service, the tension between religion, culture and duty, the conflict of loyalties so clearly portrayed by Sebastian Barry in the character of another policeman in *The Steward of Christendom*. One is struck by the essential humanity and common-sense with which he discharges the role of policeman in Northern Ireland, and the equanimity and total lack of bitterness with which he faced the fact that as a Roman Catholic his prospects were severely limited.

As Director of the Northern Ireland Housing Executive, he returned to Northern Ireland and to a life of public service, but he brought to it all the skills which he had acquired in the meantime. Housing shortage, location and discrimination in allocation, had been a burning issue for decades, the one single issue which had brought people out on to the streets in protest. The Housing Executive depoliticized housing, raised standards and professionalized housing administration. To have led such an organization through a period of fundamental change, to have combined staffs from many backgrounds and to have supplied the vision and the drive which would unite them in a common purpose would have been enough for most men, but not for John Gorman.

After that there was the Institute of Directors, and after that the entry into politics as one of the few Catholic members of the Ulster Unionist Party, and that rare bird indeed, a Unionist Assembly Member who was a Catholic. In this as in his other incarnations, John Gorman has been an agent for change, with perhaps less of the aggressiveness which toppled the Tiger tank, but with no less courage and exuberance. He brought a new civility into the political discourse, an ability to listen to the other person and to afford respect, and a willingness to act as a bridge between classes, traditions and cultures.

In all his life, private and public, John's religious faith has been very important to him and has pervaded and guided his life and actions. He remains a family man, the quintessentially good officer, loyal to the regiment, respectful of tradition and caring for his men. His spirit remains undaunted, a tank officer who was a cavalryman (or a cavalier) at heart. He might have been at Agincourt with Harry, he should have ridden with the Light Brigade at Balaclava.

Oddly enough, I think he would have survived both, with a good story to tell!

I never now drive past Caen without looking for a signpost to Cagny and thinking of John Gorman. I have found him, however, in many other settings, as I hope many, many readers will find him in this, his own account of himself.

Maurice Hayes
October 2002

Chapter One

FAMILY AND SCHOOL

A trench-coated figure knocked on the gates of the Phoenix Park Depot Royal Irish Constabulary. It was Michael Collins, Minister of Home Affairs of the new Free State Government which he had negotiated with Lloyd George, the British Prime Minister, through the Irish Treaty of 1920.

The Adjutant of the RIC Depot, my father, Major J.K. Gorman MC, rode across the square to meet him, dismounted and symbolically handed over the key of this bastion of Britain in Ireland. The Depot was part of Robert Peel's plan for Ireland, which envisaged a national police controlled from Dublin, employing a Constabulary trained and disciplined through a military-type Depot. Two weeks later the British Army handed it over.

My father, John also, usually known as Jack, except in his close family where he was Johnny, was born in 1890. The Gormans owned a substantial farm, Gurtishall (sometimes aggrandized to Gurtis Hall), near the village of Ballyporeen, Co. Tipperary. He was the eldest of six children of Patrick Gorman and Kathleen from Scotland. He had a happy childhood, was clearly bright, outgoing and athletic and was much favoured by his uncle, also John, who was Chief of Customs in Dublin. Uncle John put him down for Blackrock, a leading Irish public school, and contributed substantially to the cost of this. He did well at Blackrock, was head of his house and played rugger and cricket for the school. Appointed Personal Assistant to the President of Argentine Railways, he sailed for Buenos Aires in 1908. This swift appointment of an 18-year-old no doubt owed much to the benevolent Uncle John. Life in South America for a young Irishman at that time was exciting, and the charm and good humour which characterized him made him a popular figure, besides which he clearly excelled in the post, despite his youth and lack of knowledge of the railway business. There was an Officers Training Corps in the substantial British community which

1

he joined without hesitation, as there was, and is, a strong British Army tradition in the Gorman family. One legend concerns a "Peggy" Gorman who was a drummer in the 87th Regiment and lost his leg at the battle of Barossa, fighting for Wellington. Despite having only one leg (thus Peggy) he remained with the 87th. On return to Tipperary, he fathered a large family, and his sons and grandsons served in the Army, which at that time had a very large Irish Catholic contingent, over 50%.

Jack's carefree existence in Argentina came to an abrupt end when the First World War broke out in 1914 and, amid emotional scenes, a ship carrying several hundred men sailed from Buenos Aires, all of them with only one worry, that the War would be over before they could take part. He had trained as an Artillery officer and was sent to the Front, where he soon showed prowess as a Forward Observation Officer. The FOO's job was to be with the leading troops and to call down fire from the batteries further back, fire close enough to destroy the leading enemy (or at least to keep their heads down), but not so close as to shell our own troops.

By now Turkey had entered the War on Germany's side. Britain's ally, Russia, was not doing well on the Eastern Front, so Turkey's intervention threatened the whole Middle East, particularly Egypt and the Suez Canal. Jack was posted to Palestine and soon commanded a mounted Battery of the Royal Horse Artillery. His upbringing on the farm at Ballyporeen had given him a love for horses and he was a good rider. At the battle of Jerusalem, his daring and competence earned him the Military Cross. When the War ended he applied for a cadetship in the Royal Irish Constabulary and in 1919 returned home to take up his police career in the RIC which was spent totally in the Phoenix Park Depot. He had graduated top of the Cadets' wartime intake and was made Adjutant of the Depot after only a year in the Force, an astonishingly fast promotion. A factor in this may have been the arrangement made between the War Office and the Dublin (British) authorities in 1901 that Irishmen joining the newly formed Irish Guards who completed five years of exemplary service and joined the Army Reserve for seven years would automatically be accepted as Constables in the RIC and be posted to the Phoenix Park Depot. A photograph exists of the Adjutant with about 100 new RIC Constables which shows how closely the link had developed. It is said that the formation of a Second Battalion of the Irish Guards in 1914 was made possible because there were over 500 RIC who had done their five years and as Reservists were available. Another story, possibly apocryphal, is that the choice by Michael Collins of the name for the Free State Police, the Guards (or Gardai in Irish), came about because my father invited him to the Depot Mess, which was to be closed down the next day, and had a cellar which could not all be disposed of in the time, but in which they both helped.

A picture of Jack sitting in an open lorry with RIC men loading rifles and equipment clearly intended for travel north shows the extent of the change overnight. The dapper plain-clothed figure in the front, contrasting with the flamboyant Adjutant of the previous day, the RIC rather nervously embarking, armed, through 100 miles of the new Free State, heading for a Six-County entity which had only come into being overnight and was widely believed to have little viability or longevity, etched itself on my mind when my father showed it to me. Those whose loyalty to the Crown had decided them to throw in their lot with little Ulster had taken a brave step, especially those who knew that as Catholics they might never be accepted by Protestant Unionists or fellow Roman Catholic Nationalists.

My mother, Annette O'Brien, was also the eldest child of a family, this time of twelve. Her father, Doctor Patrick O'Brien, was the leading physician of the town of Midleton. A convinced Unionist, he played a part in the political career of St John Broderick, later Lord Midelton, a former Secretary of State for War and for India, who helped in the salvaging of what could be saved of British Ireland. He was a beloved and competent doctor who married Mary Leahy, daughter of one of the heads of the Irish fur trade, importing fur from all over the world. It was her capital which helped them to buy Midleton House, a large early Victorian mansion by the Midleton River, which fortuitously provided the water for the distillery which now provides the whiskey, gin and vodka for all the Irish brands, Jameson, Power, Paddy, etc. In those days only Paddy was distilled upriver from Midleton House, but my mother's younger sister, Ursula, by marrying Garnett Ross, the distiller, whose son Alexander Ross, followed him, made the distillery part of the O'Brien heritage. Annette had been engaged to a young officer killed in the trenches in 1916. She was fluent in French and German, having been educated in both countries. She was very pretty in an elfin way, strong-willed and a devoted Catholic. Her fiancé's death made her reject her plan to live in Ireland awaiting his return and she became a teacher of languages at Eltham Convent. It was on the train and boat journey from Eltham to Midleton that she met the handsome, charming Major returning from the War to become an RIC Officer. There were reservations on both sides. She had not got over grieving for her lost love; she suspected that she was by no means the first heart that might be broken by Jack; she soon discovered that he was by no means a firm Catholic (a process which accelerated in the RIC where he was horrified at the attitude of many priests at the 1916 Rebellion and the Troubles), and she was building a new life in England where half of her numerous siblings were doing well. But Jack was an ardent suitor and they married in 1922, in England, just before the handover of the Depot and his appointment as District Inspector Co. Tyrone. They started married life at Mullaghmore

House, a fine Georgian house rented from Pat Scott, an Army friend, and it was there that I was born on 1 February 1923.

First memories are of father and mother on horseback – she took great joy in hunting with the Seskinore Harriers – and of deep pain at the death of Tom, his pointer, whom I loved. I used to watch from my pram my father becoming a really skilled and innovative gardener, making pergolas, planting roses, building a rockery. It seemed there was nothing he could not do. My mother and he went skating on a nearby lake in a rare freeze-up. She went through the ice. There was no one to help. My father ran to a farmhouse and picked up a ladder which he slid out to her and so saved her. It was not so happy an outcome when she fell jumping with the Harriers and her horse fell on her hip, causing damage which later turned into rheumatoid arthritis. At 40 she had to have a stick to walk and at 80, still walking with great courage, she needed a built-up shoe to replace the shrunken hip, had pain which could not be alleviated and could not do all the things she loved so much – riding, dancing, walking, swimming. It was only years later, holidaying in Australia with my brother Richard (born in 1924) and his family, that she attempted swimming in the warm Pacific and found it such a joy.

Richard and I were joined at two-yearly intervals by Geraldine and Carolyn, and about this time Nonie Walsh from Midleton came to us as Nanny. She was a typical Co. Cork woman, warm, loquacious, fierce in her protectiveness of her charges. We loved her dearly and saw her as our advocate with parents and grown-ups generally. By now, because Pat Scott needed his house, we had moved to Edenderry Lodge, 2 miles from Omagh, where again Jack showed his gardening skills.

Richard and I were now approaching First Communion age, and Annette and Nonie were not going to let this fail. When we had been at Mullaghmore House Richard and I had gone to a little Nursery School, run by a Miss Olphert, where we were fellow-pupils of a little boy called Bunny Darling. As Nonie was reading us *Peter Pan* we were convinced that Bunny was Peter and would fly out of Miss Olphert's room any moment. Catechism was now part of our lives. My mother tried to make it mean something to me, so did Nonie. First Communion was not the revelation I had been told it would be and we went to the Loretto Convent to be taught by Mother De Sales, whom we soon found to be just as kind and interesting as Miss Olphert. We were now 8 and 6, and the daily ferrying required of my father (Annette never drove) was perhaps the reason for a bicycle for me and a "fairy" cycle for Richard appearing on the scene. I tried the bike and kept falling off. My mother said she would run behind me holding the saddle: miraculously, I did not fall until I looked behind to see her laughing at me, 100 yards behind. So every day we set out for the Convent.

4

Sometimes we were so cold, hands especially, that the memory of the pain remains with me. But when we got home mother and Nonie soon revived us.

The next family drama was that my father was taken ill with suspected cancer and, because of his Army background, was sent to Sister Agnes Hospital in London while we waited in terror for news. Everyone was kind, the new phone never stopped. My father came home, recovered, and all were overjoyed. We were particularly impressed when there was a message that the Governor of Northern Ireland, the Duke of Abercorn, wanted to visit him at home where he was recuperating. It became quite a familiar ceremony for a bottle of "Cream of the Barley" to be sent for, as this was the Duke's favourite.

By now I was old enough to accompany my father on his rounds of inspection. As I was myself to experience as a District Inspector, he had an obligation to make a formal inspection of each of his "Barracks", as they were then called – Stations today – and I would sit in the car while he drilled the "party", usually a Sergeant and four Constables, and held a "school", during which he would test their knowledge of the law, and the quality of the catering. In those days each Barracks had a cook, as at least half the "party" were unmarried, indeed were not allowed to marry until 25 years old. Often the Sergeant's wife would come out to the car to talk to the little boy who might be there for up to 3 hours. There was one who rather humiliated me by asking me to recite the alphabet, which I had learned by the then fashionable manner of "ah", "bu", "cu". "You can't even do your ABC," she said. I have a feeling that her husband had not done too well in the Inspection.

Promotion to Headquarters of the RUC, Waring Street then, led to a move to Balmoral Avenue, to a house I often see with its distinctive port-hole window, and school at Inchmarlo, a short tram ride. Richard and I settled into the new surroundings and learned to play Rugger. One of Inchmarlo's most enjoyable features was the annual Gilbert and Sullivan Opera. We took part in only one: *HMS Pinafore*. My father was a convinced believer in public schools from his own Blackrock time and having spent so much of the War with men who had had this experience, and was determined that he would try this for his children. He met Geoffrey Bing, the Headmaster of Rockport School, who was very encouraging, took both of us in and we had happy years at this little school, then less than fifty boys (no girls) preparing for the Imperial Service College (later to become Haileybury and ISC). The senior masters were Eric Tucker, later to succeed G.B., and Monty Weaving, the French master, who was crippled by an accident in Canada earlier in his life. All these men had a profound effect on me. Bing was a fanatical cricketer and I recall him now walking along a road practising shots with his stick. He read us younger boys Kipling's *Just So Stories* while we toasted bread at his study fire. Tucker encouraged me to sing, and I did so at Carol Services in Glencraig Church (of Ireland), and we had an Annual Singing Solo Competition.

While my father had won the day on boarding schools, my mother was determined that we should not lose our religion, so we went to Holywood every Sunday to Mass and the sacraments of Confession and Holy Communion.

Our family had a summer holiday to Tipperary and Cork most years, varied sometimes by a rented house at Rossnowlagh in Donegal, or Mullaghmore in Sligo. They were wonderful times. We would set off in the Morris Oxford open-roof car, with the hood down if possible, the six of us plus Nonie, and make it to Midleton or Ballyporeen in the day after a dawn start. Over 70 years ago, on roads more designed for horses and in cars which were still at an early stage of development, this was adventure indeed. Once I watched the speedometer creeping up to 60 m.p.h. on a straight road near Dublin. Such speed seemed close to flying. Indeed we had done so well on one journey that, at my mother's suggestion, we stopped at Mount Mellary, the Trappist Monastery in County Tipperary, and we children were enthralled by the silent monks and the fact that a meal of cabbage and bacon, with boiled potatoes, was served to us at no cost and without us asking. Arrival at either Midleton House or Gurtishall was always a thrilling moment. In the great gardens of Midleton my grandfather raised, in what seemed to a child endless glasshouses, grapes, tomatoes, cucumbers, peaches and nectarines, with the aid of several gardeners who did not seem to mind what we ate so long as we did not harm the plants, trees or shrubs. The walled gardens had many tropical features, including date palms. The river which ran past the house was full of trout and we tried unsuccessfully to catch them in our little nets. Under the bridge there seemed to be a profusion of trout, probably because they were more visible in the shade. We were forbidden to net there because grown-ups claimed we would drown.

Visits to our cousins, the Rosses, gave me my first experience of the sweet smell of whiskey, which rose from the great vats and retorts of the refinery. The distiller, my Uncle Garnet, had test-tubes of whiskey on the desk of his office, which, he explained, it was his duty to test to achieve the right proportions of a brew. It seemed the tests did him no harm as he lived to a great age.

Gurtishall was no less pleasurable for us – more so in many ways. Our grandmother loved singing and she could dance jigs and reels while she did so. The large farmhouse had a rather splendid drawing-room which we used in the evenings and on Sundays, but the real focus of life was the huge kitchen with an open fire fuelled by peat which never went out, and "cleats" – dishes and pots swung on chains over the fire. The enormous fireplace had benches running each side of the fire where the children and old men would sit to warm themselves, while Granny prepared wonderful meals. Again bacon and cabbage were favourites. She would also go up the mountain which was part of the Gorman land to pick what she called "Blaeberries" – blueberries in Scotland. There was a river running through the farm, this time with bigger trout, and Richard and I found an old badminton net which we rigged up as a fishing net by walking on each side of narrow parts of the river poling the net in the water. My father, while quite impressed with our enterprise, gave stern warnings about its illegality and the fearsome penalties if the Guards caught us. We learned to swim in the river and, since it was often early September when we visited, helped the men with the harvest. The beauty of the countryside seen from the Galtee Mountains, of which one side of the farm was part, stays with me still. As the eldest son, my father could have inherited if he had wanted to, but he had a career ahead of him and had never forgiven De Valera for overturning the Treaty, killing, as he described it, the rather heroic RIC enemy Collins and putting the Catholic Church in temporal power in the Free State. The farm went, with Dad's approval, to the kindly hardworking bachelor next son, Pat, on the death of my grandparents. Ballyporeen became famous when Reagan was President and, hearing that my family came from there, the American Ambassador asked me if I remembered any Reagans. I told him that I remembered a conversation in the farmyard, the yardman being called Reagan, when I asked my grandfather and father why a close friend with that name was called by them *Regan*. "Son," said Grandfather "Ireland is a snobbish country. Well-doing men, doctors, solicitors, whose name is Reagan are always pronounced *Regan*, but the yardman; he's *Raygen*." A few weeks later the Ambassador was recalled and, recollecting that he was going to tell the story to Nancy Reagan, I was in a panic that I had caused his downfall. There was no need to worry – he had advised the White House that Britain would not fight Galtieri over the Falklands and, like Joe Kennedy before him, had given the wrong advice.

Starting at the Imperial Service College in Windsor was quite daunting to begin with. New boys were given rather a hard time and there seemed innumerable rules about what one wore, when and where one walked and what was expected of one as a "fag". I do not believe that it was sadism, but there seemed to be a lot of beatings. The procedure was that after lunch the prefects who left the room before us lesser boys would climb to a bell-tower above the dining hall and as we poured out would call out names of the luckless offenders who would receive two or four strokes of the cane. I doubt whether it did me any harm, none of the "offences" being of substance, and it made one feel rather heroic showing the weals on one's buttocks. Smoking was serious and beyond the prefects' sentence. Six from the Housemaster was the penalty.

The school had a small number of Roman Catholics and went out of its way to ensure that we could practice our religion, though, as at Rockport, we took part in daily prayers and hymn-singing. It always surprises members of Anglican congregations that I know so many hymns, although in the new and better Ecumenical world there is little difference now.

By now it was becoming clear that the world was moving towards a Second World War. In 1938 we were put to digging an enormous trench in a field close to College, large enough to hold 500 boys, masters and families. It was with great relief that we heard Neville Chamberlain saying "Peace in our time" on his return from seeing Hitler, especially as the great trench had filled with water. We had a good Dramatic Society and Richard and I were both soldiers in *Henry IV* and had small parts in various other plays. Music was abundant, classical concerts by visiting singers (I got rather weary of Wagner), but I was in a House whose Assistant Master was a German Jew who had escaped the Nazis and in the evenings we would listen to Chopin which he played brilliantly. In sport I was not a success then; small for my age, I was too light for the Rugby scrum and not fast enough as a back. It was the same with Cricket. My poor performance resulted in a rather permanent job of scoresman, at which I was quite good but bored. An offer by Eton College, just along the river from the ISC, gave us use of several sailing dinghies, so many a happy summer afternoon was spent sailing on the Thames.

By now, the summer of 1939, the dreaded School Certificate loomed. I was taking it in five subjects and the scope was wide. For example, poetry featured strongly in English and America and Ireland in History. Charles Stewart Parnell's story was one which interested me very much – his illicit love affair with Kitty O'Shea, the class tensions which underlay much of the jealousy shown by less able political contemporaries and the strong disapprobation of the Church at the position he had achieved of dominance of the Commons through the strength of the Irish Party which enabled him to control the Liberal/Tory split in whichever direction he wished, particularly in relation to Home Rule for Ireland.

When the History paper appeared on my desk at the Examination, to my joy one of its main questions was on Parnell and I wrote furiously on the subject, answering other questions sketchily. The examiner must have had the same fascination, as I was awarded over 90% in the History paper.

At that time University Entrance was possible to students who got five Credits in School Certificate, though few would be accepted at the age of 16 which was the natural S.C. age. It was therefore a very good time to be at school for the extra year or so with University Entrance in one's pocket, as it were and with time for sport, development of interests cultural and social. A preparation, in fact, for later life.

My father was appointed County Inspector RUC of Londonderry in August 1939. We moved into Chilcoot, Prehen, overlooking the River Foyle, a charming house built by an adventurous Irishman called Hyland, who as a young man had faced the terrible journey over the Chilcoot Pass to Alaska in the Gold Rush of the early 1900s and had struck gold. He set up a packaging business in the city of Derry (as we all called it) and because it had prospered had left for England, so the house was available. All that summer holiday was spent in anxious anticipation of two things, the likelihood of war and the School Certificate results. Of the two my greater dread was failing the S.C., because, having read Siegfried Sassoon and *All Quiet on the Western Front*, I was a convinced pacifist and felt that war, if it came, would not much affect a 16-year-old.

On the same day early in September Chamberlain declared war on Germany and my School Certificate results arrived. I had obtained Matriculation with five Credits. Next day it was announced that no children could travel to school from N. Ireland to Great Britain. A period of frantic activity began then. My poor parents, having just moved job and home, had to find schools for four children, as my sisters were now of school age. It was a time of great stress for my father as Derry was clearly going to be of key importance as an Atlantic port. Derry gaol was full, with many IRA suspects interned, and he had to deal with Army, Navy, Civil Defence and RAF officers all clamouring for RUC help in setting up their forces.

He had met Ian Stuart, Headmaster of Portora Royal School, Enniskillen. Stuart asked Richard and me to become boarders and the disappointment I felt in not having eighteen months to two years of mildly prestigious existence in ISC, which had now joined up with Haileybury, did not last long. It was a good time to reinvest in my "Irishness", which several other ex-British public-school boys also experienced at Portora. John and Henry Brooke and Henry Richardson, because they lived in Fermanagh, came as dayboys to the school, and I believe missed some of the benefits of living with boys from both sides of the Border. Later I was to discuss this with the Brookes, sons of Lord Brookeborough, when we found ourselves together at Sandhurst.

Once more the question of our religion had to be tackled. Again we were not made to feel outsiders, and no one questioned our going to Mass in Enniskillen, while all the rest of the school went to the Protestant Cathedral. It gave us a rather distinctive position which was quite enjoyable. We struck up friendship with Larry Hall the newsagent/confectioner in the main street, and were in demand as suppliers of sweets, and I regret to say cigarettes. Smoking was stoutly opposed by Ian Stuart, largely on the grounds that it would spoil the fitness of his Rugby teams. Stuart, formerly a master at Eton (he always wore the dress of Eton's teachers), had himself been an Irish Rugby International and had been capped a number of times. He used to recall to us the one and only time Portora had won the Ulster Schools Cup, in 1914, when captained by Dickie Lloyd, who was later killed in France. Training for the group of boys from whom he picked the First XV was intense. Shivering in the early morning in the mists of Lough Erne, cross-country running at every chance, endless coaching and admonition from this single-minded man fired us with ambition to succeed in the Second War, as Portora had done in the past. Perhaps inherent in this too was the anticipation that we were going to have to face the greater test of service in battle, because by 1940 the war was going very badly for the British, without Allies of substance and with an Army beaten in France.

An RAF fighter pilot, son of the Portora School doctor, was awarded the DFC for destroying a Messerschmitt when his guns were ineffective by ramming it. He drove the wing of his Spitfire into the German plane, which crashed, but he managed to land his battered Spitfire. Meeting him as we did (he was an old Portoran) was inspiring and a later event in my life probably owed much to this.

The summer of 1940 passed peacefully. As a senior boy, I was allowed great latitude in going for bicycle rides with a special friend through the glorious Fermanagh countryside. We even managed to get to Garrison, where my parents later had the use of a fishing lodge, Rosskit, owned by Colonel Cutbill, one of the King's Knights of Windsor, who was not permitted to travel to Ireland.

On one of these expeditions my friend and I met two charming girls, both very pretty and so trysts were organized of a rather innocent character, viewed from present behaviour. One of my attempts to appear sophisticated was to suck on an empty pipe and it was in my pocket when I left my blazer by the lake after a swimming session (not with the girls, I hasten to say). The blazer was found with the pipe in it by Ian Stuart and there was a great furore. I went to him and told him the story. He was so pleased that I only had the pipe as a "prop" that all was forgiven. Indeed he made me a prefect.

The 1940/41 Rugby season now took on an even more gruelling character. Portora did well throughout the season. We had a good pack, but lighter than schools such as Campbell College, Methodist College, R.B.A.I., which were able to choose from numbers far greater than Portora.

The final of the Ulster Schools Cup knockout competition takes place annually on St. Patrick's Day, 17 March. I had had a reasonably good season playing on the right wing, and had scored a number of tries. Nonetheless, competition for places on the XV was intense and another boy, named Locke, was my challenger for the Wing position – I expect this was part of Stuart's psychological motivational technique – but the team was announced and I was picked.

On 16 March I found a lump on my neck and reported to the Matron. Instantly whipped off to the Sanatorium where my RAF hero's father, the School Doctor, pronounced "Mumps". He did, however, insist that a radio was made available and I lay in misery and isolation in bed listening to the great match. Fortunes swung from end to end of the field and it seemed that it would be a scoreless draw. In the last few moments Locke scored. Portora had won after 27 years. I wish I could say that I was undilutedly delighted for Locke, but there was a feeling of "There but for the grace of God . . . !"

Richard is a wonderful brother. He has all the qualities I lack – patience, gentleness, more demonstratively loving. He has always shown no resentment of an older brother who has been given more attention, but has enjoyed any success I may have had. So far in this extremely egotistical memoir he has appeared as a shadowy supporter, but he has a story of his own which needs telling. Sailing to India, with no Army training, he found himself in a twilight world of apprehension as to his acceptability as an officer and propaganda by British Indian Army officers explaining how superior the British were, and how they must have no patience with Indian Nationalists who were, anyway, quite unreliable in the war effort. He is an easygoing, gregarious man, and devoted to his family.

On arrival in India, at the Bombay Gate, he found himself in the Indian Army Service Corps, perhaps because he had distinguished himself as a driver for the American advance party to Derry before the US entered the war. Having had a few trips at the wheel of Dad's ancient Ford up the Prehen drive, he got a licence which in those days cost 5 shillings and required no test. The Americans hired him and gave him a large Station Wagon, a novelty to us. Now commissioned in the Royal Indian Army Service Corps, he contracted Yellow Fever, a most serious illness, and was in hospital for many months. He fell in love with his nurse, Sister Susan O'Leary, from Co. Galway. Letters home extolling the beauty and charm of this Queen Alexandra Sister cut little ice with Annette, especially when she worked out that Richard, then only just 20, was seriously contemplating marriage to Susan who had to be six or seven years older. Despite parental pleas, Richard pressed ahead and on his 21st birthday Susan and he were married. She had to leave the Nursing Service; he, now recovered, had only the tiny pay of a Lieutenant and before long the first of their five children, young Richard, arrived. The rift over his marriage persuaded Richard to seek his future in Australia, and when the war ended in 1945 Susan and he, now with two children, arrived in Sydney. Understandably any jobs going were for the returning Aussie Servicemen and "Poms" were not considered. He decided to become a docker or "Wharfie" and soon found himself among some of the roughest, toughest men he had ever met, hard workers and drinkers, very volatile in their Union, and not at all averse to brawling and serious fights. Richard demonstrated his calming talent and physical strength to such an extent that he was now Foreman, on a substantial salary, had much more time off and, with family now approaching three children bought a taxi. Between the Foreman hours and the taxi-driving he was working far too hard and when our Father appeared in Sydney in 1950, having just retired as Deputy Chief of the British Police Mission to Greece, he persuaded Richard to give up this profitable but killing double job and enlist again in the Australian Army. The Korean War was imminent and Dad was certain from what he had learned from the Embassies in Athens that Australia would play a major part in the forthcoming war.

It must have seemed odd to the Recruiting Sergeant in Sydney to have a former British Captain (a rank he had achieved on leaving the British Army in India) applying for the Australian Military Police as a Private. He did well, was soon commissioned and in the thick of the Korean War.

Colonel Robin Charley of the Royal Ulster Rifles fighting in Korea tells the story of asking the first Australian soldier he met, "Have you ever heard of a fellow-Ulsterman called Richard Gorman?". The reply: "I am Richard Gorman"! At the end of the Korean War Richard returned to Australia, now to Brisbane, where he was engaged in bringing the Military Police to a higher standard, as he had learned in Korea how much responsibility rests on the MPs, not only in such duties as controlling access to the front line and ensuring safety among mobile columns, but the extremely difficult job of keeping order and discipline in rear areas, where troops fresh from battle can go "berserk" and create huge problems for the civil as well as military authorities. His achievements led to his appointment as Deputy Director of the Military Police, with a strong chance of becoming Provost Marshal of the Australian Army. Then came Vietnam, and again Australia sent a large number of servicemen. This was degenerating into a humiliating defeat for the US and its allies. Saigon was filled with indisciplined drunken service representatives of the non-communist allies. Unspeakable horrors took place with ordinary soldiers becoming serious criminals. Richard, in the thick of this demoralized chaos, did all he could to keep order, discipline and justice alive, but in vain. He was dogged too by a broken vertebra in his back as a result of his jeep being rammed by a truck and, despite surgery, is still in pain.

He was evacuated from Vietnam just before the capitulation and, though promoted to Deputy Provost Marshal, retired later to civilian employment at Sydney University.

Since I have given space to my brother I am aware that hitherto this has been a male memoir, with little if anything about Geraldine and Carolyn. Geraldine was always the home-making, caring one who, after life in Greece with my parents, decided she would take a job in Australia, with the added incentive of Richard being there. At first all went well. She looked after the small children of British immigrants, who treated her well and, because she had had the training of a Princess Christian nurse, she was particularly good with infants and much in demand for new babies.

She met a young Australian Air Force man of Irish descent and fell in love. Richard was very dubious and conveyed this to my parents as well as to her. Jack and Annette, remembering how they had reacted to Richard's own romance, put this down to their old-fashioned ideas and did not do as much as they both said later they should have. It was a disaster; he was dishonest. She did have a baby which was very ill at birth and died; he was not there to help her and provided neither home nor income. Fortunately good nuns came to her aid and she was able to turn her Princess Christian training to adequate effect and made a life for herself in the absence of the roving husband.

My mother's worsening arthritis convinced me that my parents needed help and, without telling them the full details of my scheme, I sent a ticket to Australia for Geraldine to come to Carrowdore, Co. Down where my parents had bought a house. She came "for a few months", when Annette had a serious stroke, which prevented speech, and totally immobilized her. Geraldine nursed her lovingly for three years, when she died and was buried in the graveyard of the Church of Ireland which was close to their house, and near the grave of their friend Louis McNeice, the Irish poet, whom they had befriended during their time in Athens, where he was Cultural Attaché at the British Embassy. My father was lost without her and wanted anyway to leave Carrowdore where they had been so happy. Geraldine and he found a small comfortable house at Barton-on-Sea, in Hampshire, and moved there, where she looked after him until he, in his turn, died after five years. So she turned to infant nursing again and was very successful maintaining the Barton house and herself, with a little help from her siblings. It was said that few babies born into Debrett did not pass through Geraldine's hands sometime! She became disenchanted with the Catholic faith and joined Jehovah's Witnesses where she finds the support and companionship which was not evident in England. She still works looking after the children of a woman writer.

The youngest of the family, Carolyn, has had a very different life. Living in Athens with my parents from 1945-1951, and an extremely pretty and talented girl, she was much courted by the young men, Greek as well as British. There were many Army Officers there then with the Communist rebellion still going on. My father's post took him all over Greece and she accompanied him on many of these journeys, learning Greek and becoming proficient in singing to her own guitar. My mother wisely sent her to Atholl Crescent to learn more mundane things such as cooking and looking after house and family. She became a talented cook and is the author of the Easy-to-Cook Book which achieved good sales years later. After Atholl Crescent she went to London and, having acted in British Council plays under Louis McNeice's direction, tried the stage, and its concomitant, modelling, with some success. But when it was realized how well she sang and played the guitar she found herself in great demand. It was during this period that she met the charming Greek Nolly Zervudachi, nephew of President Venizelos of Greece, and became engaged to him. Carolyn and Nolly married later in Athens Cathedral under the auspices of Madame Venizelos, Annette suppressing her disappointment that it was a Greek Orthodox rather than a Catholic wedding. Nolly became Managing Director of Niarchos Shipping world-wide, based in London, and they have four children and six grandchildren. Having sold their large house in Holland Villas Road to a diplomat, they bought a beautiful house in Provence where they live.

Chapter Two

ARMY TRAINING –
TOPSHAM TO SANDHURST

Now it was time to decide the future. Despite my early conviction that the War would be over before I was of an age for service, it was clear by early 1941 that there would be years more fighting. There had been some rather sentimental objections to the fact that 18-year-old servicemen had been killed in action and a scheme to give some University education to those who were suitable for commissions was devised. This required an examination, which, if passed, would result in one being sent after initial Army training to a University for six months, after which successful students would be considered for Officer training. I passed the exam quite easily and I was posted to the Royal Artillery Depot at Topsham Barracks, Exeter. It was not an illustrious start, for, after the long boat and train journey, I slept through the Exeter stop and woke up in Torquay. However, my late arrival at Topsham was forgiven as evidence of Irish unpunctuality. Foot Drill was tough, as was Gun Drill, and our only recreation was, after some weeks, permission to go out into Exeter, where we drank cider with rather devastating results. One fellow-soldier fell into the street just as a blacked-out Army lorry was passing. He raised his legs just in time and returned to Barracks with us unscathed, but rather scared.

An incident which perhaps cancelled out my rather tardy arrival comes back to me. Entering a phone-booth I found the wallet of a Canadian Army soldier, in which was his name. It was no trouble to me to call at the Canadian billet in Exeter and return it to him. He was a delightful man, who said that everything he valued, particularly his wife's picture, was in the wallet, so we parted with mutual goodwill. Next day the parade was addressed by the Colonel, who ordered me out of the ranks. I was certain that some dreadful crime had been discovered. It all turned out to be highly embarrassing, as the Canadian soldier had written to him in hyperbolic terms, and the unimportant, but I suppose useful to him, little event gave the Colonel a peg on which to hang a homily about honesty and help to our allies. It did not do me much good with my barrack room mates!

We were then told to which University we had been allocated. Instead of Oxbridge, which I felt was my destiny, it was Glasgow. I felt cheated somehow, and the more so when the contingent from several Army Depots were sent to boarding houses near the University, with stern landladies who demanded instant obedience and produced rather poor meals – not surprisingly, in view of the severe rationing. With per-week rations of 2 oz of sugar, 2 oz of butter and 1/2 lb of meat, it must have been difficult to fill the stomachs of fifteen hungry youths. Most, but not all, of my companions were public schoolboys, and once again I found, as I had at Topsham, affinity with those who had not been as lucky as us. There was one Jewish boy whose parents had escaped from Germany and who had had experiences which we could not even imagine. He had an irritatingly ingratiatory manner and had changed his surname to conceal his Jewishness, but gradually we all came to like and respect him, and he turned out to be one of the "stars" of our intake.

Increasingly I became interested in the use of tanks, which had first been demonstrated by Fuller, the brilliant British pre-war General, but put into practice by Guderian, Hitler's Blitzkrieg exemplar. To the chagrin of the Artillery officers, I opted for the Royal Armoured Corps and was posted to its training school at Blackdown, about 20 miles from Camberley, and had my first experience of British Valentines and Matildas. They were unimpressive, slow and inadequately gunned – even at that stage in the War 2-pounders were much too small. But the teamwork of driver, front gunner, wireless operator, turret gunner and commander was a fascinating challenge, especially as a Tank Officer would normally have three or four tanks under his command. I was glad to be in a Corps where mobility, "an eye for country" and opportunism were required, rather than, as it seemed to me then, the rather static role of a Gunner Officer. Among my fellows was an Irishman, Douglas Goodbody, of the famous Irish milling concern. He had served in the ranks in the Middle East, had fought the Italians in the desert and had had heroic adventures in Greece, when Britain sent reinforcements to Greece in an effort to stem the German invasion. A disastrous step, but one which eventually resulted in Russia failing to reach the Mediterranean.

About this time I heard from Colonel Conolly McCausland, Irish Guards, of Drenagh, Limavady, that the Irish Guards were to form an Armoured (Tank) Battalion and would I be prepared to apply? When I asked Douglas Goodbody about this, he told me that he had already applied, had been accepted and would be joining the new Armoured Battalion at the end of the 6-month Blackdown course. He was senior to me by several months, so would be leaving before long. I wrote to Colonel Conolly saying that I was flattered by the offer, but had reservations about becoming a Guards Officer, not least because I did not want to ask my father for an allowance, which, even in those days, halfway through a major war, was still *de rigueur* for Guards Officers, who were expected to fund themselves adequately for dress uniforms, Mess bills and expensive conventions such as never travelling by bus, only by taxi, first class by train, and frequenting the 400 Club, the Berkeley and other such grand places. Nevertheless, we arranged to meet and I was instantly impressed by this charming courtly, rather dreamy man, whose Catholic faith was the mainspring of his life. He was the owner of one of Ireland's greatest estates and my concerns about money did not impress him, indeed were rather brushed aside. He was a fine soldier, brave and careful of his men, but rather unworldly, so I was still unsure.

The next event was the dramatic announcement that the Government intended to create a much larger tank army and was turning over Sandhurst entirely to the training of officers for Armoured Regiments. Within 24 hours all of us at Blackdown, save those like Douglas Goodbody who were nearly at the end of their training, were ordered to pack up and march to Sandhurst, which had been cleared to receive us. It was a long march on a hot day, carrying packs, but when we turned through the Camberley gates and headed up the long avenue to those great buildings in which the officers of the Empire had been taught since the 1870s, the contrast with Blackdown's plebeian starkness was stunning. And this was only the beginning. I was allocated to the Old Building, and to a room with three other cadets. A soldier servant greeted us and explained that his job as batman was to clean our room, keep it tidy, polish our belts and boots, "blanco" our web equipment and generally do for us what we had automatically done for ourselves over all the previous months. He warned us to be ready and well turned out for the dinner gong which would sound at 7.30. When this happened the several hundred mostly youthful cadets gathered in a hall, elegant and colourful with portraits of past generals, Colours, shining silver trophies and cutlery, to be served a meal by waiters, rather than lining up with mess-tins. The contrast made us feel that at least we were heading for the role of Officer and Gentleman, though many felt this to be pre-war flummery.

The next day was a rude awakening from delusions of grandeur. Our Regimental Sergeant Major, a Grenadier of formidable fierceness, RSM Lord, with a voice capable of being heard a mile away, soon made clear that whatever we thought we knew about drill we must realize that the standard required at Sandhurst was that of the Guards. Whether these Potential Officers were destined for the Royal Armoured Corps, the Cavalry, or the Royal Tank Regiment was of no interest to him; he and his almost equally fierce Drill Sergeants would see to it that no commission would be granted to those who did not, or could not, perform foot-drill to Guards standards.

This daunting entr'acte was ameliorated somewhat when we realized that a great deal of our training would be in class, with exceptionally gifted lecturers on subjects which were not at first sight too relevant, but whose importance soon became clear to us – military history, the evolution of wartime strategies, the tactical lessons to be drawn from the success of the Germans, leadership, the motivation of one's men, the code of behaviour expected of a British Officer.

Chapter Three

ARMY TRAINING –
SANDHURST TO SALISBURY PLAIN

Quite soon there was an order for me to appear at Irish Guards Regimental Headquarters, Birdcage Walk, to be interviewed as a Potential Officer. Wearing my smartest battledress, with boots gleaming (thanks to the splendid batman), I presented myself to the Regimental Lieut. Colonel, Colonel Sidney Fitzgerald CVO, MBE, MC, and the Adjutant, Major "Moose" Alexander. In a Guards Regiment the ethos, traditions, discipline, recruitment standards, postings, promotions, indeed reputation, are all the responsibility of the Regimental Lieut. Colonel. He is the most important man in the Regiment and, despite the fact that many Generals, even Field Marshals, are senior to him, none would dare question him on matters regimental. This is true of all the Household Brigade – the five Foot Guards and, at that time, the Life Guards and the Royal Horse Guards.

Colonel Sidney, "Black Fitz", looked the part. He barked rather than spoke, his great black eyebrows (hence the nickname) looked thunderous, even when he perhaps thought he was being benign. It was clear that the Sandhurst revolution presaging tank supremacy over foot-soldiers (the Guards being the world's best infantry) did not fill him with pleasure. My own background, whilst not unworthy, did not contain Eton, a country estate, or indeed any Irish Guards merit, save, to me rather oddly, that I had been recommended by Conolly McCausland as a strong Catholic and the Irish Guards prided itself on being a predominantly Catholic Regiment. For example, all padres in the "Micks" were Catholic.

Rather to my surprise, towards the end of the interview Colonel Sidney said, "Conolly tells me you are concerned about funding yourself. Things are much less financially demanding for wartime Officers. If you are accepted I am sure you could manage on a hundred or two a year."

I left his splendid office with mixed feelings – the smartness of the Guardsmen at Wellington Barracks drilling in preparation for Trooping the Colour, the feeling that if one was to be in the Army it would be best to be part of the best. Most of all it had been observing in the Irish Guards NCOs and Guardsmen not only their pride in their appearance, but also the banter and "craic" in their Irish voices which spoke of more than brute militariness, but of loyalty and companionship. But where was I to find £100-£200? Not from a father who had sacrificed to send us all to boarding schools. I was certainly not going to ask Dad, as he would have told me to go ahead, and it was in this spirit of uncertainty that I learned a week later that cadets who applied for the Irish Guards were to parade to be interviewed again by Colonel Fitzgerald that afternoon.

Poor cricketer though I was, I had been picked to play for my Company (there were six at Sandhurst), so I changed into whites and was fielding when the RSM himself, looking even more terrifying than usual, paying no attention to the match in progress, strode across the field towards me. Halted in front of me, "Mr Gorman, *Sir*, you are absent from your Regimental Lieut. Colonel's parade. Go there at once, *Sir*, dressed as you are."

"Black Fitz" and "Moose" were waiting for me. With them was my Company Commander, Captain Tyler, also Irish Guards. "What the hell do you mean by not parading for me this afternoon?" Haltingly I tried to explain that I did not want to offend anyone, that Colonel Conolly McCausland's commendation of me was a great and undeserved honour, that just that hour or two at Birdcage Walk had shown me how great a Regiment was the Irish Guards, but that I could not, and would not, ask a father who had done so much for me to produce £100 a year. The Colonel seemed lost for words. Eddie Tyler spoke up: "I have succeeded since I transferred to the Irish Guards [he had earlier been a Naval Officer] in surviving on my pay alone. It is not easy, but it can be done. I think Gorman is a Mick and we could do with him." I was told the interview was over.

Next day Eddie (as I came to know him) sent for me to tell me that I had been accepted, and should go to Keenan Philips, the regimental tailor to be fitted for uniform. He then told me his own story. A Naval Cadet at Dartmouth, he had never had any family finance behind him. He had had a good career after commissioning as a Sub-Lieutenant, particularly because of his aptitude for radio, radar and codes. He had the great honour of being appointed to the Royal Yacht, but all the time he had no money and his contemporaries, without flaunting it, were able to live appropriately on an income which was taken for granted. In 1938 he tired of the effort to keep up appearances and resigned from the Navy. This caused great fury in the Admiralty and he was refused permission to resign on the grounds that to do so when a war might take place soon was cowardly. His uncle, Stafford Cripps, later Chancellor of the Exchequer, heard about his nephew's request and Eddie's resignation was accepted. Ironically, in 1939, when war broke out and Naval reservists were being called up, the Navy refused to have him back. He applied to the Irish Guards, stating his Signals background, was accepted at once and lived on his pay, even though he had married his beautiful and talented wife Pippy during his 18 months out of the Services.

My whole ambition now was to justify my selection. The work at Sandhurst became intense. We would go out on exercise in all weathers, sometimes with tanks, sometimes just with small vehicles known as Pick-Ups which were driven by young women ATS. Looking back, it makes me wonder why none of us, so far as I know, ever took advantage of these youngsters, for often we would be one cadet with one ATS practising radio, map-reading and mobility all through the night.

Occasionally we had genuine tanks to train on in countryside exercises. To be the Commander of a three-tank Troop was rare and only happened when one was close to Passing Out. As Troop Commander, I was led into an ambush of enemy guns and tanks (all simulated). The proper course of action was to reverse, get into firing positions and by use of mobility get behind the enemy. This is what I had been taught, and it was right, but some demon in my mind made me take a different tactic, to charge. Our three tanks drove over the ambush at such speed as we could muster. A flustered Exercise Officer expostulated and told me that the "Charge of the Light Brigade" was nothing to this. My reply was that, just as cavalry had revolutionized infantry warfare, so the speed and surprise of tanks would, if used aggressively, sometimes win the day. He was not convinced!

We were shown our reports before Passing Out. Mine said I would be a good officer with Irish soldiers, but was impetuous and likely to cause casualties if not kept on a tight rein.

Passing Out is a famous ceremonial at Sandhurst. After a parade usually inspected by Royalty, in our case the King, the now-commissioned officers march up the steps of the Old Building to the music of a Guards Band and go to their rooms where they dress in the uniform of their new Second Lieutenant rank. The change from drab khaki to the resplendence of a uniform, in my case with two rows of four buttons and a star on one's shoulder, was thrilling.

My father was there, in his uniform of County Inspector RUC, and with him was Richard who had been accepted as an officer in the Indian Army and was to sail for India at once.

After a short leave, and now resplendent in my Service Dress with eight buttons and an evening Blue uniform, again with the buttons and a scarlet stripe down each leg, I reported to the Irish Guards Training Battalion at Lingfield. Another rude awakening. The Adjutant, Major Guy Tilden-Wright, met us new arrivals from Sandhurst. They included James Chichester-Clark, later Prime Minister Northern Ireland, Lord Edward Fitzmaurice, later killed in Normandy, Keith Bryant, a rather surprising Irish Guards Officer, with whom I was to share quarters, who had been a journalist and had written a book about Marie Stopes, the birth-control proponent, Lord Mount Charles, now Marquess Conyngham, of Slane Castle, and Pakenham McCorkell, of Derry, son of Sir Dudley McCorkell. I was to see Packy killed in Normandy, in a horrifying incident. There were several other, who went to the 1st Battalion, then in Tunisia, ten men in all.

The Adjutant, a distinguished Irish Guardsman who had served in the Great War, soon disillusioned us about what we could now expect as "Ensigns", as Second Lieutenants in the Guards are called. We would have many hours every day of foot-drill, not ordering others about but learning it again ourselves. He did not believe that Sandhurst drill was anything like good enough for the Micks. So at once we were on the square. Drill-Sergeant McComish, from Belfast, and Sergeant-Major McGarrity, from Kerry, gave us a really hard time. We were told the story of James Lees-Milne, later famed as writer, broadcaster and National Trust head, who went through this same testing time at the Training Battalion in 1940. A scare that German invasion was imminent led to the whole Training Battalion being sent to man Dover Castle, one of the Channel bastions. Lees-Milne had reached the stage at which he was being trained to drill a Platoon of Guardsmen. The morning after the sudden move to Dover Castle, the Commanding Officer, Lord Gough, had ordered early morning drill. James found that the Castle Square, high on the hill, had no barrier between it and a steep drop of several hundred feet. There was a thick mist rolling in from the sea. The Drill-Sergeant, after several "on the wrong foot" commands, halted the Platoon, about thirty men, and said, "The Officer is just testing you. When he gives a command on the wrong foot, he expects you to ignore it. Just march on." The unfortunate James L-M now realized that the mist was getting thicker and that all depended on him getting "Halt" as the right foot passed the left. He marched the Platoon towards him and at last got it right. Then he was able to give the "About Turn". The mist became thicker. "Quick March," he ordered. The Platoon disappeared into the mist. "Halt," he cried; the footsteps grew fainter; "Halt" again and again, still the tramp of feet. Then silence. At this moment Lord Gough and the Adjutant appeared on the square. A gibbering Ensign rushed up to them. "Sir, I have killed my Platoon." The mist cleared to show grinning Micks climbing up on the square, having clung to scree over the edge. The relieved James Lees-Milne was indeed relieved of active Irish Guards service as of that day. He was appointed Railway Transport Officer for a London station and survived the war to become one of the outstanding literary figures of his day.

The glamour of our rank (and uniform) was unavailing of anything except a narcissistic dressing for dinner, and soon we found ourselves invited to the NCOs Dances and Bingo nights. The Drum-Major was an Ulsterman called Cherry, who had at the camp a very pretty daughter. We found a lot in common, I sat out many dances with her and walked her home to the Drum-Major's quarters. There were numerous Guardsmen saluting and giggling slightly, and the next day the kindly and wise Adjutant sent for me to say that this would not do and that the Drum-Major had confirmed what had happened. To modern eyes this must seem an extraordinary event – a pretty girl, herself an ATS, and a young soldier – but in the Guards the system is geared to a division between officers and men. Officers are expected to have their own lifestyle and not to take any advantage, because of rank and uniform, of Other Ranks.

Drilling and infantry exercises occupied the weeks and at last we were declared fit to appear in public and given weekend passes. I went up to London with Michael Cole, later Lord Enniskillen. He was a splendid dance-band drummer and introduced me to the 400 Club, where he was greeted as an old friend and fellow-professional by the band. It was an intriguing evening, ending in The Bag of Nails but I realized that without money it would be disastrous to take on this lifestyle. Fortunately this was not an option, as we were shortly afterwards posted to our Battalions – the First to Tunisia, the Second (Armoured) to Salisbury Plain and the new Third Battalion to Scotland.

When I arrived at Warminster on the edge of Salisbury Plain I was given command of No. 5 Troop of No. 2 Squadron of the 2nd Battalion. Four elderly and unreliable Covenanter tanks were my charge, with crews who had been supplied by the other four Troops of the Squadron. The idea was to increase the number of Troops by one in each of the three Squadrons. My Squadron Leader was Major John Madden, of Hilton Park, Clones, Co. Monaghan. He was a large restless man, a professional soldier who had seen pre-war service in Egypt and had been at Boulogne and the Hook of Holland in the last stages of the Battle of France. As a novice officer I was much in awe of him and when, after a few days during which I tried to get to know my four Sergeants and sixteen Corporals and Guardsmen, and to bring the Covenanters into running order, John Madden sent for his five Troop Commanders and gave us orders to entrain at Warminster station the next night to load our tanks on flat wagons to be conveyed to our exercise, I felt that at least I did not have to ask where the railway station was.

I mounted the turret of my tank. My driver was Guardsman Goulding from Goole, Yorkshire, and there was also the Front Gunner, Turret Gunner and Loader/Wireless Operator. Through my internal circuit I gave orders for "engine start-up" when No. 4 Troop's blacked-out tank lights passed. "Engine won't go, Sir," Goulding's despairing voice. "Try again." Minutes passed, the starter grinding, when to my huge relief the engine started. By now the dim lights of No. 4 Troop were far out of sight, so we set off for the station, my three other tanks following mine. Racing into the round courtyard which I remembered from my arrival, I realized that there must have been an entrance for goods vehicles which I had passed. By now all four tanks were in the courtyard and poor Goulding had an irascible commander who ordered him peremptorily to reverse, which he did with such vigour that the courtyard wall was knocked down. "Driver advance," I shouted. At this moment a small van raced into what was left of the yard, with two agitated Staff Officers sent to find out what was happening. The Covenanter had a habit, when put into forward gear and with acceleration, of rising in front. This one did so and we landed on the bonnet of the little van, crushing it. When No. 5 Troop eventually reached the tank transporters No. 2 Squadron found the story hilarious and my nickname "Blockhead" was coined.

No. 2 Squadron, for some reason which I connect with the personality of John Madden, had nicknames for all its Officers. Madden's own was "The Jumper", John Dupree, his Second-in-Command, was "Two-Three" (the Guards' pause between drill movements), Vivian Taylor was "Tinker", Hugh Dormer was "The Birdman". The most unusual was that of Tony Dorman, known as "Dipper". He was a keen naturalist and had started studying for the Veterinary Service; after the War he attained the post of Head Vet of the United Nations. Fishing in the Wiltshire River Nadder he was disappointed not to observe dippers, and wrote a letter to *Country Life* in which he said that it was his observation that dippers were never to be found on chalk-stream rivers. This caused a flood of letters to *Country Life,* such as, "I have fished the Nadder for 50 years and have never failed to see dippers," signed _____ Col. Retd. After a few issues there was the notice "This correspondence will now cease. Signed Editor."

Hugh Dormer, "The Birdman", was our Squadron hero. He had volunteered for Special Operations and had on several occasions parachuted into France with the object of destroying German installations such as large factories, work requiring bravery and presence of mind beyond most of us. Every moment he was in danger, through betrayal by French quislings or by some clue which he gave to the Germans who stopped him frequently, especially after his bombs had done their work. On the third such venture he managed to escape over the Pyrenees to Spain, with the Germans hard on his heels, and get back to England. He was awarded the Distinguished Service Order, after the VC the most coveted decoration a service officer can win. He returned to No. 2 Squadron as a Troop Leader. The experiment of the 5th Troop came to an end (I often wonder how much I contributed to this) and Hugh Dormer went off on another death-or-glory venture, so I inherited his hand-picked and splendidly trained No 4 Troop. I shall not forget sitting round a campfire just before he left with all twenty men around us while he talked to us all about his pride in us, and hopes for us, and had something to say to every one of his, now my, men, with never a word about what he had gone through and was destined to go through again.

Salisbury Plain became the training ground of the 5th Guards Brigade, the Armoured force of the Guards Armoured Division. The lessons learned in the Desert War were studied for clues as to tactics of modern Armoured formations, and many parallels were drawn between Naval fleet operations, where speed and mass could outflank and overcome an enemy and, with the addition of an "eye for country", beloved of the hunting fraternity, could bring the Germans to defeat. We perfected the "hull-down" ruse, which enabled tanks to position themselves just below the crest of a hill and, by firing High Explosive shells with a trajectory which brought the shell over the hilltop without hitting it, would enable us to achieve hits against an enemy who, even if he knew where the shell was coming from, could do little about it. My Artillery training came in handy here, but, as we had few guns which fired HE, there was little chance to practise the cunning stratagem.

My troop was distinguishing itself in many ways. They had the highest level of comradeship of any men I had ever met. They looked after each other, and me, in a most generous way. We always seemed to have time for a quick "brew-up" of tea (not the later slang word for a burning tank). The outstanding character was Corporal James Baron, my driver. One of the Desert War lessons was that a tank crew had a much better chance of survival from night attacks by shelling, or bombing from the air, if it dug a large hole capable of holding five men packed together like sardines in a tin and had the tank drive over it. We practised this on our exercises and it gave me a whole new understanding of the values and attitudes of these good men. The contrast between the elegant officers pacing up and down in front of their serried ranks of Guardsmen, the saluting and deferential mode of address, where a Guardsman, charged with some minor offence, such as passing out on parade, had to preface his excuse with the words, "I thank you Sir for leave to speak", and us sharing blankets in a trench sometimes filling with water could hardly have been more calculated to bring us all into dependence on each other. It was a revelation to me to have to censor their letters and to learn for sure what I had been wont to deny indignantly, that I snored vociferously!

The Brigade consisted of Armoured Battalions of the Grenadier, Coldstream and Irish Guards, a Motor (lorried) Battalion of the Grenadier Guards and a Reconnaissance Battalion of Welsh Guards. We shared a comfortable Mess and got to know each other. This was a crucial part of our development as a Division, but there was a serious deficiency which was to dog us later. The 32nd Brigade, the Infantry arm of the Division, did not train with us. The Coldstream, Welsh and Irish foot-soldiers were separate from us and many friends from Sandhurst and the Training Battalion were out of reach. Whether it was because training implying the Normandy Bocage would have alerted spies to D-Day's intentions, whether it was to wish-fulfil those experts, like our own Commanding Officer, Lieut.-Col. Kim Finlay, who believed that we would fight over the plains of France, Belgium and Germany, we had little to do with our infantry brethren. How differently it would all work out in reality.

Chapter Four

ARMY TRAINING –
NORFOLK TO ARNHEM

Our next move was to Norfolk, near a village called Shakers Wood, 20 miles from King's Lynn. By now we were expert in loading our tanks on to rail flat-cars, or on to tank transporters, which appeared in greater numbers now, as did a newer tank, the Crusader, with a six-wheel bogie, as opposed to the Centurion's five bogies. The Crusader had the world-beating Rolls-Royce engine which powered the Spitfire, and for speed and versatility it seemed a war-winner, but the tank itself was a disappointment. The armour was thin, the gun (6-pounder) small and, proud as we were of our Rolls-Royce Merlins, they were high-bred technical marvels, not altogether suited to Guardsmen who a year before had had little if any contact with an engine of any sort. Fortunately we had a Technical Adjutant, Major Ronnie Robertson from Dublin, whose patience, encouragement and ability to instruct the most clod-hopping crew were outstanding. When a Squadron of Crusaders moving at 30 m.p.h. across the Norfolk countryside was able to wheel and retreat, advance and change direction at the command of the Squadron Leader, one almost felt that this "Corps de Ballet" would sweep past its bemused audience of beaten Germans. Little wonder that Colonel Kim had such devotion to the desert/navy tank philosophy. Many a Norfolk asparagus farmer must have cursed us as we left tracks across his precious fields.

We had now a small Mess and got to know each other much more closely than we had in the large Warminster Mess. Terence O'Neill was our Intelligence Officer and he and I dined together quite often, though he was considerably my senior. He was a charming man, whose ideas for the future of Northern Ireland were far in advance of this time. He agreed with my view, echoing my father, now County Inspector of Co. Londonderry, that the gerrymandering of a Unionist majority on the Council, by stretching the political area into places miles outside the City to achieve a Unionist majority, was the antithesis of democracy. His view of the Orange Order was not favourable. He was never belligerent and when Packy McCorkell joined us, whose views supported his father Sir Dudley's, he never argued with him. Terence was not a "clubbable" man. He was no joiner of noisy parties or given to the tittle-tattle of Army gossip. He took his Intelligence role very seriously and gave us brilliant talks on German plans and likely wartime developments. A highly intelligent, rather diffident Ulsterman, whose love of his country was sincere, his distance from the ordinary people of his Province made him easy prey for Ian Paisley after the war.

One evening we had as guest Oliver Chesterton, who had just returned from Tunisia, where our 1st Battalion had achieved immortal fame by its capture of Hill 212, the key to the mountains held by Rommel's Army which was trying to get home to Germany after Montgomery's victory at Alamein. After dinner Oliver recounted the story of the 800 Irish Guardsmen attacking entrenched crack German troops holding this hill, in daylight, with precious little support. He described the Irish Guardsmen, of one Company of which Major Chesterton was Commander, marching through tall corn (it was autumn) and every time a comrade fell, wounded or dead, his neighbour would go over to him and thrust the bayonet of his rifle into the ground beside him, so that stretcher parties might find him. Then, with numbers dwindling all the time, came the ferocious assault on the hill, driving the Germans back over its brow and as night fell, the Micks digging in for the assault which was bound to come at dawn. When it did the Guardsmen fought hand-to-hand with the Germans, both sides using the bayonet and hand-grenades. The enemy was repulsed. Lance-Corporal Kenneally, believed then to come from Co Tipperary, a Bren-gunner, decided that he was not, in this position, able to play much part in the hand-to-hand battle, where he was as likely to kill his mates as the enemy. He could hear, over the hill, a German Officer haranguing his men, psyching them up for the next attempt to drive the Micks off Hill 212. Quite casually Kenneally rose from his shallow slit-trench and, holding this ground-intended machine gun in his arms, walked over the brow of the hill. The Germans were as astonished as were his own fellow Guardsmen and even more so when, from the hip, Kenneally disposed of nearly 100 enemy. Then, equally coolly as had been his appearance, he disappeared.

Some reserves of water and ammunition were got to the little group holding the hill tenuously, but tenaciously, throughout the day. Before dawn the next day it was clear that a larger number of Germans were now again preparing for a final assault. Because he had been wounded in the leg, Kenneally this time asked a Sergeant from the Reconnaissance Regiment to help him and, supported by Sergeant Salt, he did exactly the same thing as the day before. This time the Germans had posted guards. He emptied a Bren magazine, thirty rounds, into the SS Officers' group and coolly changed the magazine, taking on the guards who were now firing at him. Sadly the Sergeant was killed, but Kenneally hopped back. The hill had been saved. The Germans withdrew and within a few days Rommel's Army surrendered to Field Marshal Lord Alexander, Commander of the First Army and himself a distinguished Irish Guardsman. Kenneally was awarded an immediate VC by Field Marshal Alexander at the Victory Parade at Tunis shortly afterwards.

Another change. We were now to move to the Yorkshire Wolds, where the charging, swooping tank formations could more appropriately practice their mass movements over the hills and dales of the Yorkshire countryside. We had had little contact with Norfolk people and they were probably relieved that sixty tanks were no longer wrecking their cultivated fields and hedges. Most mornings we had seen the return of RAF bombers from European targets. We had heard the confident noise of the massed bomber squadrons just after dark on their way. Then crippled aircraft, some with only two engines in action, with tails in rags and able only to fly just above stalling speed, brought home to us the sacrifice that others were making towards victory. The Battle of the Atlantic was going badly and the image of seamen dying in the icy Atlantic to bring the food and fuel to us to have us fit for the Second Front was another reminder that we were elite troops being prepared for our own trial.

It was on the Yorkshire Wolds that at last the 2nd and 3rd Battalions started to train together and we in the 2nd got to realize how important fellow-soldiers were other than tank crews, namely the infantry of the Guards. The 3rd Battalion Commanding Officer was Colonel J.O.E. Vandeleur, a distinguished Irish Guardsman who had served in Palestine before the War and also as an officer in the Sudan Camel Corps. He was a peppery, staccato man, devoted to the Army and his wife, Felicity. His Second-in-Command was Conolly McCausland, his senior Company Commander Basil Eugster. We set up a Mess marquee and dined together nightly by the dim light of oil-lamps. A resemblance to Colonel Joe resulted in my being mistaken for him sometimes and I discovered that he always came into the Mess at the same time. Walking with his characteristic short quick step, I made my entrance; all got up from their seats, as was the convention. When they realized that I had fooled them, my brother officers gave me a "duffing-up" and there were no more false-pretence Colonels.

Joe Vandeleur now began training us in earnest as Tank and Infantry troops. At the same time our Crusader tanks were replaced by Shermans, the American battle-tanks; so Joe insisted that a box holding a telephone be fitted at the rear of every tank to enable the foot-soldiers to speak to the tank crews. He would tirelessly conduct TEWTs (Tactical Exercises Without Troops) with all ranks present to show how infantry/tank co-operation, right down to an individual section of seven infantrymen and a single tank, could together achieve what neither on its own could, how the use of infantry mortars and anti-tank weapons such as Piats could help us and how the close relationship between Infantry and Artillery and later close-support aircraft could often be better controlled from the ground than from the inside of a tank. One was conscious of the difference of approach of our own C.O., Kim Finlay, whose more grandiose *masse de manoeuvre* was in contrast to the smaller battle-plans of Joe Vandeleur. We were not to know which was to be the principal battle mode. Most of us tank men hoped it would be the former, when, like cavalry of old, we would sweep all before us.

The Sherman was a delight in comparison to the Crusader. Its engine was simple and almost foolproof. It consisted of five Chevrolet motors arranged around a main drive shaft, producing huge power to drive the 40-ton vehicle, capable on the road of over 40 m.p.h., and with tracks incorporating rubber which gave them much longer life than the British all-metal ones. Its gun, at 75mm bore, was considerably bigger than the 6 pounders we had had and so the howitzer theories which I had brought from my Gunner days could now be put into action. The armour-piercing quality of the anti-tank solid shot was then, in 1943, not at first seen as inadequate, though later one tank in every four was fitted with a British 17-pounder gun capable of penetrating the latest German armour – of that time.

Scarborough was about 20 miles away, so we young officers would go to the Pavilion Hotel on Saturday nights to dance and meet the local talent. The hotel, owned by Charles Laughton's family, was welcoming and the dances were an opportunity for us to get out of battledress and become part of non-military life for a while. John Madden decided that we should have a Squadron series of exercises, so he organized a tented camp at Robin Hood's Bay and his wife Nita joined us. It was a happy time. The Guardsmen enjoyed nearby Scarborough. We improved our tank handling and co-ordination – particularly in the use of radio. The "Jumper" went off in his 4-wheel-drive jeep to the grouse moors and invariably came back with several brace. His technique was to steer the jeep with his large left hand and hold his shotgun with his right hand. When grouse rose in front of him he would invariably bring down a brace. I was invited to join him for one of these forages and saw the tactic in action.

Radio was a great boon. The No. 19 Set, British, was a brilliant invention. There was an "A" Band, giving good transmission up to 20 miles, a

"B" set with a useful range of a mile or so, and an Intercom, enabling the Tank Commander to speak to his crew. The three separate nets were operated by a switch close to the Tank Commander's hand. In a Squadron situation with about twenty tanks tuned to the "A" net it worked perfectly. Using code-words – Commander was "Sunray" for example – the Squadron Leader could control the action of all twenty of his tanks, which could also if necessary speak to each other. A Troop Commander had his own "B" set, enabling him to speak to his three other tanks. The intercom was the most used part of the set, enabling all the crew to be in communication with each other. The trouble was that in a tank bumping and rolling across country, even without enemy, Commanders were apt to speak on "A" when it was Intercom they needed. A Brigade exercise on Salisbury Plain was set up to show how an Armoured Guards Brigade could give an example of "wireless discipline", with nearly 200 tanks all with the 19 Set able to hear the Brigade Commander co-ordinate and direct the operation. Brigadier Billy Fox-Pitt, a charming, rather elderly Grenadier, got on the air at the height of the cavalry-type tank sweep across the Plain. "Driver, whoa," we all heard; "Driver whoa," rather less patiently; "Driver stop, you bloody fool; we are going to go over the edge of a quarry." It was not long afterwards that Norman Gwatkin, a dashing Welsh Guards Officer, became our new Brigadier. I do not remember hearing him on the "A" set.

Wireless discipline, which sounds as though it should be easy for Guardsmen used to obeying orders and to speaking only when spoken to, was very difficult in practice. It was frequently the case that a tiny error in tuning would result in a station able to speak but unable to hear, drowning out others who could not silence the interrupter. Furthermore, when large numbers of stations were on the air together those on the periphery of the group could hear but not be heard. Irritating when on exercise, disastrous when in action.

Life went on very actively and I got to know my Troop and brother officers really well. A new responsibility was imposed on us by the Army Bureau of Current Affairs. ABCA had been set up by Government, it was said by Labour members of the Wartime Coalition Cabinet, as a means of educating forces members in politics. Every week a manifesto would arrive outlining the options to be considered when war ended – National Health, National Pensions, public ownership of the means of production and distribution, of transport, energy and ports, Trade Unions and their role. It was rather daunting for young officers to be expected to lead discussions on all this and to create an educated electorate when several million servicemen and women found themselves required to vote at the first post-war election. Many of us were content enough to trust that Churchill would lead us as successfully in peace as in war, but we found, especially from the many

Merseyside Irish Guardsmen, a totally different attitude. Many had experienced poor education, dreadful public housing, serious poverty and heavy unemployment. They were not looking forward to going back to this and not a few were quite open about lauding Communism. After all, Russia was an ally, led by the benevolent Uncle Joe Stalin. In common with my brother officers, I decided that it was the Guardsmen who were educating me rather then the other way round. From then on I found myself interested in politics.

The winter of 1943/44 was particularly tough and I had an attack of pleurisy, which resulted in our kindly Adjutant, Major David Peel, packing me off to Hampton Court where my aunt, Dr Katherine Fraser, lived in a Wren house. She was a doctor with a large practice, including the many Grace and Favour occupants of Hampton Court Palace. A week of her convalescent treatment, which included large meals, produced, despite rationing, from gifts of food from grateful patients to her soon had me well again. An invitation to Queen Charlotte's Ball arrived and I was to have my first experience of the pre-war Social Season, with several hundred debutantes taking the floor together to curtsey low to Princess Marina. The setting of Grosvenor House, champagne supper and dancing until near dawn, was a revelation of the good life for those who could afford it and one wondered whether such extravagance would continue after we had won the war, which we had not by any means done by then.

As the spring of 1944 passed without the D-Day we had all expected, and as training and keeping up the morale of our men became more routine in the one case and difficult in the other, we worried that the invasion, when it came, would be rather an anticlimax and that the great victories of Russia at Stalingrad and at the gates of Moscow would result in our facing triumphant Russians across the channel.

Field Marshal Montgomery came to visit us on an airfield. He arrived in an open jeep laden with cigarettes, to find the 5th Armoured Brigade drawn up in perfect Guards ranks, at attention. We had no rifles, so a "Present Arms" was not possible. He drove to the front of the 2000 men. A high voice called, "Gather round me, men". No such order was known in the Guards, so the Brigadier gave each Colonel an order to march his Battalion round the Field Marshal's jeep. This had to be conveyed down the ranks until it reached the Sergeant Majors. It was not the tidiest of exercises and there were loud complaints from Guardsmen who had turned out expecting an inspection. However, Monty did, I think, realize that he was not appealing to the ethos of the Guards and got on with his briefing about the forthcoming invasion, though giving us no clue as to its location or timing. Brigadier Norman Gwatkin ended by calling for three cheers for our Commander-in-Chief, and the little Field Marshal, with the funny beret on which he wore two insignia, drove away smiling, still with the cigarettes undistributed.

Now the pace of training accelerated. A British Army invention of making our tanks waterproof, so that they could wade ashore having been unloaded by landing craft in water up to the top of the turret, gave endless hours of work to achieve the sealing of the hundreds of orifices on our armoured vehicles. Some tanks were in fact modified to "swim" with pontoons attached to their sides and enable them to use their guns whilst swimming ashore. Others had flails, cylinders fixed in front of the tank, with heavy chains to beat the ground in front as the cylinders rotated. Thus they blew up mines which would have disabled the tanks. Some were modified to act like bulldozers, others had huge baulks of timber strapped together so that a deep tank-defensive ditch could be filled and the tanks got across. These were all British rather than American devices, and I saw in this the ingenuity and inventiveness of our country, but, sadly, it was the American genius for mass-production and engineering excellence which had provided the great bulk of our equipment.

In May the long-awaited movement order arrived. We were to travel to holding areas in the South of England close to, or on, the coast. The Southern Counties were to be closed to nonessential civilians, such as holidaymakers. After long train journeys carrying our vehicles on flat cars we arrived at Hove. It was a bizarre sight to see rows of tanks outside the gracious Edwardian Terraces with the coast of France visible on clear days, and we were in a high state of anticipation of what was to come after all the years of preparation.

Soon the first V.1 pilotless bombers started. The Buzz-Bombs, as they were called, made a distinctive whining noise, which it was important to listen to, as when the noise stopped the bomb would descend. It was thrilling to see the Spitfires chasing the V.1s and often shooting them down by tipping the wing of the V.1 to make it fall in countryside rather than London. This was of a piece with my Portora RAF hero's ramming exploit.

After the isolation of Yorkshire the delights of Brighton, next to Hove, which the Guardsmen took little time to discover, made for a spirit of light-hearted revelry. We were ready, our tanks were ready; all that was needed now was the order to embark. The days and nights passed, and at last on 6 June the invasion took place. It did not need a radio bulletin to tell us; all night bombers had roared over us and we could hear, from far out to sea, the booming of naval guns. There was much speculation that the Normandy landings were a feint, to draw the enemy away from the more direct landing-point in the Boulogne/Dieppe sector. Indeed it emerged much later that the allied deception plans, involving a "ghost army" in Kent, had fooled Hitler – and us too.

Eagerly we stood to daily, expecting to be on our way; then the news that bad weather had wrecked much of the beach landing facilities led to a stand down and we soon reverted to the festive Brighton life. Every night was like the Eve of the Battle of Waterloo and the little night-clubs of Hove and Brighton were packed with young Guards Officers and the young ladies of the war zone, which the area had become because of the ban on non-essential travel. At one of these "boites" I met a very pretty girl, whose husband, she informed me, had been shot down in the RAF. We saw each other almost every night and became lovers. It was only after this that she confessed that he was not dead, but was a POW. It would be nice to be able to say that I brought the affair to an end at once, but it would not be true. I was behaving dishonourably and my conscience was bad. Sheila, for that was her name, was of Irish descent and was probably feeling as guilty as I was, but somehow the imminence of battle and the high emotion of the early days of a first affair kept us from facing the dishonourable truth.

Suddenly the move was upon us and the Battalion set out for Southampton, not, as we first thought to embark, but to be billeted in a tented camp outside the port. Once again we found ourselves waiting, waiting. The tension everyone was feeling communicated itself by people, normally good-humoured, becoming angry and irritable. I went to Confession to the young Irish priest who had replaced Dom Julian Stonor, the Benedictine who had been with the Second Battalion in France and Holland in the 1940 retreat, but was now, to his and our sorrow, not fit enough to continue with us. The effect of some of the weight of guilt had fallen from me – the selfish consequence of the act of Confession – but it was only the knowledge that if killed I had the chance of eternity that bore me up. I was still unsure of how I would perform under fire.

Gertrude Lawrence, Noel Coward's partner in so many of his shows, came to sing to us in the camp. Her songs, some trite and sentimental, nonetheless gave all of us in the Battalion a wonderful send-off, as next day we set off for the Tank-landing ships at Southampton. At dusk we sailed and the coast of Normandy became visible in the early morning light. It was now over a fortnight since the landings, so it was not surprising that there was little to be seen of the fighting. A mass of ships of all sorts surrounded the huge temporary port which had been towed across the channel; barrage balloons clustered in the sky to prevent low-level air attacks; on the beaches were many wrecked tanks and other vehicles, and the German defences of wicked-looking steel girders, with mines attached, stretched along the miles of beaches, with gaps where the invaders had succeeded in breaching them. There was, as we got closer, a rumble of far-off fire, but it seemed unreal to be driving our tanks down the ramps onto the sand and climbing up the dunes to roads controlled by red-capped Military Policemen. Then to our harbour near Bayeux, in peaceful wooded country, with little to indicate that furious battles had been fought nearby. We were in waiting yet again. Even now, training was still going on apace. The tank lessons of fighting in the Normandy "bocage", small fields with banks and high hedges, began to come home to us. The Third Battalion had been in action at Carpiquet Airport and Colonel Joe Vandeleur, his usual ebullient and rather dramatic self, came to tell us about it. He was particularly critical of officers walking about unnecessarily when under fire. What had been a good example given to their men at Oudenarde and Malplaquet was not appropriate to Guards Officers in modern war. "If you hear a mortar shell coming towards you, dive for cover," he cried. Now whether it was by accident or design there was a large pool of muddy water in front of him and he threw himself into it, emerging dripping and with his immaculate uniform a muddy mess. It was a lesson none of us forgot! There is a time for sang-froid, there is a time for self-preservation.

Still the days passed. The news was of stalemate, with no sign of a break-through either on the Caen salient nor the American Mortain front. Heavy fighting to capture Cherbourg was taking place, but all the talk was of a massive German counter-offensive using the reserves sitting in the Pas de Calais awaiting the real assault which Hitler still believed was to come there.

We visited Bayeux Cathedral to see the Tapestry and the Micks challenged Bayeux to a football match, which the wily Frenchmen won. We had, in typical Mick fashion, found sources of fresh vegetables, wine and, best of all, cheese. The 14-man pack which provided rations for 14 men for 1 day, or 1 man for 14 days, or variations on the 14 to 1 theme, was not exciting, and supplementing this with a fresh chicken or a piece of beef was luxury indeed. But the best of all was the supply of potatoes, which to Irishmen were the staple. Remember that in England potatoes were dried and issued in packets; cooked with added water, they tasted of cotton wool. The Normandy cheeses, Camembert, Pont l'Eveque and Brie, were still being produced and sold by the Normans. The older men told us that eating chalky Camembert the day after it was made was uncivilized, but that did not stop us from enjoying it. One drink which I abhorred was Calvados. Years later in Quebec I was offered a glass and said to my host, "No thank you. It has a slight aftertaste of something very like gasoline". I tried it and found it and its cousin Armagnac delicious. Of course the reason for the aftertaste was that Calvados was being supplied to the troops in jerricans, the 4-gallon American petrol container, and washing every petrol vapour from such containers was not possible.

We were deluged by anxious letters from families at home. How were they to know that the Guards Armoured Division, which had trained for three years for this, was in such a peaceful, idyllic situation? Censoring my men's letters, I could see that they felt they were frauds and some, by hints of "security", tried to convey that they were in action.

By now Hugh Dormer had rejoined us. As usual there were no details of what he had been up to, but there was great joy in No. 2 Squadron to have him with us again. I feared to begin with that he would take over No. 4 Troop from me, but he soon reassured me that he had been promoted to Captain and would be commanding his own tank as John Madden's Headquarters Officer. When I brought him to the Troop that first evening, they were preparing their evening meal and were overjoyed. We ate the food they gave us and Hugh talked of what he hoped the world would be like for us all when the war ended. He talked of Ireland and the need for Catholics to forget the old hurts and to stand up for values which he believed the Church epitomized – tolerance, honesty, honour, courage.

Years later I talked to Cardinal Basil Hume, a master at Ampleforth who had known Hugh. He told me that he was an outstanding head of his house, was a dedicated Catholic and, with high intelligence and love of people, would have very likely become a priest. When I said "Perhaps your successor, Your Eminence?" he said "Perhaps. God's hand is unpredictable, but he would have been as outstanding after the War as he was in it."

Hugh's presence raised the spirits of No. 4 Troop, particularly mine, and when, at long last, we were called to hear Colonel Kim Finlay's orders I felt as I suppose soldiers from time immemorial must feel, dedicated, trained, shrived and confident. Crusaders must have felt like this.

Colonel Kim told us that next night we were to take part in what could be one of the key battles of the War. The Guards Armoured Division, the 7th and 11th Armoured Divisions were to take part in the first big armoured battle since the invasion. We were to travel all night over tracks laid down by others to Caen, to use the bridge captured by the Royal Ulster Rifles over the River Orne to hit the Germans at the hinge of the planned breakout. Kim saw this as a way in which his ideas of cavalry tanks, using the Sherman's speed, could surround and overcome the static enemy. To us young officers who had spent three years preparing for this moment it was inspiring.

The drive to Caen on tracks which were now deep in dust, requiring us to tie handkerchiefs over our faces to keep the dust out of our mouths, and the anxiety lest a breakdown could result in missing "Goodwood" – the name of the battle to come – made the night drive unpleasant, but over it all, for all of us, was the feeling, "Will we be able to do what the whole free world expects of us?"

We came to the bridge just before dawn broke. As we came into our positions on a hill overlooking this single fragile Bailey bridge, which was to take nearly 2,000 tanks over it to break the Normandy stalemate, a roar in the sky showed us the first of 1,000 bombers which were to open a way forward for us. It was an unforgettable sight. They were quite low and we could see the bombs falling. The whole corridor which was blown for us was erupting; for 10 miles there seemed no chance of anyone surviving this lane of destruction. However, quite steady anti-aircraft fire was hitting the RAF bombers and we watched the crippled aircraft crews parachuting down to what was bound to be a hostile reception. There were many others which crashed, without any sight of the crew baling out. The 11th Armoured Division started to pour across the bridge and fan out into the open flat country which stretched east from Caen. The dust and smoke raised by the 1,000 bombers created a pall over the battlefield, but there seemed no enemy response, and the 200 tanks of the leading Brigade seemed to us to be "swanning", the word for free movement which we used then. The 11th tanks were followed by what seemed an endless procession of scout cars, tracked ambulances, even 3-ton trucks. At last the flow stopped and we awaited the order to advance to our first battle. The minutes passed, then we officers were called to our "O" Group, where our Colonel told us that the 11th had been badly held up, that there was a serious danger of us all getting mixed up together, and that our debouchment over the bridge was delayed for an hour. The one hour became two. By now old soldiers like Corporal James Baron had got a brew-up going for breakfast and once again the Guards Armoured Division seemed set for an "in waiting" role. Kim Finlay's advice to us was to the effect that radio was impossible because there were so many sets tuned to frequencies close to ours that there was no chance of "A" set communication and only a slim hope of "B" set. He said that there had been a message that the village of Cagny, 5 miles ahead on a rise, was defended and that the Irish Guards, when released for action, would be directed onto it. Very helpfully, he told us that a line of electricity pylons, running at an angle across the plain, passed close to Cagny, so that, if we were in map-reading doubt, simply following the pylons would get us to Cagny. *At last* the order to move. Over the bridge we went, the Shermans running perfectly. No. 4 Troop was off to victory at last! I took position as planned and, leading my foursome, went straight into a greensward which turned out to be a deep bog, impossible to see, and famous, as I learned later, for sinking cavalry in a medieval attack by the Huns on Caen. I managed to direct Troop Sergeant Evans to go on with our Firefly 17-pounder tank, but the faithful Sergeant Harbinson, in my fourth tank, I kept to help get us out of the quagmire. After what seemed hours, but was probably half-an-hour, a combination of good driving by James Baron and a steel towrope from Harbinson got my tank (named Ballyraggett) out of the bog. It seemed that my first live action was to resemble my first railway-station exercise.

By now the Squadron was far ahead and fragments of speech on my radio conveyed that the enemy was by no means obliterated. Then we came on the tanks of 11th Armoured Division, dozens of them, mostly on fire, with crews tending to their mates who had managed to get out of their burning tanks. A pitiful sight. There was nothing we could do for them and we could see that the tracked ambulances which had seemed so unnecessary in the morning were now saving lives.

Pressing James Baron on to top speed, with Sergeant Harbinson following 200 yards or so behind, and taking the pylons as my guide, I found the Squadron. It was halted to the west of Cagny and Tony Dorman, "Dipper", was on his feet, evidently wounded, but gesticulating wildly forward. Since the whole strategy of our leftwards attack on Cagny had been to take it by the speed and dash which we had learned on Salisbury Plain and the Yorkshire Wolds, I took it that Dipper was urging us on and we charged up a cornfield, towards a hedge at the top of the rise, and turned the corner into a lane which ran along the hedge. To our right was another hedge at right-angles to the first. When we swung round into the lane it was horror personified. There 300 yards ahead was a Tiger Royal; behind it and to my right were three other Tigers in support.

This is the moment to describe why the Tiger Royal was such a dreadful enemy. The Germans had gone for quality, not quantity, in their tank production. They realized that the US output of tanks would numerically swamp them. So they designed a tank with superior armour, with the famous 88mm anti-aircraft gun of 20 foot in length and the result was a tank which was as close to perfection as any produced in the War.

We had been warned of the existence of such a monster. Corporal Baron and I had discussed it. We had rather light-heartedly concluded that, if confronted by a Tiger Royal, there was only one thing to do and that was to use the naval tactic of ramming, which my Portora hero had demonstrated. Baron agreed that it would be right to use the Sherman's speed to counteract the rather slow traverse of the Tiger Royal's 88mm gun turret. We concluded that, mad though it seemed, the only hope in a 75mm Sherman was to ram. When the Tiger Royal came in view its turret was at 90° from us, with the gun towards the 2nd Battalion tanks at the bottom of the rise where I had seen Dipper. We had an HE round in our gun, as Albert Scholes, my gunner and I had earlier concluded that this would be more useful than the ineffective allegedly armour-piercing round which was the alternative. This was a lucky decision because, as Corporal Baron was accelerating towards the Tiger Royal, Guardsman Scholes from 50 yards was able to put a high-explosive shell onto the Tiger's turret. The effect of such an explosion on a crew confined in a small space is quite devastating and as we raced towards it, the Commander's head emerged from the turret. He must have been totally bemused by what was happening to his impregnable monster. Here he was, supported by three other Tigers, of almost equal impregnability armour-wise, having used his superb long-range 88mm gun to knock out the tanks in the valley, now dependent on the slow speed of his turret traverse to shoot at an enemy by now only yards from him. The Sherman crashed into the left rear of the Tiger. The German tank crew started to evacuate; the three supporting Tigers were clearly aiming at us. I ordered "Bail Out". The Germans and ourselves were trapped in the little space between the two tanks. At this moment Sergeant Harbinson emerged from the hedge corner and with incredible bravery took on the three supporting Tigers. "Run, sir, run," cried Corporal Baron, so I led my crew along the hedge, turned the corner into the tall cornfield and we made a sort of nest there. Passing Sergeant Harbinson's tank, we saw it had been hit at close range by the Tigers and we concluded that all five crew must be dead. While we were discussing this, a figure suddenly jumped into the "nest". It was Guardsman Agnew, our front gunner, who had been trapped by the German gun above his escape hatch. When I ordered "Bail Out" he found himself having to crawl along the belly of the Sherman in a lengthy escape procedure. When he got out of the turret he glimpsed a number of men running to his right along the hedge, so he followed and jumped into a ditch where they were sheltering. They were the Tiger Royal's crew; he gave them a hasty salute and ran the other way, by luck finding us.

My feelings at this our first action were certainly not of triumph that we had at least decommissioned the only Tiger Royal seen on the Western Front. They were more that it was a job only half-done, and, having ordered Corporal Baron and the three Guardsmen to stay where they were, I ran through the cornfield towards some woods at the bottom of the rise, about 400 yards away. As I got closer I found there was a Firefly on its own, with apparently no one in it. I climbed on the turret and looked in. There was the body of Sergeant Workman, headless, spreadeagled over the gun, with the gunner and wireless operator in a state of shock. Obviously a shot from the Tiger Royal had been high and had taken off Workman's head shortly before we had come on it, at right-angles to us. The crew helped me to get the body out and we hurriedly cleaned up the gun-sights and periscopes. There was no hesitation when I ordered the driver to advance over the corn-field to the tall hedge which had been on our right when we turned into the lane and saw the Tiger Royal reversing into the lane, its turret at right-angles to us fortunately.

By easing the Firefly gently into the tall hedge we were able to see the three ordinary Tigers, still in the same positions, and the Tiger Royal and Ballyraggett locked together. Our first shot was at the Tiger Royal, but it was high; the gunner was shaking. His next one hit the Tiger Royal and we got another shot into Ballyraggett, so that it could not be towed, or driven away, by the enemy. The guns of the three Tigers were now pointing towards us, so we went 100 feet further along the hedge and pushed into it again until we could see the enemy. By now they were pointing to their front and we were able to get away four rounds, two of which were hits. Once again at least one of the Tigers was traversing towards us, so we withdrew towards the lane, intending to try the same tactic again. By now we were close to the blazing Sherman and to my joy, three scarecrows, on fire, their clothes burning and long strips of skin hanging from their bare arms, emerged from the ditch. It was Sergeant Harbinson, with his two turret-crew members. We got them onto the flat deck of the Sherman and at full speed headed across the cornfield again, through the wood, and found the Regimental Aid post and our Doctor Ripman, with his team. They dealt with the three casualties, and got Pat Harbinson away that night to the famous burns hospital at Lingfield where Mr McIndoe, the plastic surgeon, operated. Harbinson lived for nearly two weeks, was able to talk to his mother and sister, but as more than 50% of his body was deeply burned he died, as did so many others who experienced the Sherman's flammability. We cooked on a stove known as the "Tommy Cooker". The Germans made this grim joke about the Sherman – they called it the "Tommy-Cooker".

By now the 3rd Battalion had arrived at Cagny. There were dozens, indeed hundreds of tanks, Cromwells (the British fast tank), Churchills (the heavier armoured but slower British tank), and the ubiquitous Shermans all over the battlefield, some still burning, others blackened hulks. The great naval-type sweep across the only flat plain in Normandy had failed in its object of piercing a possibly mortal salient in the German front. It was now an infantry battle, in our case, to secure Cagny, and this our 3rd Battalion did that night.

It had been a salutary lesson to all of us who had dreamed of the massed "cavalry" sweeping the enemy from our path. Failure to achieve, in full, a military objective is not necessarily disastrous. Indeed, looking back, particularly at the Arnhem operation, the "Bridge Too Far", it seemed a failure, because the grand plan was not achieved. But war is about combat and casualties. Operations such as "Goodwood" did thrust a salient into the German front. It resulted in the rushing of German armour from the US front at Mortain to hold the salient at Caen. It led to heavy losses of men and material which could not be afforded by the enemy. The further small-scale field-by-field fighting led to the Mortain breakthrough and the closure of the Falaise Gap, resulting in the capture of German soldiers and armament, including tanks, totalling 400,000 men.

Nearly 50 years later, as a result of the efforts of the Irish Guards, historian/archivist Major Tony Brady and I travelled to Frankfurt to meet General Von Rosen, a retired NATO chief, who had been a young officer in the 204th Heavy Tank Battalion of the Reichwehr. He had fought in Russia, where the Tiger Royal had first been used, and told me this story.

His Battalion had been in reserve but German intelligence had deduced that a massive British breakout from Caen was imminent, so the 204th Battalion was sent to the ridge which ran from Cagny northwest towards Caen. The 1000-bomber raid hit them and some of the Tigers were blown upside-down by the heavy bombs. He described one occasion when, after the raid, he took for granted that a Tiger upside-down in a huge bomb-crater was destroyed, but he heard calling from inside it and managed to extract the crew, who were only shaken, and by using towropes they righted the Tiger and made it fit for action.

The Tiger Royal had just been delivered and he was delighted to welcome it and looked forward to commanding it. To the fury of the 204th Battalion, whose officers were all Prussian "Vons", an SS Officer was sent to command it. Remember it was at about this time that Von Stauffenberg and other aristocratic German officers tried to assassinate Hitler. Von Rosen believed that giving command of the great tank to a loyal Nazi was the High Command's way of warning the "snobs" that they were under observation. The SS Officer was not seen again in 204 after the ramming.

Von Rosen told me that after the War he had been invited on many occasions to conduct battlefield tours to enable bodies such as the British Staff College to study "Goodwood" from the German side. When the tours reached Cagny he would recall that his Commander, Major Von Luck, saw an 88mm anti-aircraft battery of half-a-dozen guns, doing nothing as the flood of British tanks passed in the valley below them. The gunners were in slit trenches. Von Luck ordered the officer to depress the guns and shoot the tanks. When he answered "I am an Anti-Aircraft officer, not an Anti-Tank officer," Von Luck pulled out his pistol, pressed it into the reluctant gunner's neck and said, "You will be neither if you don't depress your guns and fire on the British."

Van Rosen said that for years he had claimed that the Irish Guards at Cagny had a secret weapon, because one of his tanks, at least a mile away, was destroyed by a single shot. It was only when he met a survivor of the anti-aircraft battery that he learned that the shot had come from them. Whether in reprisal for the officer's humiliation in front of his men or from a genuine failure to identify the difference between a Tiger and a Sherman will never be known.

Ballyraggett and the Tiger Royal were still there a year later, locked together. Sadly no one thought to photograph the sight, though Tony Brady has spent years looking and has an RAF photograph which shows a large "blob", but which does not give a picture when enlarged. Recently, however, a German photograph has been found.

The day ended for us with withdrawal to Colombelles, the industrial estate on the edge of Caen. We were still in Sergeant Workman's Firefly, its turret still covered in blood, now sticky and smelling, and we set to work with hot water and rags to clean it. During the night as we lay in our "grave" beneath the tank, a little Breton spaniel crawled in with us, absolutely terrified by the bombing and shelling which had taken place. I christened her Colombelles and she stayed with me, riding on the tank of my soldier-servant's motorcycle, which she loved, or in a lorry. It was always a delight to see her at the end of a period of fighting. The motorcycle was made for me by Lieutenant Billy Clark of Upperlands, a mechanical genius who constructed it out of the wrecks of bombed or shot-up Nortons which were to be found easily on the battlefields and roads of Normandy.

The day after the Tiger Royal battle John Madden came to see me with the remains of No. 4 Troop; he told me that Corporal James Baron was being recommended for the immediate award of the Military Medal and me for the Military Cross. The bad news was that we were both being "left out of battle", L.O.B. as it was called, for a period. We were both upset at this, but more probably in shock, as it is called now. In fact, returning to the rear, to the Forward Delivery Squadron, was very useful, since it was the job of the F.D.S. to have tanks and crews ready to deliver replacements for tanks knocked out or broken down. We were able to identify a fine new Ballyraggett and returned to the Squadron in it.

Now the thrust of the battle altered. The Guards Armoured Division moved northwards to the hilly ground and small fields near Estry, overlooked by a high hill called St Martin des Besases, which had been captured in a particularly bloody and difficult battle by the 6th Guards Tank Brigade, in Churchill tanks. Fellow Troop Leaders in this Brigade had been stationed at Warminster two years earlier and among them were William Whitelaw and Robert Runcie, with both of whom, one Deputy Prime Minster to Mrs Thatcher, the other Archbishop of Canterbury, I was able to reminisce many years later.

Now we had infantry in the shape of the 5th Coldstream, wonderful soldiers but not Micks. It was puzzling to us all that the Division did not put Grenadier tanks with Grenadier infantry, Coldstream tanks with Coldstream infantry, Irish Guards tanks with Irish Guards infantry. The ways of the Army are sometimes hard to understand and it was not until we fought our way to Douai, weeks later, that we came together as the Irish Guards Group, commanded by Colonel Joe Vandeleur.

Now began the steady war of attrition which was the very reverse of the more glamorous "sweeps" which we had expected. Each time a tank pushed through a Norman hedge, and, because of the bank, lifted its front so that its bottom was exposed, there was a strong danger that the weak bottom armour could be penetrated by quite a small anti-tank weapon or a Panzerfaust, which was the German equivalent of the PIAT. Subsequent evacuation because of the immediate fire in the Sherman resulted in many casualties, so officers did their best to reconnoitre before exposing their tanks.

Hugh Dormer DSO was one of them. I had seen him earlier on the day of his death, in fact got into his turret to discuss the plan for our "laager", the bringing together of the Squadron at night. His turret was full of flowers, which he had picked in an interval in the day's fighting. It was typical of this great man that he was civilized enough to want to bring some beauty into the crudity of our lives then. It was getting dark. I went to back to No. 4 Troop and led my tanks to the laager. There was a loud explosion in the adjoining field, followed by the typical exploding holocaust of a burning Sherman. Next morning we found Hugh, shot dead on the ground nearby, a field's length ahead of his tank. Clearly he had been reconnoitring on foot to test for German presence to try to avoid the all too frequent ambush into which his men might be lured. His death caused great sorrow throughout the Battalion, nowhere more than in No. 4 Troop, where tears were shed. He had picked them, trained them, loved them. Had always joined us when he could for the evening brew-up. It had always been a strength to me, his inadequate successor, that he was so totally supportive. I had lost an admired friend and a much-needed philosopher.

Almost every day brought casualties. We moved to La Maviendière, a similar area of small fields, hedges and banks. The 5th Coldstream lost five Commanding Officers during this phase, though one of them, believed to be dying, eventually recovered and, years later, I was to have much to do with Michael Adeane, the Queen's Private Secretary.

The L.O.B. system resulted in No. 4 Troop being behind the front line when an urgent call came for ammunition and fuel for No. 2 Squadron which had fought its way to the top of a ridge overlooking an important road used by the Germans. We set off, two tanks in front of four 3-ton trucks containing the fuel and ammunition, and two tanks behind. A Military Policeman warned me that a German mobile anti-tank gun positioned on a hill still held by the enemy had fired accurately at vehicles attempting to cross the valley and climb the ridge. Of course the trucks had to use the road which meandered through the valley and up the hill. I warned the truck drivers of the risk – the greater because of their loads – and told them that we would cover them as best we could, but that their best hope was to put their foot down and drive like hell, one at a time. They managed to beat the Germans every time and it was with some complacency that I delivered the loads to the Squadron. It was getting dark and I wanted to see the Infantry Commander, Major "Feathers" Steuart-Fother-Ingham, commanding a Company of Welsh Guards, sent in to reinforce the 5th Coldstream, which had suffered so many losses. I got out of my tank to search the hedgerows where I knew "Feathers" had his Command dugout and, with unforgivable carelessness, took my shining map-case in my hand. After a few yards there was a loud "crump" and the unmistakable noise of six Nebelwerfer shells dropping. The Nebelwerfer was a particularly horrible German weapon, with six barrels fired simultaneously and very accurately. Clearly a lookout had seen someone with a map-case (normally an officer) and thus a valuable target. I hurled myself into a small depression in the field and, miraculously, although covered with earth, I was not hit. I started to make a run for it. At once the six shells came at me again. Once more they were all around me. My instinct was to try again for the "safety" of Feathers' dugout, but prudence dictated that I wait for darkness, so I lay there praying hard and hoping that the Nebelwerfer team would think me dead. I know that "foxhole" conversions are highly suspect, but when yet another salvo with its eerie whistle approached I promised the Almighty that, if spared, I would serve Him better than I had done so far. By now it was dark and I ran unscathed to the dugout where I found a furious Feathers who had looked out earlier and seen this "bloody fool with a map-case" drawing down fire on *his* position. A swig or two from my hip-flask soon got him into his normal good humour, but it was evident that it would be mad to attempt to return that night, so No. 4 Troop took what cover it could, dug its trench-bed and awaited the dawn, at which time tank crews climb in and await attack. This dawn brought the Nebelwerfer again and Sergeant Jennings, one of Tinker Taylor's No. 3 Troop, was killed. Tinker set off to clear the ridge of Germans, now clearly reinforced. He had a hard battle, losing many of his supporting infantry, but none of his tanks. It was a thoroughly professional and effective action and played a part in the MC which he was deservedly awarded. He has since the War kept up with members of his old Troop, and they with him, and I try to do the same for my old soldiers of No. 4 Troop. There is no doubt that No. 2 Squadron of the Second Micks is in a class of its own. Every year the Dublin, Belfast and Liverpool Annual Dinners have more old comrades from No. 2 Squadron than any other part of the Regiment. Having taken this hill, we were directed to the next one. Here there had been an earlier troop attack by four Royal Armoured Corps

Shermans. It was a macabre sight. All four were in a perfect row and, when we had fought our way to the top of the hill, we were able to have a look at the Shermans. All four must have been hit simultaneously and suffered the flash fires which we dreaded. There were five neat dwarfs, shrivelled men, burned where they sat on their tank seats. At least death must have been quick for them.

During that day's battle another macabre occurrence sticks in my mind. My close friend Packy McCorkell's troop was fighting up the next hill in front of my troop and the Nebelwerfers were putting their six close shells all around his tanks, when suddenly we saw a body, arms outstretched, rising from his tank, which had erupted. A mortar shell had fallen through the Commander's hatch, exploded in the turret, killing all in it and resulting in poor Packy's body being thrown high in the air.

By now one was getting the understandable dread that one's luck could not go on. Of the thirty-five officers of the 2nd Battalion over half had already been lost and the odds for survival of the rest were even money and reducing. After days of fighting – little battles compared to Goodwood – but important in grinding down the enemy, we were delighted, Dipper, Tinker, the Toddler (Hugh McDermott) and I, to hear John Madden on the "A" set calling us to an "O" Group in a lull in the fighting. I remember that I had captured a German officer's sleeping-bag, which I had laid out on the flat engine-cover of Ballyraggett. When Corporal Baron saw this he said, "Sir, you must be mad. I've always told you you were mad, but sleeping there will kill you." As always, I did as he said and spent the night under the tank. In the morning a few shattered strips of cloth were all that were left of the sleeping-bag.

To return to the story, the Troop leaders, Dipper, Tinker, Toddler and I got out of our tanks and very carefully ducked among the hedges and ditches to reach our Squadron Leader, who we had not seen for several days. Corporal Lees, John's driver, had brewed up and there were six mugs on the back of his Sherman when John Madden welcomed us with John Dupree. We started a happy chat about what was going on when John said, "*Go, Go*. I am not happy about this. We may be under observation." We put down our mugs and rather bolshily walked away; the scream of Nebelwerfer bombs filled the air and in a split second the salvo struck where we had all been gathered. John Madden was lying there, his left leg shattered. It was amputated later, and so the Jumper had to face a lifetime deprived of the mobility which was so precious to him. He never complained and Nita was a wonderful companion. He was able to do remarkable things, such as sailing a little boat, a Snipe, on Lough Erne. The way in which, without his artificial leg, he managed to manoeuvre himself and the boat, without sinking it, or inconveniencing his crew-member, was remarkable to behold. He was able to drive a car and on a post-war tour of the place where he lost his leg, he took several of us, and Nita, across country away from roads and even lanes. He truly had "an eye for country".

The sudden instinct which caused him to send away his officers just as we had arrived demonstrated, I contend, the difference between the professional soldier and us amateurs, just as James Baron's strong advice to me over the sleeping-bag showed how he, a regular pre-war soldier, had the same instinctive quality.

Major Edward Tyler replaced John Madden and, after our contact at Sandhurst and later in the Battalion, I was very happy to see him with No. 2 Squadron. Eddie's style was quite unlike John's. He was not as blunt or decisive, but he had that other gift of leadership of making his subordinates believe that they had themselves thought of an idea or plan. Eddie had already won an MC as 2nd-in-Command of No. 1 Squadron and he was to earn a Bar later.

Field Marshal Montgomery decided to hold an investiture and those in the Guards Armoured Division gathered in a field behind the line. Some years later, dressed in the uniform of a District Inspector of the Royal Ulster Constabulary, I met him at a Royal Warwickshire Regiment ceremony at Ballykinlar. The RUC Officers' uniform resembled that of the Rifle Brigade and as a District Inspector, I had a Major's crown on my shoulder. Monty came up to me and asked what a Rifle Brigade Officer was doing there. He was discomfited when I explained that he had mistaken my uniform. "Well," said he, "you have the Military Crawse [his pronunciation]. Where did you get that?" "In Normandy, Sir, from you." "Oh, I don't remember that. Remind me of the occasion." "In a field behind the lines when a number of us from the Guards Armoured Division were decorated." Monty, "What did I say to you?" Me, by now rather irritated by the cross-examination: "You told us that the War would be over by Christmas." Monty: "Can't remember saying that. Anything else you remember of the occasion?" Me: "Yes, an Auster [reconnaissance plane] kept buzzing round over our heads, interrupting you; you ordered your C.R.A. [Commander Royal Artillery] 'Shoot it down!'" Pause: "Did he, did he?" My intended joking reminiscence fell on stony ground and he moved off.

He was a remarkable man, a total egotist, cunning and professional, with a single-minded determination to succeed, but never, if he could possibly help it, taking more risks than he judged wise in relation to his own career. The contrast between him and our "own" Field Marshal Earl Alexander could not have been greater. Alex, the youngest ever Commanding Officer of an Irish Guards Battalion, in France in the Great War, was a superb athlete and Army champion in the mile. Such charm had he that he was able to co-ordinate armies of different countries, all with different objectives, without compromising the objective. It was he who defeated Rommel in North Africa and, with General Mark Clark of the US, invaded Sicily and Italy, keeping the vast army of the enemy engaged at a time when Russia needed every possible distraction of German forces.

The Battle of Normandy was coming to an end. The US Army breakthrough at Mortain had enabled General Patton, their colourful commander, to sweep over the Seine, and the road to Paris seemed clear. We found ourselves on the tank transporter being ferried across the Seine and then charging through the old First-War battlefields of Arras, Cambrai and Armentières, thinking wryly of the ghosts of our forebears who had died in France for possession of these small towns.

By now the demand to have us linked up with our Third Battalion had resulted in General Alan Adair, the GOC of the Guards Armoured Division, a Ballymena man whose family agent was to be my future father-in-law, George Caruth, agreeing, and so we formed the Irish Guards Group.

Our first action together was the capture of Douai in north-west France. We had been driving through French villages with the populace cheering and the Resistance doing their best to demonstrate their effectiveness against the Germans. This was frequently the cause of pushing shaven-headed Frenchwomen to the front of the crowd, pinioned by men whom we suspected of having done a bit of collaborating themselves. We became wary of pleas to divert to places in which it was claimed that we could capture enemy troops and material pinned down by the gallant Resistance. These claims usually produced a few frightened Russians or Poles, forced by the Germans to join up for menial tasks.

As Douai approached the excitement of the crowds increased. We were aware that it was at the English College in Douai that the 18th Century English priests had been trained to return to the Reformed England, usually to face the rack, the priest's hole or the gallows. The welcome we had had en route was nothing to what we were given in Douai. The crowds were ecstatic and wanted to show their appreciation by giving us wine saved up "*pour le jour de la liberation*". Babies had to be kissed and, most significantly, the early crop of plums had to be offered. They were not fully ripe and we were to pay the penalty. In all this hilarity there was a ghostly reminder that the Germans were not beaten. A troop of SS Panzer tanks, supported by infantry retreating from the coast, took on Lieutenant John Swann's troop which had been directed to protect the western side of Douai. There was a fierce but brief battle, in which the Wehrmacht was driven off, but not before Swann and his crew were hit and burned. Yet another outstanding officer and crew lost.

The result of the Irish Guards Group formation was that Colonel J.O.E.

Vandeleur, the senior, was now joined by his nephew Colonel Giles Vandeleur, who had replaced Colonel Kim Finlay. Relations between these two men were of the closest and both Battalions looked forward to even greater Irish Guards successes. They discovered a brilliant and beautiful young lady, Mademoiselle Nicole Courtille, whose English was impeccable and who was the interpreter for the formal proceedings with the Douai Mayor and Council that night. Fifty years later she was to play the key role in the Irish Guards reunion with Douai.

The night was short, as during it we were ordered by our Corps Commander, Lieutenant General Sir Brian Horrocks, to move to Lille, from where we were to capture Brussels. Euphoric as all the celebrations of liberation had been, it was a sobering thought that next day we were to advance over 100 miles and capture one of Europe's great cities. What was left of the night was not only spent in contemplation of this task ahead but dealing with the effects of unripe plums, on top of large quantities of wine.

Before dawn on 3 September 1944 the whole of the Guards Armoured Division was on the move, on two routes to Brussels. The Household Cavalry – the Life Guards and the Blues – in their tiny scout cars were in front, giving us warning of German concentrations on our route. The competition between the two routes to be first into Brussels was intense. By now wireless discipline was so much improved that we were able to hear at once of any hold-up. There were dozens of battles some quite fierce, others rather token resistance. The French "underground" were even more in evidence and now seemed more genuine, especially in routing us past enemy defences. The day wore on and the conviction that we could achieve the longest advance in a single day of the whole War filled our minds. As it became dusk we could see the outline of Brussels and the Palais de Justice on a hill, which the Germans had fired to prevent the documents which were stored there, and which would reveal war crimes, being captured.

We were there! The crowds now dwarfed anything we had seen on the way and the Municipality turned on the city's lights. "*La guerre est fini*" was the cry and it was almost possible to believe this. The Irish Guards Group was directed to a Flemish suburb east of the city called Auderghem. Here we were to position ourselves to fight off any attempt by the enemy to retake Brussels.

Again the people of Auderghem surrounded us all in a sea of happiness. An elderly lady, a Flamande pointed to the words "Irish Guards" on the shoulder of my battledress and, through another woman who spoke French, I heard that she had gone to get me a present. She returned with a copy of *Some Experiences of an Irish RM* and told me that this had been left behind in her parents' house in 1914 by a British officer billeted on them. I have the book still.

We were drawn up at the edge of a large area of allotments and, as always, stood to before dawn. I was able to make out movement on the far side of the allotments and warned my Troop to be ready to fire the Browning machine guns which were mounted on the turret and the co-driver's side of the hull. These guns had a high rate of fire, over 200 rounds a minute, and eight of them were devastating. As the light improved we could see German helmets in the woods and then a mass of soldiers debouching from the wood, over the allotments, about 300 yards away. I gave the order to fire and it was slaughter. Only when a few pathetic white handkerchiefs were waved from the ground was one able to order "Cease Fire". The many hundreds of German soldiers were what is known as Corps troops, clerks and non-combatants of all sorts, who had been collected by Nazi officers during the night and ordered at pistol-point to attack us. It was not a happy occasion and I often think of it.

Next day we learned that the whole champagne stock of the German Army was stored in railway tunnels under Brussels and we were at liberty to send a truck to draw whatever we wanted. I was in charge of our little Squadron Mess, so it fell to me to do this. A 15 cwt truck seemed appropriate and when I arrived at the Arches I was met by a German soldier, whose only concern was to get my signature for what we were taking. As far as the eye could see there were crates upon crates of Piper Heidseck. It looked as though the whole 1944 vintage was there. We took what the truck would hold and went back to Auderghem, where we started to distribute the bottles to the Squadron. Some were so enthused by this surfeit of champagne that (it is said, but I saw no evidence for it) tank gun ammunition racks were emptied and bottles of Piper Heidseck put in each shell rack. But it could not last and a rather unsuccessful attempt by Colonel Joe to repeat some of the achievements of his ancestors who had been heroes of the Battle of Waterloo was a serious failure; a larger German force fleeing across the battlefield knocked out two tanks and killed a number of Guardsmen.

After only two nights in Brussels we were off again, heading north for Holland. By now the champagne had lost its attraction and many a Guardsman was heard to say, "Give me a cuppa instead of that old fizzy stuff".

The first important objective was the Escaut Canal, a wide waterway running to the Scheldt and carrying freight in bulk. The canal marked the border between Belgium and Holland.

German resistance to our northward drive was hardening all the time. The War was by no means over and Irish Guards actions at Beeringen only succeeded in clearing the route after fierce fighting and losses of men and tanks. Beeringen was a coal-mining centre and the enemy made clever use of the mountains of coal to set up observation posts giving a view for miles around.

The Welsh Guards, whose tanks were Cromwells, the successor to the Covenanters and Crusaders, were now in front and making good progress. The tactic was that these fast, low-slung, highly manoeuvrable tanks would probe enemy positions, and if they seemed strong, bypass them, leaving it to their "heavy friends", which was the codeword used on the air to describe Shermans.

Late one evening after a day's fighting Eddie Tyler told me that the Welsh Guards were running short of petrol and ammunition, so would I please escort five lorries to them, 10 miles ahead at a village called Elst. The theory was that, if we drove fast, the German fire might not be too intensive and any roadblocks could probably be pushed aside. Off we went and what had promised to be a risky enterprise came off splendidly. We used the tactic of firing at points which *might* conceal enemy positions. Quite often this resulted in the hidden guns or tanks giving their positions away by returning fire or coming out of cover. It was dark when we reached Elst and I was given a warm welcome by the Welsh Guards C.O. Colonel Windsor-Lewis, as his tanks were seriously short of fuel and would have been unable to go far the next day.

We were preparing a meal prior to getting some sleep when I was sent for by the Colonel. He told me that Belgian resistance had given information that a large formation of enemy with tanks and anti-tank guns had been seen on the far side of Elst. Clearly a determined effort was to be made to halt the British advance. He really seemed to believe that the Shermans were more capable of taking on such a task than his Cromwells, so he ordered me to set off at dawn through the village and to engage the enemy on our own. His Battalion would follow my Troop, but on reaching the crossroads would turn left, hoping to bypass the enemy position.

It is part of the strength of the Guards system that orders are not questioned, but I felt that at least my own Battalion should know that the Welsh Guards were using an Irish Guards Troop, which had been sent on a defined replenishment mission, for a totally different purpose and I suggested to the Colonel that he should at least radio my Colonel to tell him of the plan. He was not pleased by this and said he might not be able to raise the Irish Guards, which were of course on a different frequency to his. I was to take it that if I heard no more I was to be on my start-line before dawn to set off when he ordered us to do so. We were on the start-line at the required time when a Welsh Guards officer climbed on Ballyraggett and told me that the attack had been called off and my Troop was to return at once to rejoin No. 2 Squadron. Some very relieved soldiers set off at speed southwards.

It seemed that Colonel Windsor-Lewis had spoken to Colonel Giles, who knew him well, and had made rather light of what No. 4 Troop was to do. He kept using the "heavy friends" phrase which alerted Giles to the suspicion that he wanted to use us to save casualties of his own. Colonel Giles, having consulted Eddie Tyler who was even more suspicious that "Jim Windsor-Lewis is chancing his arm", gave the order to return. Later it was indeed confirmed that a heavy well-armed ambush was in position. Four Shermans without cover from ground or air and unsupported by infantry or Cromwells would have been easy targets.

We were now within 20 miles of the Escaut Canal and the Irish Guards Group took over the lead, with No. 2 Squadron in the front. Our maps, which were pre-war, had not been marked with the forest of conifers which had been planted afterwards. They were now up to 12 feet tall and a network of "rides" ran in every direction. A young Belgian volunteered to stand on the back of Ballyraggett to guide me. By now, because of casualties, I was second-in-command to Major Eddie Tyler and was to lead and control half the Squadron on a mission to find a way through the new forest, which might with luck bring us to the Escaut. I put Charles Tottenham, a bright young officer, into the forest first, with the second troop following me. All went well to begin with. My guide was invaluable and it seemed too good to be true. Suddenly German armour and infantry were all around us. My brave young guide had to jump off, as bullets were flying, and we were lost, as was Charles Tottenham's Troop. By radioing him to fire Very light flares I was able to locate him and asked for the help of the Reconnaissance Troop, commanded by my friend Charles Warren. They were in Honey Tanks, very lightly armoured but extremely fast and manoeuvrable, and so small as to make a difficult target. Shells often passed through the light armour, emerging the far side, and quite a number of lucky soldiers had had this experience. We began to fight our way out of the forest and could see German anti-tank guns trained on the exits. A Honey raced out of cover so fast that the Germans could not get him; the commander was Sergeant Barnes and he drove at speed in the open, the German gun trying to alter position to aim at him. This exposed the flank of the gun and its crew and a high explosive shot from my gun knocked them out. The Honey, having done this brave decoy act, ran into a bog, like the one I had encountered near Cagny. It was totally stuck, so I ordered Barnes and his crew to run for it while we gave them covering fire. They all got away. In the meantime Charles Tottenham was dealing with larger numbers of enemy most successfully, but we were now far ahead of our infantry, in the unmapped forest, and we withdrew, picking up my brave Belgian guide.

Whilst we were doing this – it was now late afternoon – Charles Tottenham came across a more substantial road than the rides we had been using; this road and a railway track beside it seemed to him to be running in the direction of De Groot Barrier where there was a bridge over the Escaut. On hearing this Colonel Joe sent armoured cars to find out where the new road (like the forest, unmarked on our maps) ran. The Household Cavalry reported that indeed the road did run to the village and the bridge was intact, though heavily guarded by a number of 88mm guns, some actually positioned on the bridge itself. By now a typical Vandeleur action was in being. A Troop commanded by Lieutenant Duncan Lampard, an Irish Guards Platoon commanded by Lieutenant John Stanley-Clarke and an Engineer team were being hurried to the village along the new road. There appeared to be none of the scattered enemy left who Tottenham, Barnes and I had been fighting. The inference was that the Germans were withdrawing over the Escaut Bridge and that it was wired up with explosive to be blown when all the troops, tanks and guns south of the Escaut Canal had got away. Speed, timing and surprise were the essential elements in the "Joe's Bridge" plan. As it was getting dark Colonel Joe's little force was in hiding close to the bridge when he decided that the moment had come. Lampard's Troop, closely supported by the Irish Guards foot-soldiers, broke cover, raced through the little village and turned right towards the bridge. The 88mm guns both on the bridge and north of it got some hasty shots off, but Lampard's men were over and taking on the enemy on the far side. Now it was the turn of the Royal Engineers and their officer, Captain Joe Hutton, who climbed the steel girders searching for the central wires which, at the depression of a plunger, would blow the Escaut bridge high in the air, taking with it the men, guns, tanks and Engineers. He found many wires running under the bridge and cut them; detonators in the piers were also removed. By now a full-scale battle to retake the bridge was being launched by the enemy and the Irish Guards, reinforced as the rest of the Battalion hurried to the scene, held on grimly. As the minutes passed, the odds against the bridge being blown up lengthened and Captain Joe Hutton began to breathe more easily. At last it became clear that this daring exploit had succeeded. The delight at the capture of this precious bridge, which was to be the key to the Arnhem operation, was being conveyed to the Irish Guards from Montgomery downwards.

All the other bridges over the Escaut had now been destroyed and we stood to before dawn in the confident anticipation that enemy still south of the bridge must make a determined effort to take it back. Sure enough at first light many enemy tanks were seen moving towards the village; gun battles between the Shermans of the Irish Guards and German Panthers and mobile anti-tank guns were in full swing. Our Adjutant, the greatly-loved David Peel, realizing that a tank was without its Commander, got into it and took it into action. Sadly the tank was hit and all the crew, including

David Peel, were killed. It was a violent enough battle, but without supporting infantry, air cover or back-up artillery, the Germans had little chance of repeating the Irish Guards coup of the previous night and what was left of them retreated, leaving numerous brewed-up armoured vehicles.

Now the spotlight turned to the north and the tiny bridgehead which had been captured the previous night had to be expanded not only to make it more difficult for an enemy counter-attack to capture the bridge, but also to ensure that concentration of artillery did not succeed belatedly in destroying it. Barrage balloons were soon protecting our prize from air attack and fierce fighting took place, which pushed the Germans further and further back, creating a bridgehead which was deemed adequate. It was now that we became aware of a formidable weapon, the rocket-firing Typhoon. This aircraft, evolved from the Spitfire, had been equipped with ten rockets. A rocket's trajectory is quite flat, unlike a bullet fired from a gun. Thus a diving Typhoon pilot could aim at a ground target, release one of his rockets which, under its own propulsion, would hit the target aimed at. This sounds easy but there was a big snag. To identify his target, to line up his aircraft so that it was flying/diving directly at it, was to present the enemy with a superb opportunity to shoot down the Typhoon. The pilot had to be very brave and determined to fly to within a few hundred yards of the targets, where he could expect a torrent of fire from ground troops who were shooting for their lives. Now we saw this new weapon in action. There was a tall warehouse in De Groot Barrier which gave a view for miles around. Each time a German field-gun opened up, a Typhoon from the "Taxi-Rank" would heel over, dive on the gun and destroy it and the gunners. It was by no means one-way; several Typhoons were hit and the pilot had little or no chance of bailing out, because of the low-level flying required.

A big conference was called by Sir Brian Horrocks, our Corps Commander, to be held in a cinema in the village. By now I was a Captain, so was senior enough to be present. As many saw on television after the War, Brian Horrocks was a natural actor. His stage presence was drama personified. On stage with an enormous covered map behind him he started to speak: "Gentlemen, how would you like to have this all finished by Christmas?" The cheering from his audience gave him his answer. Slowly he pulled up the cover of his great map; first, the battle for Valkenswaard, 20 miles north of the Escaut, then one after another, five in all, bridges across rivers culminating in the two bridges over the Rhine which divides in two entering Holland, the bridges of Nijmegen and Arnhem. As this fascinating story unfolded, in a prodigious feat of memory, he described how three Airborne Divisions, the American 82nd and 101st Airborne, and the British Parachute Division would be dropped simultaneously on the

Grave, Nijmegen and Arnhem bridges. Each of the five bridges had its own plan of attack, to take the bridge intact if possible, but to have enough bridge-building capacity to repair or replace damaged or destroyed ones. It was the most inspiring address I had ever heard and when it was ending he strode to the edge of the cinema platform. "Now you must be wondering who is going to have the honour of leading this great dash which may end the War". Pause . . . "THE IRISH GUARDS". A voice, mine, was heard "Oh, my God, not again!" He told me after the War that he had heard me, but said it had not annoyed him. He knew the Irish Guards would take the lead superbly. As all who read or saw *A Bridge Too Far* will recall, his great worry was that German tank reserves might be located somewhere on the route and that the final bridge at Arnhem might not be captured, or if captured, not held for the six days which was the planned time limit. Several days passed as hundreds of guns, some of very heavy calibre indeed, arrived around us at De Groot Barrier. All our vehicles were overhauled, guns polished, maps studied and letters written; the build-up of tension was close to that we had experienced before D-Day.

If all went to plan, the British Army would debouch over the Arnhem Bridge towards the great plains stretching east from Apledoorn right into Germany. We would be across the Rhine, with no serious barrier to prevent us from the capture of Berlin, ahead of the Russians, who were now, after the heroic stand at Stalingrad, beginning the push which was, in the end, to get them to Berlin before us.

On Sunday we celebrated Mass and at midday the guns opened up. The noise was terrifying and poor little Colombelles, who had survived so much since Caen, slipped out of my trench and ran away. No one ever saw her again. It was not a good omen, but I hoped that Guardsman Clarke, my soldier-servant, still with Billy Clark's motorcycle, would find her. No. 1 Squadron was to lead the Battalion and all sixty tanks rolled forward over the Escaut Canal. The barrage was now lifting towards the extreme range of even the heaviest guns, but the reassuring sight of the Typhoon "Taxi-Rank" could be seen high above us. As so often, the start of the battle was smooth and No. 1 Squadron's twenty tanks were over the bridge, and on the raised road running straight towards Valkenswaard. There was a hump in the middle of the bridge and I was on it, held up by the line of No. 1 Squadron Shermans in front of me. Suddenly a tank erupted in flames, then another, and another, and another. Burning men tumbled out of the tank trapdoors, seldom the full crew of five. I counted nine burning tanks in front of us. There was nothing we could do. We were virtually nose-to-tail and could not see from where this lethal fire was coming. Then the Typhoons came in, again and again, the rockets streaking in the flat trajectory we had already seen, stationary as they left the Typhoon wing and then accelerating with flame belching from their tail, straight at the chosen target, while the pilots, rockets away, hurled their Typhoons around the sky to evade anti-aircraft fire. Several failed to get away and crashed in flames. I saw no pilot eject. Now the surviving tanks threaded past the nine wrecks and the 3rd Battalion Infantry, sweeping the ground on each side of us, kept flushing out hundreds of Germans from their trenches and dugouts. Their faces were deadly pale, with little flecks of blood. I often noticed this effect of continuous heavy shelling. We could now see the destroyed tanks and guns, victims of the gallant Typhoon attacks, and the pace of advance quickened; by evening we were in Valkenswaard, but, alas, this time the bridge was blown and trucks full of the parts of the Meccano-like Bailey bridge were hustled past us as we took up positions in the captured town. News of the 101st and 82nd American Divisions and the British Parachute Divisions was awaited anxiously, but now the first inkling of what was going on behind us reached the Battalions. Supplies for the whole Army were still having to be trucked from Normandy, nearly 600 miles away. An unexpected enemy benefit of Hitler's delusion that the "real" invasion would take place directly across the Channel was that many divisions of well-armed Germans, who had not been subjected to the horrors of Normandy, were now able to be directed to cutting our over-extended supply line, mostly dependent on single roads. When these were cut, not only were badly-needed supplies not available, but planning for such a massive operation as we had embarked on was made almost impossible. Furthermore, troops who should have been fighting at the front now had to be sent back along the supply-route, creating more chaos and delay, as serious pitched battles had to be fought against determined, well-armed Germans eager to get home to the Fatherland.

Hard work all night had the Bailey bridge up and operative early next day and we pressed on to S'Hertogenbosh and Grave, where the 82nd Airborne had achieved complete success. We had had no contact with US Airborne troops until then, indeed little with any Americans. These soldiers created a great impression. They were tall, fit, well turned out, extremely friendly and obviously interested in the famous Guards. Many of them had Irish ancestors and were astonished to meet the Irish Guards. They found it confusing that so many of us were Irish Catholics and from Eire, as they had supposed that De Valera's neutrality would have prevented his people from joining the British Army. The days passed with progress being made, but not as fast as we had hoped. Disturbing reports reached us from Dutch Resistance that there were indeed tanks somewhere between us and Arnhem. We found that the BBC gave us better up-to-the-minute information than we were getting from the conventional Army sources. It was clear that at Arnhem there was serious trouble and that at Nijmegen there was little progress in the capture of the half-mile-long bridge over the Neder Rhine. At last we were into Nijmegen. The Irish Guards tanks were given the task of getting to the Rhine downstream of the road and railway bridges, and we managed that. The 101st US Airborne were to carry out a river crossing. Where were the collapsible boats? Stuck in a break in the supply line, broken again by Germans retreating from the coast. At last the trucks arrived. These folding boats were British. The Americans had never seen them before. They were just canvas, with a folding skeleton frame, and could hold ten men. On the bank of the Rhine, we, who had never seen the folding boats before either, did our best to help the Americans put them together. About fifty boats were assembled. All the while the menacingly fast river and the rattle of machine-gun fire from the opposite bank made it clear that anyone crossing this greatest of European rivers was going to have a mission of suicidal proportions. In fact many of us Micks expected the rather mad, to us, river crossing in these little boats to be cancelled. Not a bit of it; 500 soldiers set out, paddling furiously, and we concentrated all our fire on likely or even unlikely places across the river, which might give cover to German machine-gunners or marksmen. We used smoke shells to blind the enemy of targets. Despite all this, the fleet of little boats, pulled downstream by the current, kept paddling. Many sank. A bullet or two holing the canvas was enough, with the weight of ten men, to fill the boat quickly. We saw many soldiers struggling in the water, many not able to make it to the far bank. Then a number of boats reached the north shore, the soldiers leaping from their craft and running towards the rise in front of them from which the enemy had been shooting. There was then an extra-ordinary sight. The 101st had ordered that each boat which had survived the crossing should return with two paddlers to take another boatload across. They did this. It one of the bravest sights of the whole war. Men who had survived the first onslaught struggled to get the flimsy craft back again to take another load. By now the first soldiers had disappeared over the rise and we took it that they were fighting their way to the end of the vital road bridge. Suddenly there appeared on the *railway* bridge a horde of soldiers, some of them with field guns towed by horses, all wearing what we, who could see them, took to be German helmets. Some cautious senior officer ordered the Irish Guards not to shoot. It was galling to see the enemy, probably not of the highest calibre, crossing the railway bridge to the same bank on which the US soldiers were fighting for the road bridge. After some time the cautious prohibition was removed and Charles Tottenham, who was closest, was ordered to fire at the stream of soldiers which by now had several more field-guns towed by horses. We noticed that he was, with great accuracy, hitting the guns with solid shot. I radioed him to ask him if he realized that he was using the wrong shells, "Yes," he said.

"If I used High Explosive it would hurt the horses." He was a great animal-lover.

Now a dramatic denouement to the river-crossing beckoned. The Americans signalled that they had captured the northern end of the bridge, and so an operation rather like Joe's Bridge but on a much larger scale was mounted by the Coldstream Guards Group, a combination of a Troop charge across the bridge by Peter Carington, later Lord Carrington, British Foreign Secretary, supporting Infantry of the Coldstream Group, and Royal Engineer bomb-disposal experts, resulted in this, one of the great bridges of Europe, being captured intact. The stage was now set for the final bridge, Arnhem. During that night the Irish Guards crossed the Nijmegen bridge, marvelling at its length, its height from the river below and the many steel arches towering above us, suspended from which could be seen the bodies of German snipers, tied to the girders to fire on us.

Colonel Joe was in his usual dynamic form and we were in an upbeat mood when the order to advance was given. Then things started to go wrong. The road was 6 ft above the low-lying boggy fields, the cloud-base was very low and the Typhoons could not operate. Worst of all, Tiger, Panther and mobile Anti-tank guns, dug into commanding positions, were reported by our leading Troop, commanded by Tony Samuelson, whose own tank was destroyed. Infantry attacks across the boggy flat fields were suicidal, especially as there was little or no supporting artillery, which could at least have provided the cover of smoke shells. All day we probed for any weakness in the German defences. A troop of Household Cavalry Armoured Cars, using their great speed, managed to find a circuitous route of little farm roads, which eventually took them to the bank of the Upper Rhine near Arnhem, and some British Parachute Division men got across using ropes to prevent them being swept downstream. We had heavy casualties from each attack, heroically carried out by the small groups of tanks and infantry which was all that could be used in this impossible battlefield. One outstanding feat was performed by William Harvey-Kelly, who marched up to a German tank and, standing beside it, knocked it out with a PIAT, the small British hand-held anti-tank weapon. As a result of his bravery, his Platoon of the Third Battalion overran this key German position and we made several miles of advance. I have always felt it unjust that William, later to command the Regiment, was not recommended for the Military Cross. I suspect that the sudden departure of Colonel Joe to take command of another Brigade was the reason for this. By now night was falling, we had little to show for the day's fighting and were 10 miles still from Arnhem, from where we heard that the bridge there was not in our hands, despite the incredible bravery of Colonel Frost and his men who were still holding one end of it.

A troop of tanks from a British Cavalry Regiment appeared beside us on the main road. The young Lieutenant asked for briefing for his Troop and a platoon of infantry which he had crowded onto the engine covers of his four Shermans. He told me that his orders were simply to put his foot down when it got darker, to charge straight to Arnhem and hope to make it over the bridge. I did not want to discourage him but the road ahead was littered with knocked-out tanks, still burning. We could not believe that the Germans would not have anticipated such a charge, with the Escaut and Nijmegen bridges captured in this way so recently, and with 10 miles of hostile road ahead, defended, as we had learned to our cost, by many tanks, guns and infantry enemy. We pointed out to him the strong-points which we had at a cost identified during the day. He was a brave chap, and the infantry officer with him, who was William Deedes, later Lord Deedes of *Daily Telegraph* fame, did not hesitate in their determination to "have a go". Just as the moment when what would have been a suicidal, almost kamikaze, mission was about to set off, an order came through cancelling it. The Troop and Platoon returned the way that they had come and we were relieved for them.

Next day a Brigade of Polish Parachutists was dropped ahead of us. We could see the figures falling from the quite low-flying planes and watched with horror the blazing aircraft, hit by enemy fire, crashing. We could not see whether anyone got out, but doubted it. The brief improvement in weather which had enabled the Polish drop to take place did not last long enough for our Typhoons to operate, so the slow progress against heavy opposition had to be mostly by foot-soldiers, with tanks in support. It all seemed snail's pace and our dream of the strike which would have seen us in Berlin was fading fast. The next bad news was that our hero, Colonel Joe Vandeleur, was promoted Brigadier and would be leaving us to command a Brigade in another Division.

The advance reached a stalemate. Again and again our supply lines were cut. Opening dykes and flooding the low country, the Germans were able to make Antwerp virtually unusable, and the Reichwald, the long strip of land, part Dutch, part German, running beside the Rhine, was under water for much of its length. Winter was upon us and the only good news was of Russian advances.

Chapter Five

HOLLAND / GERMANY – 1944/45

Colonel Giles Vandeleur, still our 2nd Battalion C.O., sent for me when we had been withdrawn from our efforts to reach Arnhem and told me that as I was one of the few officers who had been in continuous and unscathed action since Normandy and, as he was certain that there would be a lot more action in the New Year, he wanted me to take a week's leave and go home to Fermanagh, where my parents now were. This was wonderful news and I got a lift in a returning supply truck to Brussels, and another in an RAF Dakota to Heston, with another helpful RAF flight to Sydenham, now Belfast City Airport, catching the train to Enniskillen. A hurried phone call to my astonished mother was all I had time for, to learn that my father was out shooting snipe, but would come for me as soon as he returned.

I was still in my tank-suit. This was a splendid off-white type of padded "Siren Suit", much like the non-padded version which Mr Churchill wore. It was waterproof, with a hood, and was claimed to have some fireproof qualities, though I never saw proof of this. The welcome of the Enniskillen people who saw me waiting at the station was particularly warm. They had all learned of our adventures, which were widely reported in the Enniskillen paper *The Impartial Reporter*. Many of them had known me during my time at Portora. The delay after the 24-hour journey from Nijmegen gave me an opportunity to take in the peace and tranquillity of Ulster, the War becoming a distant memory. A very happy week followed. My two sisters and my mother made a great fuss of me and I went shooting with my father, also on leave for Christmas, every day.

It seemed only a short time before I was on my way back. No RAF lifts this time, but a crowded troopship from the Port of London which ran aground on a sandbank in the Thames Estuary, where we were stuck for two days, until a higher than normal tide floated us off. While this rather boring and uncomfortable incident was going on (no bunks and only stale sandwiches), the Germans attacked through the Ardennes. The swing in public sentiment from the euphoric period of the advance through France, Belgium and Holland of the apparently unstoppable Allies to the knowledge that a surprise attack on a rather second-rate American Division stretched along the Rhine to hold off attacks through the Ardennes Mountains had succeeded brilliantly caused a drop in confidence which was quite appalling. Even the BBC sounded doleful to us in our stranded troopship and the grounding of close-support aircraft, such as the Typhoons, gave a great advantage to the Germans. Tales abounded of Germans dressed in US Army uniform or disguised as nuns having penetrated US lines, causing death and destruction to the unblooded Americans.

When we landed at Ostend Captain Lord Rupert Neville of the Life Guards and I, the only Guards Armoured Division Officers on the stranded ship, were sent directly to the Ardennes to join the Divisions which had been rushed by Montgomery to the north side of the German salient, while our old friends the US 101st Airborne Division had been sent to the south side. I got there as No. 2 Squadron was preparing our attack, and it was pleasant to be welcomed by Eddie Tyler, Tinker Taylor, Dipper and my old troop, No. 4. We captured a mining village, badly bombed and wrecked in the fighting. All the inhabitants had fled and Guardsman Clark, my indefatigable soldier-servant suggested that he might be able to fix a bath for me. One of the ruined houses had indeed a bath, but no water. Clark told me to undress (it was freezing cold, with snow on the ground) while he brought food containers filled with hot water from the cookhouse nearby. Several of these produced rather a lukewarm shallow bath, but he promised that a really hot container was ready and started to pour it into the bath, which I had got into. He had not checked and the container was full of the rather glutinous peas which are a favourite dish for the Army. But it was hot, so I told him to go on pouring and had a good bath, even if I emerged a rather pea-green colour.

Several days of strenuous fighting in bitter weather followed and I began to have difficulty breathing. Billy Clark, my friend of the motorcycle (which Clarke was still riding), appeared. When he saw me looking very sick and struggling for breath, he went straight back to the Medical Officer, Hugh Ripman, who took one look at me and had me in an ambulance at once. It was a serious attack of pleurisy, both lungs badly affected, so the closing stages of the Ardennes took place without me. The shaky beginning of the operation ended in a brilliant victory for the Allies, who closed the salient, resulting in another rout of the enemy, who lost thousands of high-quality men and hundreds of tanks. Hitler's mad gamble had not come off and the prophets of doom were silenced.

For some weeks after I returned, recovered, to the Battalion we concentrated on training the replacements who were reaching us from England. The effect of conscription had resulted in the best being recruited first and many of the Guardsmen who reached us were small, unfit and quite unsoldierly by the standards we were used to.

When we crossed the Rhine and captured Cologne, heading for Hamburg and the Baltic, I found myself in the Forward Delivery Squadron with Joe Saville, a 2nd Battalion friend who had lost an eye in Normandy but had insisted on returning to the fight. The F.D.S's job was to have tanks and their crews in good shape to fill the gaps caused by our tanks and crews becoming casualties. Naturally two Irish Guards officers were particularly sensitive to the quality of Mick replacements. I was furious when a tank driven by Guardsman Charlton, its guns in charge of another Irish Guardsman, both from Liverpool, appeared. It seemed to me, in the presence of Grenadier, Coldstream, Scots and Welsh Guards, that the tank was dirty, guns and equipment ill-maintained, and that the two Micks responsible for it must be made an example, so, standing on the back of the tank, I demonstrated for all to see what a horrid pair these were. They looked chastened and promised to do better. How much better I was to learn later.

The War in its last stages, we passed through Hamburg, towards Denmark, capturing a Concentration Camp, Sandbostel, en route. Descriptions of such places have been made so often that I shall not go to any lengths to describe the horrors, or the brutality and inhumanity of those running it. We put them to work, women as well as men, to bury the dead, clean it up and help save the lives of the many close to death.

Almost on the last day before the German surrender the Germans put in a fierce attack on a troop of our tanks, which were overwhelmed, and the tank which I had excoriated in the Forward Delivery Squadron, driven by Charlton, was hit, though for once did not catch fire. The officer and his crew baled out. A field's length away a mass of German infantry could be seen advancing, so understandably the officer ordered his crew to retreat as fast as possible, to the comparative safety of the three remaining tanks of the Troop. Having had some trouble getting his escape hatch to work, Charlton did not join the others as they ran back. They heard the sound of shooting as they ran and reckoned that Charlton must have been doing his best to cover them, as the Germans did not seem to be coming on as fast as before. The rest of the Troop were able to contain the attack and there the matter seemed to end.

A few days later the Unconditional Surrender of the Germans on their

Western Front was signed by Admiral Doenitz in the presence of Field Marshal Montgomery. The War was over at last. We had a monumental party and, rather hung-over, set off for Rhineland, to a little town called Gummersbach, where the Irish Guards were to be stationed for the rest of 1945. Our joy in victory was rather moderated by the knowledge that we were going to be sent to the Far East to finish off the Japanese. Tinker Taylor, by now Adjutant of the 2nd Battalion, was sent on leave and I was appointed Acting Adjutant.

Consulting those who knew what Charlton had done (they were not quite sure what exactly) to enable the rest of his crew to escape, we decided that there was enough evidence of his behaviour to recommend him for a Mention in Despatches. His body had been found when the disabled tank's position was retaken. This citation was on its way to London when I had a message from two SS Officers who were prisoners of war, having just been captured. We interviewed these men, ruthless Nazis, unlikely to wish to ingratiate themselves with us. Their story was extraordinary. It seemed that when they knocked out the Sherman and saw the crew running for cover they could easily have caught up with them or shot them. They saw Charlton getting out of his driver's seat, then getting back in again and re-emerging with the front gunner's Browning machine gun. This he set up on a gate and fired at the by now closing Germans so effectively that they threw themselves to the ground. A burst of fire from a German sub-machine gun shattered his right arm. They could see him transferring the Browning to his left arm, his useless right arm hanging from his shoulder, until his renewed firing led to a better-aimed enemy burst which killed him. The two SS Officers agreed to write sworn affidavits of their evidence and this was enough to authenticate a citation for the Victoria Cross. Charlton's was the last VC of the Second World War. We forgot to cancel the Mention in Despatches, so he was awarded this too. I often think sheepishly of the humiliating treatment I meted out to him and his promise to do better.

Chapter Six

RUC – ENNISKILLEN –
NORTH ANTRIM – MARRIAGE

The Royal Ulster Constabulary decided to reintroduce the system of commissioning Cadet Officers which had been used before the War for half the Force's officers, the other half being commissioned from the ranks. Naturally this procedure was not universally popular. It limited promotion for those who had joined as Constables and moved upwards to the ranks of Sergeant and Head Constable. There were, however, many in authority who pointed to the "fast track" system of commissioning in the Forces and to the RIC/RUC tradition which has resulted in younger high-ranking officers, often with higher education and other experience which brought benefit, so what turned out to be the last "tranche" of Cadet Officers were chosen by interview from those who volunteered.

I was uncertain about volunteering. The Irish Guards were keen for me to become a regular soldier and I had been happy in my five years in the Army. On the other hand to achieve the rank of District Inspector, (junior Superintendent in today's structure) at the age of 23 would be an achievement, so I applied, and was interviewed by the Inspector General, Sir Richard Pim, who had himself served as a Cadet Officer at Phoenix Park under my father, and who had later joined the NI Civil Service and the RNVR. Sir Richard had been called up into the Navy at the outbreak of war and had been chosen by Winston Churchill to set up and develop his "Map Room", which gave the Prime Minister a graphic picture of events all around the world. It can still be seen underground at Whitehall and Pim set up Map Rooms at all the great conferences, at sea and on land, at which the Allies strategy was decided.

I found him a really impressive person, tall, slim, extremely friendly and informal. He had a mass of information about me, including a wonderful commendation by Major John Madden, written from Hilton Park, Clones. He explained the delicacy and difficulties of being the Chief of Police in Northern Ireland, where there was at that time so little that could be done to prevent a Stormont Minister from ordering the RUC to take actions which in a British situation would require the approval of the Police Authority and would certainly be debated in Parliament. Looking back, it was a great honour to be confided in like this, and it gave me an insight into the profound problems of policing in a country as polarized as Northern Ireland.

Five of us were accepted: David Corbett from Fermanagh, a Household Cavalry Officer with whom I had served in the GAD, and Michael Magill, who came from Co. Down and had had a distinguished Naval career, Willy Moore an Irish Guards Lieutenant, with the Military Cross, with whom I had had many experiences in the latter stages of the War and whom I liked very much as a kind friend and great company. Nigel Spears was an RAF Bomber Pilot who had flown sixty missions, and had survived against the odds. The fact that three of us were sons of serving Senior Officers was not the cause of any comment or criticism. How different it would be today! One can just hear the comment, "Nepotism is alive and well in the top echelons of the Royal Ulster Constabulary"!

We assembled at the RUC Depot at Enniskillen, still wearing our Service uniform. A good omen for me was that this was on 1 February 1946, my 23rd birthday. It was a challenging regime. In six months we had to learn enough about Criminal Law and Court Procedure to prosecute cases before the Resident Magistrates. The history, ethos and regulations of the RUC were drummed into us by highly proficient instructors. Motor cars were now coming onto the roads and streets in numbers and a whole new aspect of policing was evolving. We were given instruction in high-speed driving under the system devised by Lord Cottenham, which must have astonished the good country people of Fermanagh as we drove at 90 m.p.h., did skid-turns and high-speed reversing on the roads around Lough Erne and to Garrison on Lough Melvin.

There was again a lot of foot drill and physical training which we enjoyed, particularly as it brought us into close contact with the recruits, many of whom were ex-Servicemen. One man I remember particularly was Denis Malony, who joined the Force as a Constable and, despite many oppor-tunities for promotion stayed in that rank. He was the first Ulsterman to run 100 yards in under 10 seconds. He was killed, holding his wife's hand, in the British Midland Kegworth crash. His daughter, Dr Maria Malony, was my key Public Relations Officer years later in the Housing Executive.

The months passed quickly and our Passing Out was looming. This depended on a final examination in all the subjects in which we had been instructed. The Depot Commandant was Tony Peacocke, later to become Inspector General. A very clever man and an international-class Bridge player, he spent a lot of time with us giving us the background information and experience which we would need when we passed out. He was also the Chief Examiner of the board which was to judge whether we were fit to take on the responsibilities of a District, with, on average, about 100 policemen. The final exam showed David Corbett top, with me second, the others not far behind. David was very properly seen as the star. He was bright, ingenious and, furthermore, married, so it mattered more to him to pass, and pass well.

The Commandant gave us the news that Princess Elizabeth had been invited to the Passing Out, not only of us five Cadets but the 100 recruit Constables. A lavish ceremony with the RUC band, in the presence of the Prime Minister, Sir Basil Brooke, the Minister of Home Affairs, Edward Warnock, and a great number of notables, was planned.

Tony Peacocke was keen that we five should mount a demonstration of an activity unique to policing in Ireland, and, under Willy Moore's leadership, we decided to build a potheen (illicit liquor) still. We built a V-shaped hut and then used peat "bricks" to make it look like a turf-stack. It even had a hidden door. Inside the stack was the still, consisting of a barrel of "wash", a mixture of molasses and other ingredients, a paraffin cooking stove and the "worm" (a long coiled pipe) inserted in the "cooler", which converted the steam from the "wash" into liquid by cooling, resulting in a drip of highly alcoholic liquor into the final vessel. We had practised the operation and, when each of us had been presented to the future Queen and congratulated on being commissioned, wearing our Guards, Navy and Air Force uniforms, we hurried to our rooms, donned dirty dungarees and got the potheen still into operation. Princess Elizabeth was taken on tour of the Depot, which ended with the novel exhibition of a working potheen still. She came into the "turf-stack" with her Lady-in-Waiting to see these greasy rascals at their illegal work and I heard for the first time her girlish laugh, which I was to hear many times in the future.

She was being escorted to her waiting Rolls-Royce by the Prime Minister, the Home Minister and the Inspector-General, when out of the crowd stepped a rather eccentric but highly intelligent Head Constable Instructor, who presented her with a bottle, tied with a green ribbon, saying, "Your Royal Highness, perhaps you would like a drop of the potheen". She accepted it rather gingerly, handed it to the Lady-in-Waiting and departed. There was a frightful row. Poor Peacocke accepted the blame for the demonstration still; we took responsibility for presenting a far more life-like demonstration than he had understood us to be arranging and the Head Constable was upbraided by everyone. Then the real trouble began. Ian

Paisley, just back from Bob Jones University in America, where he had been ordained in the fundamentalist religion which developed into the Free Presbyterian Church, had been at the presentation of the bottle of potheen and, although he was not then an MP at Stormont, he had many supporters who were able to raise the matter to the embarrassment of the Government.

Before taking up my commission, we had a visit from my mother's sister, a nun with the title of Sister Veronica. She had stayed with us often before the war and had made a great impression on me. Her wartime story was amazing. In 1940 when visiting her Midleton home, she met Frank Duff and Edel Quinn who were the chiefs of the important Catholic lay order, The Legion of Mary. They persuaded her that since she had been educated in France and was fluent in French, she could serve God better by developing the order in that country. She left at once, and began her mission in May 1940, in the Midi where she found a Bishop of Irish descent who helped her to get started. The Germans were now in possession and control of the country, and Veronica, travelling all over France, was constantly arrested by them as she carried a British passport, issued before partition. The Germans let her go despite this and she developed her campaign into Spain, the Netherlands and Belgium, where, in Brussels, she met Bishop Suenens, a Fleming who spoke little English, who asked her to teach him. Suenens, who narrowly missed becoming Pope, introduced her to King Baudoin of the Belgians, who became a close friend. He asked her to find him a wife and she suggested the Spanish Countess Fabiola. Baudoin and Fabiola fell in love and the courtship took place in Veronica's flat. When it was announced that the shy King had found his beautiful and lively wife, all Belgium was delighted. Suenens, later to become Cardinal, wrote two books about Veronica, *The Hidden Hand of God* and *The Hidden Life*. Veronica made a deep impression on all who met her. She had leadership qualities of a high order. She certainly impressed me, and had no inhibitions about my marrying Heather, though she could not come to our wedding because of her duties in Europe.

My District was North Antrim, based at Ballymoney, and covering Portrush, the Giant's Causeway, Bushmills, Ballycastle, Loughguile, Armoy, Cloughmills and Rasharkin. My deputy was Head Constable Isaac Keightley and there were about 100 Sergeants and Constables. I had been found lodgings with the Land Steward of Benvarden, the largest estate in the District. Mr and Mrs Willy Lyons were wonderfully kind and welcoming and I was very well fed by the motherly Mrs Lyons. Benvarden is owned by the Montgomery family and they treated me as one of the family. Jack and Nanette Montgomery were there at weekends. It seemed an idyllic life and my hesitant efforts at prosecuting twice a week at Petty Sessions did not go too badly. The local solicitors were a decent bunch and as long as I gave them a reasonable chance to defend their clients, and in particular did not spring new evidence on them which they had no chance to refute, the courts were not places of bitter rancour.

As always in my life, just when everything seemed set fair, and I was probably getting a little complacent, I was sent for to be told that the Route Hospital, Ballymoney, was very concerned about a girl called Eileen Bowden, who had been brought into the hospital by relatives, was in a dying condition and it was clear that an amateurish abortion had been performed on her. I went straight to the Route and saw Dr Bill Belford, the Senior Physician, who told me that Eileen was conscious, but dying, and her septicaemia was too far advanced for even the strongest antibiotics to do any good. Sergeant McDowell was in charge of the case and, as, at the Depot, we had been taught of a rare Criminal Justice procedure, the Dying Declaration, I suggested to him that we (he!) should carry this out. Politely, he pointed out that, as the senior, it was more appropriately my job. With the Doctor and Sergeant I went to her room. A pretty young girl, 18 or 19, deathly pale with huge eyes, she was conscious. With my voice choking I told her that she was dying and had no hope of recovery. I said that the law provided for someone in her position to state in a Declaration what had happened and that, in the event of a trial for murder, the Declaration could be given in Court. I had expected her to protest, cry, even faint, at being told of her hopeless situation, but she was absolutely calm and grateful, she said, to be given the truth. She asked that what she would say be written down, so I wrote:

"I, Eileen Bowden, with the fear of death before me and no hope of recovery wish to make a statement." I read this out and she asked to sign it.

She then described how she had slept with her boyfriend and become pregnant. They did not want to marry and he told her of a chemist in Belfast who would abort her. Her mother had known nothing of this and she had had to borrow £100 to pay the "chemist" who was to do the operation. With the boyfriend she had travelled to Belfast and gone to a dirty room near the city centre where the abortionist had first taken and counted the money, and then, without any discussion, washing of hands or sterilization of the instruments, produced a rubber tube, inserted a wire into it and thrust it into her vagina twice. It was very painful and she was bleeding. He thrust them out of his room, warning them menacingly that it would be the worse for them if they told anybody. She said the pain increased daily until she was unable to bear it and went to the Route. She did her best to exonerate the boyfriend, but it was clear that she believed the "chemist" (who turned out to be a salesman of male catheters, used for clearing male urinary tracts) had behaved very badly.

During that night she died and a pathologist carried out an autopsy in the Route morgue at which I was required to be present to take charge of exhibits. I had had experience of hundreds of bloody scenes in the war, but the dissection of a young girl who had given me the statement the day before was an awful moment. Her womb had two incisions confirming the double penetration she had described. It was now my job to find and interview the "chemist". News travels fast in Northern Ireland and he was waiting for the police, quite coolly. "Yes," he said, after I had cautioned him, "the girl did come to me. Her man friend did give me some money, but the briefest of examinations made it clear to me that she had been the victim of a botched abortion, and I told them that they should never have come to me, that I did not do abortions, and that she should go at once to hospital." We seized a number of catheters, for forensic examination, but did not find wire.

The case came to Court at the Antrim Assizes, before Mr Justice William Lowry, father of the Lord Chief Justice of Northern Ireland of recent times. Defending was Mr Lance Curran KC and prosecuting Cyril Nicholson KC, father of Lord Justice Sir Michael Nicholson. I had never given evidence in Court before. The charge was murder and giving evidence in the absence of the Jury to establish the admissibility of the Dying Declaration was not too difficult. The hard part was when the Jury was recalled and I was subjected to skilled, stern cross-examination by the famous Counsel who tied me in knots and, indeed, even planted in my mind the possibility that the "chemist" had turned away Eileen because she had already had an abortion, which was botched, and that he was being prosecuted for someone else's crime. The man friend, who had not been charged as an accomplice because it was believed that he would be a useful prosecution witness, changed his evidence to infer that Eileen might well have organized an earlier abortion and had been keen to visit the "chemist" to clear up her symptoms. It was a bad moment and I have often sympathized with police witnesses who have to put up with cross-examination of a pitiless character. The "chemist" was convicted of manslaughter. This was a relief as in those days murder carried the death penalty. I have always believed that the death penalty inhibits convictions for murder. Witnesses, even police, are reluctant to help send an accused to the gallows and juries are certainly inhibited by the thought, which may even result in jurors, fully believing in the guilt of someone accused of murder, refusing to convict.

It was only a short time after this experience that the five new District Inspectors were invited to attend the trial of Ian Hay Gordon, an RAF Aircraftsman, for the murder of Kim Curran, the daughter of the KC, Lance Curran, who had been my skilled tormentor in the Bowden case. Gordon had been befriended by the Curran family and was a lonely, backward and inarticulate Glaswegian, a rather odd friend for the cultured Curran family. Kim Curran's body had been found on the long avenue to the large Curran home. She had been stabbed many times. She had been seen walking with Gordon earlier and he had returned to his station that day in an agitated state. He had taken his uniform to be cleaned by a local laundry.

The chief evidence was a statement made after caution to a Scotland Yard detective, Superintendent Capstick, who had been brought into the case because of the unusual nature of the circumstances. By now Lance Curran was Mr Justice Curran, a High Court Judge, and his elder son had become a Catholic priest. Rumours abounded. Capstick was grilled as I had been. Gordon's case was that Capstick had scared him into confessing, that he was innocent and that it was coincidental that he had sent his uniform to be cleaned. No knife was found and there had been no clear evidence of sexual assault on the girl.

The case came to an abrupt end when the Jury returned to their hotel that night to consider their verdict and, despite the Judge's admonitions, had visited the bar and, though they denied it, had spoken about the case to people in the bar. At a re-hearing Gordon was found guilty of manslaughter on the ground of temporary loss of sanity and mental inadequacy of personality. He was sentenced to a long term.

One of the big events in the life of a North Antrim District Inspector was the North-West 200. This international motorcycle race, with dozens of entrants, brought very large crowds to Portrush and Portstewart. The race was at speeds of over 120 mph on public roads closed for the day and it was important to stop people, and dogs, getting on to the course. About 200 police were drafted in from Counties Antrim and Londonderry to help marshal the race. It had not been run in 1947, my first summer in North Antrim, so in 1948 I was looking forward to seeing my first North-West 200. Having briefed my police, I took up position at the corner which, rounding a sharp bend, would take the racers towards Portstewart. The "Road Closed" car raced past; at that moment the Earl of Antrim, accompanied by his small daughter, Christina McDonnell, appeared on the opposite side of the road. "John," he called, "I need your help." I was in uniform; blackthorn stick in hand, I strode across the track intending to tell Ran (short for Randal) Antrim that there was no way they could cross when I was made aware of a beautiful girl standing beside him. "This is Heather Caruth, she has just been invalided out of the WAAF [Womens Auxiliary Air Force] and is Christina's governess." Somehow my stern intentions were forgotten and I escorted them across the road.

The Antrims played a prominent part in the life of the county. Lord Antrim, later Chairman of Ulster Television, had given his family a powerful voice in the affairs of a Province in which they had been prominent for hundreds of years. His wife, Angela, a Roman Catholic from

69

Yorkshire, took a leading part in the cultural life of the Province. I had met them both shortly after arrival in Co. Antrim, before Heather came on the scene.

One of Angela Antrim's loves was drama. The strange polarity of Ulster and the absence in those days of TV, led after the war, to a blossoming of Drama Groups. Ballymoney was in the van of this, because in the 20s and 30s there had been a thriving Literary and Debating Society, which had produced plays as well. When I appeared on the North Antrim scene Winifred Belford, wife of Dr Bill, had invited me to join the Drama Group and I was delighted to do so. The rather austere life of a District Inspector in his own District meant that there were some rather boring evenings for a 23-year-old. Soon I found myself on the stage of the Ballymoney Town Hall, as the elderly Rector in *The Holly and The Ivy*. This was followed by Blunchli in *Arms and the Man* by Shaw. Every year there was an Ulster Drama Festival and Lady Antrim was President. I got the prize for Ulster's leading actor from her hands and it turned out that she had designs on me to raise funds for the Ulster War Memorial, the appeal for which she chaired, and we got to know each other quite well.

Though it happened two years later, it is worth recalling my next contact with Ian Paisley. We had had the ambitious idea of producing Christopher Fry's remarkable play, *The First-Born*. Nanette Montgomery had given me this to read. It is a verse-play about Moses and had to me a passion and a faith which made my part, the cruel Seti, scourge of the Christians in Egypt, an arresting challenge. The Bangor Drama Festival was then, except for the Grand Opera House final, the apogee of the Amateur Drama world. We were picked to play on the last night, a Saturday, and had some confidence of a major success. Ian Paisley, starting his mission of fundamentalism, decided that he would book the Ballymoney Town Hall for a Protestant Rally, at which, said the ads, wafers would be passed around to prove that the absurd popish belief that God's Body was in the bread and His Blood in the wine was to be exploded as nonsense, because sanctified bread, wafers, *not wine*, would be passed among the audience to sample. It was not a hard decision. Seti, who had been my concern, took second place, but it was galling to leave my wonderful cast, including a soprano, a young girl from Ballymoney who achieved opera fame later.

They got back from Bangor very late. I was asleep but they called me to come to the party. *The First-Born* had won everything, best production, best set, best players. But the main prize had been won by Edward Gordon, the bachelor Headmaster of Dalriada School, a brilliant actor and producer, who had learned the quite difficult part of Seti in 24 hours. I have always given a hard time to Ian Paisley for denying me this triumph. He says, "Are you sure you would have been better than Ted Gordon?" I am certain I would not. This man was an actor who could have been in the Richardson/Gielgud mode had he not been devoted to his teaching job. I produced him in a part called *The Tempting of Brother Dominic* in which a most beautiful and seductive woman, Gwendoline Perrott, and he gave a one-act performance which touched the heartstrings. I believe neither ever married.

My mother had decided that, with the two girls at school in England, she should be back in Ireland to make a holiday home for them. Our Fermanagh house was on the market, so when I suggested that she should housekeep for me she accepted. I found out from Nanette Montgomery that a charming old home, Ballyhivistock, a Stewart-Moore (Nanette's family) place, might be interested to let. I got in touch with the owner, Professor Purser of Trinity College.

Ballyhivistock is a typical Irish small country house, surrounded by beech trees, with a walled garden. My mother, who had come back from Greece to reopen Cultiagh House near Lisbellaw, was charmed to find herself the temporary chatelaine of such a house. She brought with her Martha Gilroy, from Derrylin, Co. Fermanagh, who had been our cook for many years. Mary Chestnutt from Dervock came to help, which was particularly happy as her brother, Drill Sergeant Chestnutt, had been one of my torturers on the drill-square at the Irish Guards Training Battalion.

I suppose subconsciously I was trying to establish myself as a person of consequence in Co. Antrim and it was not long before I had got in touch with Heather Caruth. An invitation to the Route Hunt Ball, at the Northern Counties Hotel, Portrush, was the means of getting in touch again. Heather was just as beautiful as I remembered and the Ball was memorable. We seemed to have much in common, both having served in the War, both involved in the law, in her case her father, George Caruth's busy practice, Caruth and Bamber, in mine the RUC. She seemed to me to epitomize those qualities which I admired in women, beauty, intelligence, modesty and interest in people.

Ballymena friends, solicitors particularly, told me of their affection and respect for George Caruth, but warned that he, a Presbyterian, had married out of his "tribe", by choosing Ethel Pryde of the Church of Ireland. The Prydes were descendants of a French Huguenot family of that name, who, after the St Bartholomew's Massacre in France in the 17th century, had taken themselves off and had brought their linen skills to Northern Ireland, together with their Huguenot distaste for papists. My Ballymena friends made it clear that I would have to face a lot of serious opposition if I was to succeed in getting Heather to agree to marry me. As she had shown interest and friendly feelings towards me, but no more, I could see that there was to be much difficulty.

Several factors were on my side. Angela Antrim, a Catholic of the Sykes family who I had met in Yorkshire, was very fond of Heather and had made clear that she would help us if we married. The Ballymena ex-service people were supportive. My opposite number in Ballymena, the DI Jack Dobbin, had given me a week's instruction when, aged 23, I was posted as his neighbour to North Antrim. He used to take me for walks in and around Ballymena and I had remembered him saying as we passed the Caruth house, Drumard Cottage, on the Galgorm road, "That is George Caruth's home, a respected solicitor and great horseman, with four beautiful daughters". I had no doubt of the one I was obsessed with and told Jack so.

By now my mother had returned to Fermanagh to get Cultiagh House ready for the imminent leave of the Deputy Chief of the Greek Police, my father. Heather and I spent several weekends there. My little car, a Standard, which broke down often, was our transportation, and she seemed to enjoy my repertoire of Irish songs. After several such occasions, she had what I described as a "pretty precipitous dither" and agreed to marry me. Heather's mother, Ethel Caruth, was rather cool and asked me to talk to her brother-in-law, Captain Bob Pryde, who had served in the Great War. He was pleasant and talked of his own military background; he had been a prisoner of war during much of the 1914-18 War and had had a dreadful time. He lived in a large house in Ballymena, as did several of his brothers and sisters. They were all descendants of the French Huguenots who had brought the linen craft to Northern Ireland, but were now feeling the cold wind of competition from Belgian, French and other flax producers. He asked me about my financial prospects. I had £360 p.a. pay, £120 p.a. car allowance and a tiny amount of savings. He was kind, but dismissive. The Army background, and my own Irish Guards career, were praised, but were treated as irrelevant to the main points which were:-

I was a Roman Catholic
I came from Southern stock
My financial prospects were limited.

It was a thoroughly depressing interview, which I knew had been rehearsed with Ethel Caruth.

I was bidden appear at Drumard Cottage. I had an inkling of what was afoot, so appeared in uniform with my dear little cocker spaniel, Penny, to be told by Heather that she was not happy and was breaking off our engagement. She was leaving that day for Dublin, where her Uncle Richmond Pryde and his wife Katherine, were staying at Bray, on leave from Ootacamund, South India, where he was a tea-planter. That was it.

I was desolated. Returning to Mrs Lyons, my landlady, I was reminded by the pile of wedding presents that I must now return these. The presents were all despatched to the donors with a note of thanks. Several replied with reassuring messages to the effect that "It is all for the best".

Daily letters to Bray asking for reconsideration produced no reply, but I learned from Thirza Brodie, her sister, that Heather was due to return on an evening train which would get into Belfast before the ballet *Romeo and Juliet* at the Grand Opera House. I bought two tickets and wrote saying I would leave hers at the box office if the train was late. It was, so I went to my seat. By the end of the first act the ticket had not been collected, the ballet was disappointing and I retired to the bar. At the ballet's end there was Heather in the lobby. I was overjoyed and we travelled by train to Ballymena, where I left her off and went on to Ballymoney. Next day I took delivery of a Vauxhall Wyvern, the "state of the art" motor car of 1948, and drove it to Ballymena. Now Heather, having had several weeks of thought about the situation and with more sympathetic and enlightened relations to advise her, told me that she wanted to revive our engagement, but would not become a Catholic. I was overjoyed. I had never pressed her to "turn". It was quite understandable that her Huguenot mother and her family could not look equably on a daughter marrying a Catholic. George Caruth, whom I never met, would I am sure, have taken a different line, but he was dead.

I now went to see Bishop Mageean of the Down and Connor Diocese, to seek permission to marry Heather in a Catholic Church. He was adamant that he would not give permission. He said it would create "scandal" amongst the faithful, and that no diocese in Ireland would marry us. He was not unsympathetic, gave me a glass of sherry and escorted me to the door of his Palace. There in my shining new Vauxhall sat Heather. She rolled down her window as I introduced them. "I see what you mean," he said. "Maybe you have some connections in England to settle this?"

I wrote to Katherine Frazer, my aunt. She had a substantial practice at Hampton Court, as a doctor, and had always been a great supporter. She said she could arrange for us to be married there. Heather's mother wrote to her family friend General Adrian Carton de Wiart, VC, who had commanded troops in Northern Ireland with his base in Ballymena, to ask him to give Heather away. We arranged to be married at Hampton Court, at the Catholic Church on 23 October 1948.

Three days before, Heather and I flew to London, she to her sister Jill Style, then married to Sir Godfrey Style, now Jill Langdon-Down, and me to my aunt. She introduced me to the fatherly parish priest and took me to the office of the Registrar of the County of Middlesex. It all seemed so simple. I asked to see the Registrar; his secretary, learning that I wanted his approval to marry in two days time, gave me a form to fill up, which I did.

She had told me, in a voice like thunder, "You can't marry here, coming from Ireland. The earliest you can do so is after three weeks residence in the country." My answer to "How long resident in Middlesex" had been two days. I could now see disaster ahead. After all this, to tell Heather that, through my incompetence in not checking what the legal requirement was, we had now to return to Co. Antrim, and come back in three weeks, was, I was certain, the end.

I sat there in the Registrar's outer office in total misery. The secretary was adamant that the Registrar *never* flouted the rules which he was employed to observe. A dapper figure walked past us and into his office. "Is that him?" "Yes, but it will do you no good trying to get him to break the law." "Please tell him that I would like to see him."

After some minutes she came out of his office looking enigmatic, and ushered me in. A figure was standing looking out of the window.

He said, "Mr Gorman, a great Englishman, Horatio Nelson, turned a blind eye to a disobliging message. Coming up to the date of Trafalgar, your wedding day, I am proposing to do the same thing. Please correct the mistake on Question 6. As to your residence in Middlesex, you meant to answer 2nd October."

I sat at his desk, corrected the form and, thanking him profusely, took it away to the waiting car. I never saw the Registrar's face, but it is Englishmen like him, who make Irishmen, like me, like them.

The wedding was a quiet one. Ethel Caruth did not come, nor did my mother; the General, Heather's sister, aunt and Katharine and her husband Richmond Pryde, and my father, just back from Greece, were there.

Chapter Seven

RUC – NORTH ANTRIM – ARMAGH

After nearly a year of marriage Heather became pregnant and our daughter Angela was born at Ramore House, Portrush. This was a fine old Georgian house on the sea-front overlooking Portrush Harbour. Charles Lever, the Irish novelist (often called the Irish Dickens) had lived there, and wrote *Harry Lorequer* there. When Heather and I returned to Ulster, having been away for nearly twenty years, for me to become head of the Housing Executive, I thought it would be a romantic gesture to take her to see Ramore House where we had started our married life and where our first child had been born. We drove down the main street of Portrush to the harbour. To our horror Ramore House had disappeared and in its place were several maisonettes of utilitarian design. There was no trace of our charming old house. I had a lot to say to my Directors of the Northern Ireland Housing Executive about the destruction of a fine old house.

Ramore House was let to holidaymakers in July and August when we moved into a flat in Victoria Street owned by Noelle Wells, a school teacher (and an excellent actress), who had holidays in those months. The main Ballymoney builder, Hugh Taggart, told me of a plan to build two houses on the Newal Road, one for his son Hubert, and the other, if I wished, for us. It was thrilling to see our new home rising from the little hill, and at last to feel that we were going to put down roots. Hugh and Hubert were helpfulness itself in taking us into the picture, and we had discussions about the bathroom tiles, the use of polishable wood flooring, the cooker, Raeburn not AGA, and the whole question of furnishing, carpeting and curtaining our little house. Becoming householders made an indelible impression on me. It was an experience which helped me later as head of the NI Housing Executive.

Finally the house was complete and we moved in. It was rather bare, so

I entered the Ballymoney Technical School to learn how to make furniture. It caused a few raised eyebrows among the young apprentices to have the DI attending lessons with them in woodworking, French polishing and use of tools. My ambitions were low; I just wanted to make this little house *ours*. It had a semi-circular bay window to the sitting-room, with a small flat roof above. I had the idea of making window-boxes to sit on this flat space. A very simple carpentry job, but choosing the right wood, getting the angles right, learning the best joints to use to avoid rust of screws or nails, drainage, all had the need for study and advice. The window-boxes appeared and I was now required to find the right plants, which started my gardening career. Delighted with this, I became ambitious. My mother had lent us a Sheraton half-table, so I took this to the Tech. and asked the instructor to help me copy it. He was rather dubious about my ability to do such an imitation of a classic design and called my teenage fellow-pupils into a discussion about the project. They were all favourable and the work began. It is now a treasured piece which I love pointing out to visitors. It is an exact replica of Mr Sheraton's work of 1750 or so, and, typically, I swank about my carpentry skill. The truth is that the young apprentices did it, with me getting humble jobs like sanding and polishing the table.

The life of a District Inspector was pleasant. It was not desperately hard work. We had a good social life, lots of sport, and crime was not terrorist, although many people, such as my father, warned me against complacency about the IRA.

My job was to lead and train 100 policemen in carrying out the enforcement of the law, in prosecuting wrongdoers, in investigating "outrages" (as quite minor crimes, by today's standards, were called), and to take a lead in "community policing", which was intended to keep harmony among all sections and classes of the people. One duty was to visit my eight stations at varying times of the day and night. To ensure that patrolling by foot and bicycle was going on methodically, one was expected to follow the declared route of a patrol, find the Constable and talk to him about what he had observed and what he had heard from people he had met on his way. It was quite astonishing what information was obtained this way. The patrolling Constable was not seen as a threat, rather as a friendly confidant, and innumerable scraps of gossip put together patiently would reveal facts of significance in the prevention and detection of crime.

Every month there was a formal inspection. One was expected to spend two or three hours on this. It started with a drill parade in the Barrack yard. The Constables had .303 rifles, as well as revolvers. Drill may seem to modern eyes completely antediluvian, but it gave an opportunity for those involved to look their best and to take part in an activity which gives the participants the inspiring benefit of the feeling of working together. After drill would come an inspection of the Barracks, as Police Stations were known. This was not as fierce as in the Guards, but it was important to ensure that the conditions in the quarters of five men should be spotlessly clean, hygienic and reasonably comfortable. A key part of Barrack life was the standard of food. Each Barrack had a cook, paid for by the men, but required to keep good standards of cleanliness and order. Usually they were married women whose children had grown up and who took a motherly interest in the "party", as it was called, and they did a wonderful job in feeding hungry young men.

Part of the inspection which I increasingly enjoyed was the inspection of the garden. Most RUC stations had quite a large back garden – for vegetables – with a smaller flower garden in the front. The Sergeant and his men generally took a great interest in this. Enough potatoes for the year, carrots, beans, cabbages, broccoli, leeks, lettuce, all were of high quality, if they were cared for, and eaten, by skilled gardeners. It was a lesson to me and I looked forward to the time when I might have my own garden.

At Bushmills there was a fine, older Constable called Adam Bustard who kept several beehives in the Barrack garden. This fascinated me, as at Rockport one of the masters, the crippled Monty Weaving, had enthralled us with his story about bee-keeping in Canada. When my mother and I moved into Ballyhivistock with its walled garden, this was the chance to start my bee-keeping career, and I bought two C.D.B. hives (the Irish hives which were designed after the Famine to give food and occupation to the poor in the Congested District Board areas throughout Ireland). It was very satisfactory to be able to produce my own sections of comb honey and compensated for the inevitable stings.

The Sergeant at Bushmills, Sergeant Davidson, was a keen fisherman on the River Bush, which provided the precious water to make the world's oldest whiskey, "Old Bushmills". A crop of flax was grown on most farms and in the autumn the bundles of flax stalks were "retted" (rotted) in flax-dams, usually made by blocking a stream to provide enough water to fill a dam, which could be 50 ft long, but never more than 4 ft deep. Here the flax rotted, or rather the outer case of each stem did so, leading to the next process, "scutching", that is cleaning off the rotten remains of outer cases and revealing the flax stems which provided the fibre which made Irish linen and provided thousands of jobs. The whole process had developed in Ulster because of the Huguenot "pogrom" in France in the 17th century.

Sergeant Davidson explored every stream and rivulet feeding the River Bush. He explored right up into the Antrim Hills, round Loughguile and Armoy, and he discovered over 100 farmers whose flax-dams were empty, many of whom admitted releasing the poisonous water. Since all these offences had been committed at about the same time, in September, it made sense to bring them all to the same Petty Sessions in Bushmills, which had an old Court House reminiscent of that in the TV series *The Irish RM*.

The Resident Magistrate was Major "Fritz" McLean. He was a kind man of few words, who had been a prisoner-of-war of the Turks in the Great War and had suffered grievously. He drove a stately old Citroen car very slowly round his ten Petty Sessions Courts which were always furnished with three chairs on the raised Bench, one for him and one each for his two dogs. When Major "Fritz" entered the Court, all rose, to watch respectfully as the RM took his seat, and the dogs, both whippets, sat on their hindquarters on theirs. The dogs had a peculiar sneering expression, especially, I thought, when I was on my feet introducing cases (there could be fifteen or twenty at a time), examining prosecution witnesses, cross-examining defence witnesses and defendants, re-examining, summing-up.

On this Bushmills Petty Sessions day I arrived with over 100 prosecution files to find a large crowd gathered outside and within the Court House, and, to my horror, the eminent King's Counsel, Mr Cyril Nicholson, in wig and gown with a bevy of solicitors behind him.

The RM and the sneering dogs took their seats. "Your Worship," my faltering voice started, "I have brought over 100 farmers to your Court today, to prove to you a serious conspiracy to release poisonous flax water into the Bush River has taken place. I see Mr Nicholson here, and believe he represents all 100 defendants. Perhaps he wishes to address you."

"Your Worship," said Counsel, "I am not going to have the District Inspector tell me how I should conduct my cases. I suggest that he call his witnesses to attempt to prove the serious allegations he has made against my clients."

With a sinking heart I called Sergeant Davidson to prove the first case, realizing that no matter how succinctly he gave his evidence, this could be challenged, especially on the "conspiracy" issue which I had, with some foolhardiness, introduced. Davidson gave his evidence well and said that the farmer had admitted releasing the flax-water, explaining that the noxious smell and the need for the farmer to get into the dam made it highly unpleasant if the dam was not emptied.

Cyril Nicholson rose to his feet. "Your Worship, I come here simply to defend over 100 farmers for an offence which, though serious, is very common at this time of year, given the conditions in which flax farmers have to carry out their work. In introducing the word conspiracy the District Inspector has given a different slant to the matter. I cannot accept the word conspiracy, but since there has indeed been a collective action by all these farmers on the River Bush and its tributaries, I am obliged to produce a document which is over 100 years old, which shows that in the honourable

78

cause of protecting the purity of the Bush water, all the farmers, and their fathers and grandfathers, have had a solemn compact with the distillery to empty their flax-dams at the same time, so that the late autumn run of Old Bushmills distilling, has no danger of being polluted."

Major McLean fined all the farmers one shilling each, to cheers from the crowd. When the Court cleared he invited Nicholson, Sergeant Davidson and me to join him in "The Widows" for a glass of Bushmills.

Flax has almost disappeared now from Ulster farms, but nearly 50 years ago, the consensus, even among the most avid anglers (as I am), was that the old "covenant" to rid the river of poison, much of which would anyway have entered it through dam leakage, made sense. A proviso was accepted by all, farmers and fishermen, that the quasi-legal release should be timed to coincide with heavy rainfall to wash the flax-water quickly into the sea.

Rathlin Island was part of my District. This rocky outcrop is one of the great bird sanctuaries of the British Isles. Laurens Mackie, a scion of Mackies, the engineering firm of world-wide fame, was the leading bird preservationist in Ulster, and the Wild Birds Protection Act, NI, was the most comprehensive in the UK. He came to see me and asked for support for wild birds, particularly in Rathlin.

The Island, which achieved fame years later when Richard Branson ditched his balloon there and was saved by the ferryman, had a population of about 100, a lighthouse and a Manor House, owned by the Campbell family, whose representative in Northern Ireland is now my friend Commander Peter Campbell. But the serious problem (to some of the Paisleyites) was the fact that it had a public house. I was for ever being charged with failing to ensure that it closed at 10 p.m.

The Sergeant in Ballycastle took the wild bird problem, and the closing-hour problem very seriously. In those days the RUC performed an important function, which was to "take the tillage". This was done as an agent for the Ministry of Agriculture and meant that the District had the responsibility of reporting the plans of every farmer for the next year. Constable Patterson of Ballycastle had spent several days on Rathlin "taking the tillage". He gave me an account of life there, of the values and attitudes of this little enclave – their hopes, indeed their dream, of being able to make this northernmost part of Ulster, a haven for Protestant/Catholic togetherness, and a place which the Rathlin young, if forced to leave for work, would still look on as home. There was an RIC "party" stationed on Rathlin in the last century and the story was that the DI in those days went out to inspect them, and found the "Barrack" deserted because the "party" had gone to Scotland for the harvest.

Laurens Mackie and I went to Rathlin and I met Tony McQuaig the publican, who assured me he closed at 10 p.m. and we saw the puffins, guillemots, Mother Carey's chickens, all nesting on the cliffs, particularly near the lighthouse.

Soon there was a press report that golden eagles were soaring over Rathlin, which Larens thought was just media hype, but then came a story that London restaurants with a post-war hunger to satisfy for plovers' eggs were sending raiding parties to Rathlin to pillage birds' eggs which would be passed off as plovers', but were, in some cases, rare seabirds' eggs. Action had to be taken and I had a message from Sir Richard Pim that he hoped I was fully in touch with the Rathlin egg situation. A message from Ballycastle that they had seized several thousand eggs brought me there quickly. The whole Barrack was filled with crates of eggs, white ones, green ones, blue ones, speckled ones. I sent for Larens. He took a little time to identify those which were "protected", several days in fact. London "wide-boys" were besieging us to release their treasure. A non-attributable press disclosure that we were about to release several thousand bogus plovers' eggs, which were of uncertain age in the nest and several days in police custody, made plovers' eggs non-flavour of the month in smart restaurants in London and the whole consignment went on to the Ballycastle rubbish dump. Rathlin Island ceased to be an egg sanctuary for chefs.

In those days there was a little railway between Ballymoney and Ballycastle. It was highly profitable in summer, but in those times of year-round employment it was kept going all year. One of the calls to me was to say that the Ballycastle train had never arrived. There were very few passengers, so I was not too worried and put it down to a 'phone fault due to lines being down. About 6 a.m. the next day I was 'phoned by Head Constable Isaac Keightley, my second-in-command in Ballymoney District, to say the train had simply disappeared. Nothing had been heard of it since it had set off the previous evening. Sleepily I got into my ancient car and drove to Armoy, through deep snow, and organized a train search party. There is an unusual bridge which takes a road over the cutting carrying the railway, and the Sergeant, a four-man party and I set off along the railway track towards Ballycastle. After a mile or so we found the train. It was completely snowed in. The crew and passengers, with ample coal (which was more than the rest of us had), had moved into the first carriage of this small-gauge railway, and by keeping the train's furnace blazing had a really cosy party going. Several of the passengers had food, which in those days of continued rationing was scarce; several others had bottles. We felt we were breaking up a happy party by rescuing them.

Not long after this the Ballycastle railway was scrapped and so was the Portrush – Bushmills tram, which had been invented by Traill, a Bushmills landowner who had harnessed the Bush River to provide enough electricity to power a train-line to the Giant's Causeway. This was a very popular tourist addition to the area, but short-sighted "bottom-line" experts put both the little railway and the tram out of commission. If they existed now, they would have paid for themselves several times over. Americans call this 20/20 hindsight!

Loughguile, high in the Antrim Hills, had the standard Sergeant and four Constables. They had an area to police which was totally peaceful. Indeed Cardinal Daly, who came from there, often talked to me about the good relationship between Sergeant Carabine, his "party" and the locals, most of whom were Catholics. The police occupied themselves in the summer, when not on duty, in digging peat from the many bogs, and in keeping alert to illicit distillation, which was prevalent. I took part in several raids and we found stills concealed in turf-stacks, in ravines and carved into the sides of turf-banks. The procedure was that the DI should, in the presence of the party, pour the potheen down the kitchen sink. Years later I heard that Sergeant Carabine had undone the U-turn plug of the sink drain and put a bucket there to catch the potheen. He was a great man, but "liked a drop". One of the Constables, returned to Loughguile by people who dumped him unconscious outside the station, was very badly injured. I interviewed him when he could talk. He was a homosexual, a gentle and unaggresive man, who did not flaunt his "gay" leanings. He had been in Belfast when a gang of louts had broken into a "club" where he had been sitting with other "gays" and beaten them up unmercifully. I had been aware in the Guards of people, sometimes brother officers, who were homosexual. We did not discuss this with them. They were not advocates for, or demonstrators of, a different way of life. They were just as good soldiers as we who were "straight". It seemed to me utterly intolerable that this poor man should have been beaten, humiliated and obliged to reveal his sexual orientation to me. There was nothing I could do. He was adamant that he would not name his attackers. He assured me, and I believed him, that he had never tried to seduce his colleagues. He wanted to be an acceptable colleague and a loyal member of a force he was proud of. I arranged for a transfer to another part of the Province and was glad to hear from him that he was happy and, from his superiors, that he was doing a good job.

In the summer of 1947 a great row broke out at Rasharkin. The Presbyterian Minster had had a dispute with his wife, who accused him, to some of her friends, of beating her. The Reverend Strong, whom I had got to know and like, was the most gentle of men and this rumour seemed to me just a little piece of tittle-tattle. Ian Paisley had just graduated from Bob Jones University in the Southern States, a Fundamental establishment which supported the Free Presbyterian Church which Paisley had founded, with his first church in Crossgar, Co. Down, a tin hut which I passed every day later.

A marquee was erected in a field opposite the Reverend Strong's church and media coverage was given to the Paisley meetings there, which were to take place simultaneously with Mr Strong's services. It was then that the media became quite excited. In those modest days the precise marital problems of the Strongs were unprintable, but "hint-hint", "nudge-nudge" soon gave the story the titillation to give it national coverage.

For several Sundays, I joined the Rasharkin police on the road outside the Presbyterian Church and the opposing marquee. From the latter, packed with the women members of Rasharkin Presbyterians, came the thunderous voice of the Reverend Ian. He has charisma. He has charm. He has an empathy with women which will get hundreds of women to work tirelessly for him, with no reward other than his warm praise and benediction.

Sunday after Sunday I watched the men leaving their wives and children and going into Rasharkin Church, while the wives went to Paisley's marquee. All this was happening in July, the flash-point month in Ulster, and there was now a great deal of political interest in what was happening in Rasharkin.

Terence O'Neill, who had been my brother-officer in 2nd Battalion Irish Guards, now announced that he was proposing to stand for the Northern Ireland Parliament for Mid-Antrim. I was delighted to hear this and went to see him at Ahoghill Rectory near Ballymena, where he had set up house. It seemed such a heaven-sent coincidence that two former Irish Guards Officers were to be involved in the North Antrim scene. Terence and I were thoroughly dismissive of Ian Paisley; after all he was only 21 and had a "degree" in a church which did not yet exist.

The Rasharkin drama ended dramatically. Mrs Strong got to her feet in the marquee (which had cost Ian Paisley a lot to rent) and said that forgiveness was what her Lord had preached. She forgave her husband for what she had alleged, and was returning to the Manse. Chaos!

Next day Ian had these problems:-

Paying for the marquee rent.

Giving credibility to the new Free Presbyterian Church, with only one hut in Crossgar.

Establishing a new fundamentalist belief for his supporters.

He seemed a solution without a problem.

Near Rasharkin there is a "sacred" well. The Catholic faithful make a procession to this on the feast of the Assumption, 15 August, to ask God's help to cure their sick.

I now quote Ian Paisley. He says: "I was at the Rasharkin Orange Hall, which I had addressed about the primitive, Lourdes-type, superstitious belief that this well had curative powers. It was a sensible, thoughtful meeting of Brethren who were not opposed to Catholics carrying out their practices, but disapproved of such pagan ideas, which the Holy Well epitomized." Suddenly, a Mephistophelan figure leapt on the stage of the Orange Hall. He was flashing the sword of a District Inspector of the RUC. I was terrified (!!). He addressed us, "Tomorrow in Rasharkin there will be a terrible confrontation. I have powers under the Public Order Act to ban the Catholic parade to the sacred well. But I am not going to do that. What I am going to do is to tell you that, if this procession is attacked, the full might of the RUC will be used to identify those breaching the peace, and to bring them to Court."

I don't remember the details of all this. My friend Ian Paisley has dined with me (he wineless) many times and told this story.

Next day, Sunday, the full might of the RUC's four policemen and me were there to keep the peace. The Parish Priest had, understandably, delegated his role to his curate, and about two dozen parishioners were there for the "pilgrimage". We had for the first time a radio-car and I reported to it that we were "going in". Shades of Normandy!

Led by the nervous curate with his shaking monstrance, we marched to the top of the hill, on the other side of which we could hear half a mile away the strong words of the Reverend Ian: "The desecration of the Sabbath day by the superstitious minions of Rome is now taking place. We must resist this with all our might." On we marched down the hill and the strident voice continued. The pace slowed; the curate seemed even more shaky. Within 200 yards Ian Paisley's voice rang out, on a new note: "Brethren, how can we stand here and watch our Sabbath desecrated by the Popish blasphemous Bread. Let us move behind our Orange Hall to show our feelings." As we walked, even slower, the crowd moved behind the little hall, and, as we passed, a few clods of earth (early ploughing had taken place) sailed over the hall without doing any injury.

Terence O'Neill was much exercised by this small incident. He had come to see me before the Rasharkin march and had been rather inclined to suggest that, as District Inspector, I should use my powers under the Public Order Act to ban the march to the "sacred well". When he realized my reluctance to do this, he abandoned it, but later told me that his application to join the Orange Order had been black-balled because of his support for my Rasharkin stand. It was essential for him to be a member of the Order to be elected as a Unionist MP.

The Rasharkin position was supported by the Inspector General, who sent me a most generous commendation about it, but I was immediately sent for by him to be told that Terence had suggested to the Orange Order that a way of solving the Rasharkin problem would be to exchange in my district, Rasharkin, for Glenarm, where Heather was living with the

Antrims. Rasharkin could quite reasonably be put into Ballymena District. I refused, saying that conceding to extremism, from any quarter, only raised its appetite. Dick Pim agreed completely.

A Reserve Force, of a rather military aspect, was formed in the RUC. Its role was to provide back-up in civil commotion, to police sensitive areas at times of confrontation, and to "show the flag" in a disciplined and impressive way to those who wished to break the peace. My friend Willy Moore, MC, a bachelor, was chosen to command the new Force. This coincided with my marriage to Heather, so I was not in the least resentful of his appointment. The Reserve Force was a great success. It had a Head Constable, John Hood, an ex-Irish Guards Drill Sergeant. It had tall, smart, well-disciplined men. It instilled respect for the law, and for public order.

After Willy Moore's death, Dick Pim sent for me and asked me to take over the Reserve Force. I had just managed to get a house, Heather was pregnant and I begged to be excused. He was not pleased and made it clear that I could not expect to go far in the Force if I was not prepared to give up personal convenience for the good of the Force. He was absolutely right – I should have preferred career to family. Instead of me a splendid DI Bob Winder, an ex-soldier of the Great War, but young-looking and fit, took on the job and did it well.

Some months later my father came home and suggested that we might drive to Greece, in a new car which he proposed to buy. Despite my having turned down the Reserve Force job, I asked Dick Pim for leave, which he agreed. We left our year-old Angela with Heather's mother Ethel and sister Anne, and set off for over a month's absence. It was a fascinating journey through France (where we saw the Cagny battlefield), Switzerland, Italy and Yugoslavia, where we were among the first tourists let in by Tito, and where we were sold Tourist Dinars which were rejected by garages and hoteliers; we had to sell clothing and whiskey in little auctions in towns like Skopje. We finally made it to Athens with worn-out brakes on our Austin A40, to a jubilant welcome from my parents and sister Carolyn. The weeks in Greece, seeing the Acropolis, Delphi, Euboea, Marathon and Lake Copais, gave us a wonderful insight into this part of Europe, in some ways the image of its westerly counterpart, Ireland.

On our return to Ballymoney a new feature of my RUC career emerged, the Public Order Act. This apparently innocuous piece of legislation was designed, it was said by its sponsors, to ameliorate the sectarian disputes, sometimes riots, which were so much a feature of life in the Ulster marching season. Every July and August politicians made aggressive speeches to commend themselves to voters who might not be as enthusiastic for them as a reading of their election manifesto had earlier given them promise.

There was one MP, Phelim O'Neill, who spoke at Cloughmills, great

McGuckian country, where the brothers McGuckian, by sheer enterprise, risk-taking and effort, had developed a pig business which was the largest in Ireland, possibly in Europe. John McGuckian was a young boy then, but has the McGuckian "entrepreneur" skills of his forebears.

Phelim, later Lord Rathcavan, made a speech which attacked the Public Order Act. He said it was a thinly-veiled sectarian effort, designed to boost the Orange Order and, by putting the decision on the local police, put them and particularly the District Inspector, who was the arbiter, in an impossible position. A Union Jack erected in a Nationalist area, an Eire tricolour in a Protestant area, was enough to cause a riot. His speech marked the end of his Unionist political career. Such views were totally unacceptable to his constituency. He was regarded as a hopeless eccentric. He was even believed to be in favour of "One man, one vote" in Derry! Local elections which put him "beyond the Pale" in Londonderry were seen as part of the Protestant heritage requiring special electoral arrangements to ensure that the Siege of Derry, endured by the Protestants, was not to be undermined by the prolific Catholic underclass of its suburbs.

I was there in uniform at this meeting and was impressed by Phelim's courage in speaking out in support of the impossible position in which the RUC was put, but was even then not so politically naive as to fail to see the implications. A disastrous political sound bite of the time was Basil Brooke's "A Protestant Government for a Protestant people".

In September 1955 an IRA raid on Gough Barracks, Armagh, produced several hundred weapons for the IRA. It was a brilliant coup. On a sleepy Saturday afternoon the IRA drove two lorries to the gates of the Royal Irish Fusiliers Depot and held up the guardroom, while members of the raiding party emptied the Armoury. Without a shot being fired, the lorries, piled with machine-guns, rifles and pistols, drove back across the border 10 miles away. The Commandant, Major Dermot Neill, was at his son's Prize Day at St Columba's, Dublin. The Adjutant, Michael Beggs was underneath his car doing repairs. It was the sort of surprise raid which the SAS had shown could be successful if carried out with speed and determination. There was a frightful row at Stormont. Allegations of disloyalty by the "Faughs", the nickname of the Irish Fusiliers, were bandied about and criticism of the RUC for not anticipating the raid was commonplace. The District Inspector, Armagh, was Jamie Flanagan. Recruited in Bangor by my father, this brilliant man had been his Staff Officer in Greece. He was due for transfer to Belfast, so it was not surprising that I was chosen to replace him.

Armagh, the ecclesiastical capital of Ireland, with the heads of both Catholic and Anglican churches, Archbishop Gregg and Cardinal D'Alton, was a District of key importance. It had a long border area, was home to the Speaker of the Northern Ireland Parliament, Sir Norman Stronge, and had the whole spectrum from Moy, the seat of the Orange Order, to Keady, which was solidly Republican. There was a nasty attitude to the "Faughs". The sort of comment at dinner-parties one heard was, "If Dermot Neill had any guts he would have shot himself when his armoury was seized by the IRA". My County Inspector was Tony Peacocke, formerly my Depot Commandant in Enniskillen. He took a calm and businesslike attitude to the Gough Barracks disaster, and the arrival of a new Commandant, Major Brian Clark, gave us confidence that this disciplinarian boss would ensure us no further such events. We stepped up patrolling, road blocks and activity by the Ulster Special Constabulary. In County Armagh there were 3,000 members, ready for call-out at short notice, a few hours, for £1 a night.

At dawn one morning I was called to be told that a Fusilier, in the guard-room because of an offence which the Commandant believed required him to be gaoled, had managed to seize a Sterling sub-machine gun and had held up the gate-sentries and escaped. A Southerner, it was obvious he would head for the Border, 10 miles away, so all the soldiers and police were put in action to capture him. We even had a helicopter, which spotted him making fast progress over the bogs near Keady. Brian Clarke and I set out for Keady and quite soon learned that the "berserk" soldier was in a lane with high banks, from which he would have trouble escaping. When we got there we found the police on one bank and the soldiers on the other, with the escapee, brandishing his Sterling, on the road. It was somehow expected of Brian and me that we should now end this affair. We found ourselves walking down the narrow road towards the soldier. Brian was the authoritarian: "Put that gun down." Then, "As your senior officer I am ordering you to drop your gun. Otherwise I will be forced to tell my soldiers to shoot you." My role was as the "soft man". I told him that his mother would be sad if he was shot, that he would be treated humanely if he surrendered, and used his Christian name, Paddy. Every few seconds he raised the sub-machine gun and pointed it at us. A burst would have finished us both. Brian became more strident, me more pleading. I could see the Fusilier's forefinger on the trigger and knew that Brian was about to order his soldiers to fire. The escaper put his left forearm in front of his gun and fired. He fell to the ground and was arrested.

Brian and I went home to Armagh. We had both been involved in a number of IRA attacks (all unsuccessful) on Gough Barracks and I thought I should honour the occasion by a toast. All there was in my drinks cupboard was a little poor sherry. I filled two glasses and said, "Brian, there is enough in this and a few other of our activities for a medal. Let's toss for it." The coin, rightly, came up for him, and I was happy to commend him for the George Medal, which he got and, with promotion, left Armagh.

He was succeeded by Harry Baxter, our friend from Athens whom we had met there on our recent visit. With his black eye-patch and rather stern military bearing, he seemed likely to be even more the "hard man" than Brian Clark. In fact he was the ideal successor, bringing about a harmonious atmosphere in Gough Barracks, improving the morale of the Irish Fusiliers, who were still smarting from the IRA raid, and with his wife Anne taking a full part in the social life of the city.

There was now, in the mid and late fifties, a real threat from the IRA – nothing like what occurred from 1970 onwards, but enough to worry peace-loving people. Several RUC men were murdered and there was a pitched battle at Brookeborough, which resulted in a number of IRA being killed and the Sergeant, Cordner, one of my men in Middletown earlier, being decorated. The differences between the 50s campaign and the later one were that the Catholic people were not in support of terrorism, even glorified as "the armed struggle". The IRA had quite limited objectives and saw Northern Ireland as a battleground stepping-stone which would soon be developed into the Republic, which they viewed with almost as much antipathy as Ulster. They were a threat, a serious threat, to Eire, but had not reckoned with De Valera, their progenitor, being utterly hostile to *their* all-Ireland plan. In great secrecy, and with only those "with a need to know", we developed the internment schedule. At that time the intelligence function of the RUC and the Gardai was highly developed. The records going back to the beginning of the century were shared between the two Forces. I showed my files to the Chief Superintendent in Monaghan and he shared his with me, when it related to what we called "Crime Special" matters. The internment plan was not something we discussed. The day arrived, one Sunday, when we "lifted" about thirty men in the Armagh area, about whom we had built up a prima facie case for believing that they were Republican activists, prepared for the "armed struggle". I was astonished to hear on the radio that across the Border precisely the same operation, on the same premise, was being carried out by the Gardai.

Predictably, there was a huge outcry. Nationalist politicians naturally saw this as Draconian law. Many were the interviews which claimed that we had got it wrong, that there was no question of their friends or family members being involved with the IRA. Because of the closeness of our relationship with the Gardai, we were now able to share the reasons why we had chosen the internees. The IRA campaign, which had begun to become very nasty, started to wind down. There were still bombings and shootings, but at longer intervals.

I was in a rather useful position to help the British Intelligence Services. Then, and for all I know, now, the Secret Intelligence Service had MI6 operating in the Republic, whilst MI5 did this in Northern Ireland, as part of the UK. Clearly there was a need for a liaison interface and Dick Pim volunteered me for this. Even at this length of time I prefer not to mention names, but people of great courage, integrity and love for Ireland were working on both sides of the Border to rid us of the IRA. A period of quite exhausting travel all over Ireland followed. My English accent and a fly-rod or a shotgun in its case gave me quite a convincing alias as a visiting Englishman, to meet MI6 contacts and to explain what MI5 in the North was about. The family, Heather particularly, were wonderfully tolerant of my sudden absences, which I could not, of course, explain.

Head Constable Alec Sterritt was in charge of intelligence for Co. Armagh. A mild, quiet, friendly man, he had the ability to understand the mentality of the IRA (Loyalist paramilitaries were unknown then). He was aware of my links with SIS and greatly encouraged me. Late one night he appeared at my door with a young man and asked me to talk to him. It seemed that Liam (not his real name) had been approached by the IRA and a mixture of blandishments and threats had been used to get him to join and to go to a training camp in Donegal. He said he was prepared to work for us. He did not ask for money. It is a familiar dilemma for policemen all over the world. Information is the lifeblood of police work, in both the anticipation and detection of crime; informers can do their work for money or for idealistic motives. They can also be extremely dangerous, leading police into traps, operating as "double-agents" and, having obtained police trust, compromising the operational and moral integrity which must buttress law enforcement. Fortunately in Ireland a great deal of experience of the pluses and minuses of the informers role existed on both sides of the Border.

Alec and I were convinced that we could trust Liam and told him so. Weeks passed and again late at night Alec and he appeared at my door in Armagh. We got into my car and drove to St Patrick's Cathedral. Liam took us to a shrubbery and we went through the tangled mass of brambles and laurels to a little clearing. Under a carpet of leaves he revealed a trap-door, which, when raised, had a crude ladder below, which he went down, followed by us with torches. A corridor ran to the centre of the Cathedral and into a large chamber which had at one time housed the heating system, now long replaced by more modern technology. Here were bunk beds, papers of all sorts and some bomb-making equipment – fuse wire, detonators and primers. As we were examining this a loud whirring scared us until, in a few seconds, the great clock struck midnight.

A typical dilemma faced us. Liam explained that when his training in Donegal, and later in Sligo, finished, his IRA Controller told him of the existence of the Cathedral hideout, that he was the only one to know of it, and that he was to return to his home and await orders to receive and help

. My grandparents, Dr and Mrs O'Brien, with eleven of their twelve children. Lulu, later Sister Veronica, is on my grandfather's knee. My mother is standing on the right.

. "A picture of Jack sitting in an open lorry with RIC men loading rifles and equipment . . ." (p. 3).

3. RUC Guard of Honour for King George VI aboard the Royal Yacht *Victoria and Albert*, Belfast, 1938. The Guard Commander was Major J. K. Gorman MC.

4. "There was only one thing to do and that was to use the naval tactic of ramming" (p. 38). "Ballyragget" is on the right. Operation Goodwood, 18 July, 1944.

5. "By now I was a Captain" (p. 53).

6. "My mother's sister, a nun with the title of Sister Veronica" (p. 66).

7. Meeting the Queen for the first time. Ballymoney, 1953.

8. "My name appeared in the New Year Honours for the MBE" (p. 98).

9. "He had with him Keith Granville, Deputy Chairman" (p. 138).

10. "He brought in a Baronet, Sir Giles Guthrie DSC, the Deputy Chairman of BEA" (p. 137).

11. "Will you accept the post of Director of Personnel?" (p. 137). I do and here I am at it.

12. "At the very top of Mount Royal was Redpath Crescent" (p. 159). We entertain in our new home.

13. "The first of these seminars I organized with the help of William Rees-Mogg, Editor of *The Times*, who got his Chairman Roy Thompson to make the keynote speech" (p. 164).

14. "The Show Tour promotion moved across Canada" (p. 163). Here Heather and I are in Halifax, Nova Scotia.

15. "Our son Johnny, a Second Lieutenant in the Irish Guards, had been awarded the George Medal - the first to be gained in the Regiment" (p. 172).

16. "I was lucky in my personal staff... Das Dang [was] an old-time stalwart of Imperial Airways and a man of ingenious talent with ability in many languages" (p. 175). Seen here with Heather and myself, Delhi, 1973.

17. Guests at the wedding of Das Dang's daughter.

18. Knut Hammersholt, Director General of IATA, Morarji Desai, Prime Minister of India, and the author (see p. 176).

19. "I was the landlord of over 200,000 houses in NIHE" (p. 180).

20. *Left to right:* J.G., Heather, head of J.G., "Victor Blease, who succeeded me as Chief Executive" (p. 183) and Carolyn Mulholland, sculptress.

21. Cooperation Ireland. The New York Marathon Team, 1991 (see p. 188).

22. "I spoke to the Queen about it" (p. 189)

23. "My friend Ian Paisley" (p. 83).

24. Mo Mowlam:
"I found her
refreshingly
warm and
chatty"
(p. 205).

25. "I rather unguardedly praised the leadership of Gerry Adams who seemed to be able to get the IRA to do his bidding" (p. 205).

26. [George Mitchell] "had enormous admiration for David Trimble" (p. 205).

27. Reunion Parade at Cagny, July 2000.

28. "Ballymena" restored. The caption on the back reads *"Après 2000 heures de travail voici le rèsultat obtenu. J'espere que vous serez satisfait"!*

29. In front of "Ballymena" with Sergeant James Baron MM and Guardsman Albert Scholes. Sadly, Baron died in August, 2002 and Scholes in 2000.

30. Heather and John, 2001.

an Active Service Unit, who were to carry out an operation in Armagh City which would require him to lead them to the Cathedral hiding-place, where they were to lie low until the hunt for the ASU died down. Liam was to lay in food for the Unit and to help them in any way they requested.

To raid the underground room, or to alert the clergy to its presence, and the use it was being put to, would have condemned him, probably, to a death sentence, so the only thing to do was nothing, so far as the Cathedral was concerned, but to step up security at Gough Barracks and at the two Armagh RUC stations, Russell Street and Irish Street. I instituted patrolling of RUC men in plain clothes and the Special Constabulary mobilized Constables, who carried Sterling sub-machine guns beneath their raincoats. We tried to use men whose faces were not familiar to Armagh citizens, but I underestimated the powers of observation of the public in what was in fact, though described as a City because of its heritage, a medium-sized town.

It was an eerie experience to attend Mass every Sunday, with our two elder children, Angela and Johnny, knowing that below us was a chamber which by now might be filled with explosives. After a couple of weeks, early one Monday morning I had a phone call from Sergeant J.J. Smyth, Station Sergeant at Russell Street. For a calm, indeed rather phlegmatic, man he sounded unusually excited and I went at once. The Sergeant was waiting in my office with three revolvers hooked on his forefingers.

He had been riding to Russell Street on his bicycle before 9 am when three young men ran across the road to the Cathedral, which he was passing, and up the 100 or more steps to the Cathedral. As he rode on he reflected on the unusual piety which would make three youths run up the Cathedral steps on a *Monday* morning. Putting down his bicycle, he climbed the steps and entered the Cathedral. He could not see the young men, but drew his revolver, as he thought he had seen movement in a Confessional at the end of the left-hand aisle. As he approached the Confessional, the curtain of the priest's booth opened and a revolver was pointed at him; there was a loud click and a young man fell out of the booth. Smyth went quickly to the other two booths and found two more young men, also with revolvers. Seizing the revolvers, but not opening them, he ordered the three to walk in front of him to Russell Street half a mile away, where he handed them over to Head Constable Isaac Keightley.

The Cardinal of All Ireland was then Cardinal D'Alton, whom I had got to know and respect. Telling Sergeant Smyth not to open the revolvers, I phoned His Eminence, who was at breakfast, and said I wanted to see him urgently. When we got there I asked Smyth for the first time to open the revolver which had been pointed at him through the Confessional curtain. There at 12 o'clock, the firing position, was a bullet which had been struck and which had not gone off – an extremely rare event, one which I had never seen throughout my wartime service.

Cardinal D'Alton did not hesitate. "There will be outcries now about the RUC violating the 'sanctuary' of my Cathedral; that the Church should give harbour to fleeing 'freedom fighters'. As far as I am concerned the hand of God has prevented murder in the Cathedral today. Please arrange for me to go on the media at once deprecating this dreadful act."

Returning to Russell Street, I found the Irish Street Sergeant, James Nethercott, "the Baa" to his friends, because of his rather high-pitched voice. It was through him that the ASU action was revealed to me. Outside this rather ancient Barracks we had erected a sandbagged emplacement, manned by an armed Constable all night, but at dawn the cold and weary man was relieved and the emplacement manned from time to time only.

Irish Street was then one of the poorest neighbourhoods of the city – small poorly built houses, crowded together, close to the walls of the Church of Ireland Cathedral, and with a high population density. There always seemed to be crowds of children about. The police "party" was at breakfast at 8.30, the sentry among them, when they heard a sharp "crack" at the door, went out and found a large suitcase inside the emplacement, (the detonator having gone off outside the body of the bomb). Electric fuse wires ran round the corner of the building. The Baa, who loved children and was very popular with all the inhabitants of Irish Street, was beside himself at the thought of what would have happened if the bomb had gone off. Minutes after the small explosion, Sergeant Harry McCullagh, who lived outside, came on the suitcase and, believing it to be a bomb awaiting detonation, picked it up and carried it to a nearby field. He was later decorated for this brave action.

Back now at Russell Street, it was essential to interrogate all three men independently. Liam told me that they had arrived from the Republic the previous day, Sunday, with a suitcase full of explosives. That night they had gone to the Cathedral underground chamber, where they had made up the bomb which was to be detonated by an electric firing mechanism. He had volunteered to place it in the sandbagged post and to return to where the other two men were waiting, when they would use the mechanism's plunger to explode the deadly case. When he got to the door of the Barracks he managed, with some difficulty because it was securely taped in, to pull out the detonator. The fact that children were in the streets going to school had been disregarded by his two companions. The plunger was pressed, but only the detonator went off and the gunmen ran off. They had seen Sergeant Smyth bicycling past the Cathedral and had run into it hoping that he would not follow. Then, after a while, they would have used the underground chamber for a day or two.

It was clear Liam had a lot more information. He had the locations of the two training grounds, and names and descriptions, not only of those they had met, but others about whom they had been told. He had managed to catch snatches of conversations and little bits of evidence which he was able to convey graphically. I had the luck to have a clerk who was a fast, accurate shorthand typist. Over thirty pages of detailed information were the result.

All three were indicted and, refusing to recognize the Court, sentenced to fourteen years' imprisonment.

My Sterling-armed police patrols were still operating. Head Constable Keightley was getting worried about them. He did not believe that the IRA and its supporters could still, after several weeks, not be aware that armed plain clothes police were on the streets. I was in Mayo when I heard on Radio Eireann that the IRA had held up and disarmed two RUC men in Armagh. Driving through the night, I was there the next day. The two men, walking separately, had been passing the wall of the Christian Brothers School when, with exact timing, a revolver was pressed into their heads by gunmen hiding behind the wall. They had no option but to put their hands up. The gunmen hopped over the wall, disarmed them and disappeared.

One was a mobilized member of the Ulster Special Constabulary – the much-maligned "B-Men". He was a bright, disciplined country lad, delighted to have the work, status and pay of an RUC man during this emergency. The RUC Constable was of the same calibre and a Roman Catholic. I was clearly at fault in insisting on this operation, though in my defence I was able to claim that, with the exception of the Irish Street bomb, Armagh had been peaceful. The reaction of members of the professional class and people whom we met at social occasions was revealing. It was mostly women who would say, "Have you checked whether your RC Constable isn't conniving with the IRA?" Others would say, "How come that the senior of the two, the RC Constable, took that route, past the Christian Brothers wall?" My reaction to these remarks did not increase my popularity. Another reaction, from the nationalist community, was, "Maybe the 'B-Man' saw a good chance of getting two Sterlings". I was equally outraged.

A Court of Enquiry was set up, chaired by Graham Shillington, later Sir Graham, the last RUC Inspector General. The Court consisted of Shillington and Colonel Bobby Scott, County Commandant of the USC Tyrone. Though the Court was not held in public, the media took a great interest and the decision that the operation was mistaken, but might have paid off, did not result in the sacking or transfer which I had anticipated. Head Constable Keightley, who could have made much of his warning, about which I had given evidence, did not emphasize this unduly.

A growing problem was the number of occasions on which Special Constabulary patrols mostly, but also RUC and Army checkpoints, were confronted by cars which drove through them. More often than not the non-stopping cars were being driven by joy-riders, drunks or men who had a passenger they should not have had. At times of IRA activity it was understandable that roadblock patrols, sometimes in danger of having one or more of its members run down, would open fire. To order that fire be directed at the car wheels was a counsel of perfection. In darkness, with all the speed, surprise and danger of a charging car, shots were highly likely to kill or injure driver or passengers. Each death led to an inquest and I became extremely concerned at the damage this was doing to the security forces and the tragedy of people, often quite young, being killed because of a moment's recklessness.

It occurred to me that a torch, fitted parallel to the barrel of a gun, would illuminate, at short range, the point of strike of the bullet. Choosing the new Sterling sub-machine gun, I experimented with this idea. Although crude, it did seem to have potential, so I consulted an electrician friend, Fred Gordon, who ran a small electrical business in Scotch Street, Armagh. He pointed out some snags:-

If the torch-beam was wide enough to show up the whole car, it was too wide to focus shots.

If the focus was narrowed, so as to have a spot on the target where the shots would strike, this would be too narrow to see the whole target.

Charging cars were not the only potential target. If it was, say, an armed terrorist, the torch light would provide a fine aiming mark for him.

Torch batteries were then of limited life.

Gordon was not a man who let problems deter him. He discovered that the latest spaceships had silver-zinc batteries, the size of a 20-cigarette packet, which were rechargeable and could provide 6 volts for 30 minutes or so. By adding a torch-sized additional light to the casing, with a second press-button switch, the beam width could be widened. By using a cinema projector bulb, a square image was drawn by the device, which, with a secure clip and adjusting screws, could be made totally coaxial with the barrel. Where the square light (1 ft. square at 30 ft.) shone, the shots would hit.

We discovered that by using a cluster of capillary tubes in front of the "torch" beam, the light was fully visible only from the front, with a glow only visible from the sides. We decided the device needed a name and called it the TIGA (Target Illuminating Gun Aimer). I patented it, which cost over £100, a lot of money for me, and Fred, who had done all this work for nothing, was clearly out of pocket, so when the moment came to demonstrate our secret weapon a lot hung on it. Sir Richard Pim was enthusiastic and recommended to the Ministry of Home Affairs that it should be made standard equipment for every patrol of the RUC and USC. This would have required at least 500 TIGAs. In true Civil Service style the Ministry turned this down, with a side-swipe at me, claiming that it was not my job to invent better means of equipping the police. As far as the patent was concerned, that had been my decision and was for me alone to pay for.

Dick Pim, despite the fact that he had himself been, after his RIC service, a civil servant in the Ministry of Home Affairs, lost no time in telling Sir Basil Brooke, the Prime Minister, about the TIGA. Fred and I had an invitation to bring it to his Fermanagh home, Colebrooke. It was getting dark when we arrived. He met us at his door, and told us that he had a herd of Japanese deer called Sikas, which were fast runners, the size of an Alsatian dog, and he had spent a lifetime trying to shoot one in the dark and had never succeeded.

With Fred looking on anxiously, I was positioned on the top of a small hill, and the Prime Minister, who had seen some Sikas in a wood below the hill, went off to act as beater. It was pitch dark, but I could hear a deer running towards me. I pressed the "torch" button and saw it running fast but veering away from the light. I pressed the other button, aimed below the left shoulder of the deer and fired one round. It dropped dead and the delighted Prime Minister informed Fred and me that he was most impressed and would tell the Ministry so.

As we drove back to Armagh, Fred and I began to believe that we were on the verge of a financial success. Indeed, after much haggling, where we managed to get our costs recouped on the first "tranche" of TIGAs, I think 100, we could look forward to a modest profit.

Happily the IRA, beaten because Catholic support, never high, had waned to zero and because the Intelligence institutions on both sides of the Border had developed so well, were obviously beginning to realize that the bogus historical "armed struggle" had been a total disaster, and were now suing for peace. Further orders for the TIGA were not forthcoming, but neither Fred nor I were complaining.

Looking back on that 1960 success, I have three comments. (A) Without the implacable hostility of De Valera, introducing internment and even firing squads for IRA volunteers, the Ulster success could never have happened. (B) The intelligence mechanisms were perfected. (C) The underclass of young non-achiever loners, who are the IRA's recruits, were then able to work, as almost full employment existed in the UK, including Northern Ireland.

It has astonished me that otherwise sensible Generals have so frequently been on the media to explain that the IRA is unbeatable and that a "political solution" must be found. The IRA was beaten in the 1950s, and could be again, especially as Northern Ireland is seen as important by the US, Europe and, of course, London and Dublin.

To return to the TIGA. The Army had been very impressed by the demonstration carried out by the RUC and I was invited to go to the Small Arms School in England. The demonstration went perfectly and the school carried out a testing programme, which included dropping the TIGA from the top of a building and putting it under water, but resulting in a favourable report and a recommendation that British troops in Cyprus, then in battle with EOKA, (General Grivas and Bishop Makarios), should be equipped with it. Fred and I discussed how we would fund a little factory to turn out TIGAs by the hundred. The Cyprus War came to an end. Makarios and the British Government came to an agreement, and the immediate value of TIGA was now reduced, so no order.

The Army suggested that their Small Arms School report might be valuable to the French, who were fighting a bitter battle in Algeria. Fred and I had our hopes raised and an invitation from the Military Attaché of the French Embassy at Hyde Park arrived, with a ticket by air to London. Alas for us, de Gaulle settled his war in Algeria, so no orders. It seemed that the certain way to bring peace was to try to introduce the TIGA!

My MI5 and 6 friends were aware that the "armed struggle" was gradually coming to an end and asked if I would be interested in anything other than the RUC, which would inevitably go through what is now called "down-sizing", given the removal of immediate terrorist threat. I discussed this rather vague suggestion with Heather. Her view was pragmatic and much influenced by what we could do for the children. Angela was now 8 and at the Sacred Heart Convent in Armagh, and doing well; Johnny, aged 6, who was born at home at Ballymoney (Heather had all four births at home) was at St Malachy's Primary School in Armagh. Heather was pregnant with Rosanagh when I was transferred to Armagh in 1954, and we had booked Nurse Pollock, the midwife nurse who had been such a treasure for the first two, and who came from Strabane. A few days before her planned arrival, a Saturday night, I had a call at my Armagh digs from Heather to say that the baby was starting, that Dr Sanderson, her doctor, was out and that she had asked a young woman, Marie Robinson, living opposite us to come and help her. I was worried and pleaded to let me call an ambulance, but Heather was adamant that she would not leave Angela and Johnny, and wanted to have the baby at home.

A wild drive from Armagh to Ballymoney got me there an hour later, to find Heather happily in bed with Rosanagh, with the amateur midwife Marie in attendance! Next day Nurse Pollock came with admonitions that if we were to have babies at this rate we need not be surprised if practice in child-birth made them arrive more quickly, so we should book her earlier!

Sadly, when our younger son Justin was born in 1959 in Armagh Nurse Pollock was not available, but again all went well and he was a welcome addition, making up our quartet.

We have been wonderfully fortunate in our family. Our eldest Angela, a graduate of McGill University, Montreal, and Goldsmith's College London, is mother of three children and a dedicated teacher at Roedean School, Johannesburg. Her husband Desmond and the children live there.

Johnny, former Captain The Life Guards, earlier Irish Guards, banker and now successful art dealer, owner of Quantum Contemporary Art, London.

Rosanagh, also a McGill graduate, and later at L.S.E. London, a successful businesswomen, happy wife and mother of two boys.

Justin, a qualified tree surgeon, is now running his own wood business and living near us, with his wife and two daughters.

With the terrorist threat reducing and our family thriving, we were able to have a more social life and a lot of this centred on the Royal Irish Fusiliers Depot, just above our house, where Harry Baxter, the Commandant, Hal Chavasse, his Adjutant, Bob and Caryl Lucas-Clements and Tony Brady and his wife Micki were our close friends. The County Inspector was Douglas Wolseley, who had succeeded Tony Peacocke, now Commissioner in Belfast.

Our neighbours were Colonel Tony Morris O.B.E., M.C., and his wife Merle. He commanded the Royal Irish Fusiliers T.A. Battalion, was a fellow Catholic and a Knight of Malta. Merle was the widow of Commander Verschoyle-Campbell, the youngest Submariner Commander in the Royal Navy, and had Dermot by him, and James and Timothy by Tony. We had happy times with them, and again later in England, and now see them in Connemara where they live, close to Alcock and Brown's first transatlantic landing place.

Drama once more played a big part in our lives and Heather did well in a production of *Autumn Sunshine,* a comedy about a sea-cruise. I was asked to produce plays and had the ambitious idea of putting on *Separate Tables* by Terence Rattigan, which required the leading actor and actress to take two totally dissimilar parts in both sections of a play about a seaside boarding house. Douglas Wolseley's wife, whom I had known for many years as Patricia Teale in Co. Fermanagh, strikingly attractive, with great poise and acting ability, took the part of the down-trodden, bullied daughter of a dominating mother, who falls in love with a pathetic fellow guest, a bogus "Major", with a criminal record for sex offences, and in the second section the part of an extremely sophisticated European wife of a rich socialite. The parts of the "Major" and the tycoon were played by Stanley Fitzgerald, who was one of the best actors I have ever come across.

One of the difficulties of amateur acting is the regional accent, which is so pronounced in Ulster, but both these splendid actors, and Mary Wilson, chatelaine of Armagh's main hotel, the Beresford Arms, had no problem about this and could be English, Scottish or American perfectly, when this was required.

There were a lot of scene-changes, handled by a dedicated team, with Reggie McEwen, a Royal School teacher, who also acted well, helping. We decided to take *Separate Tables* to the Bangor Festival, after it had been staged several times to packed houses in Armagh. The reviews in the Northern Ireland press were enthusiastic and word of this amateur production reached London. I had a threatening letter from the Company which was producing the play in the West End, which was still running, telling me that while French's, the vendors of stage scripts, had quite properly printed and sold us the scripts, copyright was still in the possession of the producing Company, which would under no circumstances permit an amateur production of *Separate Tables* until its professional run was completed.

By now the play was advertised and was one of the main features of the Bangor Festival. I had been made a member of the Council for the Encouragement of Music and the Arts (CEMA), forerunner of the Arts Council, by its Director, John Lewis-Crosby, and the Council made an appeal directly to Rattigan on the basis that a Northern Ireland amateur production of *Separate Tables*, far from taking business away from the professional tour (which did not include Belfast) would encourage Ulster visitors to go to London to see it. John Lewis-Crosby, a wartime brother-officer in the Irish Guards, an opera singer and later head of Christie's in the Province, was one of the most persuasive people I know, and he got a grudging acceptance of our breach of copyright, with stinging comments about the observance of the law. He had not disclosed that the Armagh producer was a senior police officer!

The Bangor production was very successful. TV was in its infancy and it was not difficult to get a full house for a good amateur production; but good as we were (or thought we were!) the Bangor Club was better, under its talented producer John Knipe, and Colin Blakeley, who became famous professionally later, in its production of *Our Town*, the Thornton Wilder classic. Bangor won. We were also in production of *Gaslight*, in which I acted the part of the young husband, and it was taken to the Grand Opera House, to the Finals of the Drama Festivals, where the best productions from the five Festivals were played.

We were on holiday in Rossnowlagh, Co Donegal, when we learned that I had won the Best Actor Award. It was not true acting at all. The part required that I should play the rather naive, very English, young man, deeply in love with his wife, putting on a show of courage and sang-froid to reassure her when confronted with terrifying situations. It was nice to win, though, and impressed my fellow Council members of CEMA.

The belief that the IRA campaign was virtually over was shattered when another attempt on Gough Barracks was made. For several years all the legally held explosive in Co Armagh was kept there, to be drawn when required for quarrying etc by the licensed owners. Many tons of dynamite, TNT and other explosives were stored in the Gough Barracks Armoury, and it was closely guarded, as was the perimeter of the Barracks, which had look-out sentry posts at each corner of the complex. One day a canvas holdall was found in the middle of the Armoury and the Commandant and Adjutant were called. Major Baxter and Captain Chavasse were quickly on the scene and opened the holdall. Therein was a clockwork device ticking away. Harry told Hal to get a vehicle and back it to the Armoury door. When this was done he picked up the holdall and put it in the back of the lorry. Hal drove it to open ground several hundred yards away, where they abandoned the vehicle. They had gone a field's length away when the bomb exploded. There was no doubt that had it not been for the patrolling sentry seeing the holdall and the two officers acting so bravely and immediately a huge dump of explosives would have caused death and destruction throughout Armagh.

It was evident that this was an "inside job". Only a Royal Irish Fusilier could have penetrated the Armoury, indeed only a member of a guard patrol could have had access to the locked building. There were 150 soldiers in Barracks, a high proportion of them from the Republic. Every soldier has to pledge loyalty to the Queen and I had the idea of interviewing each Fusilier, whether from the Republic or not, and asking them to sign a paper which confirmed their pledge. It was unlikely, I knew, that traitorous IRA pretending to be British soldiers would break down and confess, but coupled with confinement to Barracks, which the Commandant had imposed while police enquiries, in which the Military Police took a major part, were taking place, it seemed to me that we might at least scare the traitors enough for them to run for it. Several days later the CB was relaxed, on Sunday, for Fusiliers to go to church. All signed out, eager I suppose, to get out for a few hours. Two did not return.

Harry and I reckoned that those two had been able to get a message to the IRA, who would have got them across the Border in 15 minutes, despite the fact that every road had a patrol stopping cars from Armagh to Monaghan. Maybe we should have issued every patrol with a picture of each Fusilier, maybe we should have got Customs at each Border post to search every car containing young Irish men returning from Mass (just imagine the outcry if such an order had been given). All I know is that the whole episode once more confirmed the ruthlessness, and dishonour, of an organization which used the British Army as trainers, and disgraced a great regiment by infiltrating traitors to its ranks.

Harry Baxter was awarded the George Medal for his heroic deed and Hal Chavasse the MBE. Shortly afterwards my name appeared in the New Years Honours for the MBE. It was not difficult to arrange the Investiture on the same day at Buckingham Palace.

The Investiture of the three of us was the first time I had had more than a brief word with the Queen. After her Coronation she had visited Ballymoney and I had been introduced to her there, but had not had any conversation. This time she wanted to know more about the terrorist campaign and was clearly pleased at the good RUC/Army relationship, which we trio epitomized. My father and Heather were there and we had a celebration luncheon at the Guards Club, with Harry, Anne and Hal.

Although desultory attacks on the security forces were continuing, by Christmas 1959 there was a euphoric feeling that the "armed struggle" was ending and the Minister of Home Affairs, Ken Topping QC, visited all the Border strongpoints to give seasonal good wishes to us. Middletown was one of the most frequently attacked Barracks and I met him there. He asked to see the accommodation in this elderly building, which housed twice as many police as it was designed for. On the bottom floor were two cells, and despite rather pained looks and head-shaking from the two Sergeants there, I insisted on taking Mr Topping to see where I claimed we would put any further IRA attackers. I should have been less boastful. When I threw open the wooden door there was a large goose standing on the wooden bed, doing what comes naturally to geese. Clearly it was the "party's" Christmas dinner. There was a shocked silence. I heard myself saying, "Of course, Minister, we must remember that the geese saved Rome". Ulster Ministers, all of whom were Orangemen then, could hardly have been enthusiastic for this proposition and he left in silence.

Early in 1960 my Security Service friends told me that there was an important post in London for which they had been asked to find a suitable occupant. Was I willing to have my name put forward? Despite the rather vague offer, and a new-born baby, plus, as always, very little money, Heather was willing to take what was essentially a gamble. It would have been dishonourable to pursue this without the knowledge of Dick Pim, so I went to see him. All I knew was that it was an international job with an MI6 link and that I would have to take my chance with other candidates.

The Inspector General was marvellous. He could well have been piqued that someone given such a senior RUC post so early, who had declined the Reserve Force and who he had just put up for the MBE, should be considering leaving Ulster. But nothing of the sort; his attitude was encouraging; his lack of surprise gave me the strong impression that he knew more about the potential job than I did. He was standing up and, gesturing to his IG's chair, said, "Of course, you could never expect to sit there". At that time it was true, and it was frank and friendly of this most liberal of men, a Quaker himself, to have said so.

The TIGA did me a last good turn. The French Embassy in London sent me a ticket to discuss the device again, even though by now the Algerian volte-face had lessened the French need for it. The invitation coincided with MI6 asking me to go to London to hear what was being proposed for me. Our finances then did not run to expeditions to London! When I met MI6 it was a most exciting suggestion. The job was to be Deputy to the Chief of Security of BOAC, BA's predecessor airline. It would involve worldwide duties in the safety and security field, relating to BOAC's customers and staff, and an eventual succession to Donald Fish, the head of the airline's security function.

There were three other objectives:

To give the Board help in stopping politically motivated strikes – there was a shop steward named Maitland, who seemed to be able to get BOAC engineers to demonstrate in favour, for instance, of Russia's crude put-down of the Hungarian rising.

To bring to an end the involvement of BOAC aircrew in gold-smuggling to the Indian sub-continent.

To take charge of all aspects of a Royal Tour of nearly two months' duration to Asian countries, involving the Queen, Prince Philip and an entourage of 120. This was not just a security challenge, it also required administration and interface with the many national institutions and individuals who would be involved.

I went home with my mind reeling. Clearly there would have to be a strong rapport between Donald Fish and myself. MI6 were reticent about him. All I was told was that he had retired early from the London Metropolitan Police and that he had been a successful detective. Heather was her usual supportive self and as the months passed with no further contact with MI6 (I was not to phone them, they would contact me) it began to seem a chimera. In a familiar phrase someone was "offering me a seat in a show he did not own".

Early that summer, 1960, we went to Mullaghmore for a family holiday. We borrowed caravans from Ernest Sandford and David Corbett, as, now with four children, an au pair and Heather and me, we were a sizeable group. Donegal Bay in early summer is delightful; the water is no colder (because of the Gulf Stream) than later in the year, the fuschias are in flower and the tourists are not too numerous. We had the whole month of May and the children loved it. They would be in the water several times a day. I remember Rosanagh in a strange bathing-cap which reminded me of a rather lopsided divers helmet, running in from the waves shouting, "Its b-b-b-boiling," her little teeth chattering. One day a covey of nuns appeared on our almost deserted beach and they went into the sea with tent-like "habits", but, from the cries we heard, were having a wonderful time. Then it started to rain. It rained for days. We played "Racing Demon", we did guessing games, we got comics for the children to read. We had a radio, but seven people in a caravan all day is hard to take. We got a little respite by sentencing children who had misbehaved to the "Baddies Caravan", the smaller and older of the two, but this became less effective when the au pair, on her night off, met a handsome Mullaghmore young man, was insistent that he was the love of her life and wanted to see him nightly. We had to put Angela and Johnny, the elder two, in the Baddies Caravan, keeping Rosanagh and Justin (6 months old) with us.

I had run out of reading matter, so was reduced to the *Radio Times*. In it was a competition by Lockwoods, the tinned food company. It offered new cars, foreign holidays, cash in lieu, for anyone who could put in order of merit four slogans. My Permutations and Combinations education told me that 4 x 3 x 2 x 1 = 24 was certain to provide a correct answer, so I started to fill up the application. But this needed twenty-four copies of the Radio Times, and the Mullaghmore shop, had only twelve. We had an Austin A70, a large car, so embarked on a Donegal journey to get another dozen entry copies. Typically I had not read the small print. Each entry had to have the label of a Lockwood tin. So, seven people went round villages in Donegal to find Lockwood tins. Some rather rusty tins were produced, twenty-four in all, and we returned to the caravans. No one thought to label the tins which were now denuded of their identification, but it seemed sensible to eat some of the contents of the anonymous tins. Most of them were "Macedoine of Vegetables". Not popular with the little family, but it was all becoming quite a team effort, when, for the final time, I read the small print again. It said, "In the event of a tie, a fifth slogan will be used by the Judges to decide the winner". After the Macedoine débâcle there was derision about Lockwood's delicacies, and being told then that "Lockwood stinks" would not win, they settled for "Lockwood's taste" . . . !

Off went our twenty-four entries and delivered to the "Goodies" caravan was a letter which we were convinced would give us the news that after all this we had won a great prize. There was excitement when I opened the letter, which said we had won – an electric kettle, as there had been several hundred winners! I had some wry amusement when on buses in London I saw the slogan "Lockwood's Taste"!

When we got back to Armagh there was a message awaiting me from the Managing Director of BOAC, Mr Basil Smallpeice, inviting me to meet him at Airways Terminal in London and sending a ticket! We got on famously and, as I had had briefings on what particular issues I was required to concentrate on, it was not difficult to describe how my RUC experience would help in the Communist infiltration and gold-smuggling problems. So far as the Royal Tour was concerned, I could only offer some administrative skill and ability to get on with people.

Soon afterwards, having sent off my CV, I was called for interview by the Board at Heathrow Airport. Arriving in good time, I was intercepted by Security Officer Oliver, the first person of the Security staff I had met. He was very well turned-out, polite and intelligent, an ex-soldier. He told me that Mr Fish, the current Security Chief, would like to see me for a short chat before the Selection Board and led me to his office. Donald Fish, a tall, saturnine figure, could not have been more unwelcoming. He told me of his lack of admiration for the RUC, which he regarded as second-rate in comparison to the Metropolitan. He told me that he was totally opposed to youthful "seeded players" who achieved senior rank, by-passing people who had slogged through all the ranks. He told me that there was nothing which airline security could do to stop gold-smuggling, that it was up to Customs and police in the Near, Middle and Far East. He became rather excited and said that he had already contacted an outstanding detective officer from the Met, whom he believed would be ideal, and finally that he did not want me as his Deputy, or in any other capacity. When I could get a word in I asked if he was a member of the Selection Board, due in a few minutes. This enraged him still further, as he said he had been humiliated by being left off it. Rather oddly, I left his office quite light-heartedly. It seemed to me that, if the Board wanted me, Fish would go, and if they did not want me, then I could return to the RUC without any loss of face, as only Dick Pim knew about the MI6 intervention.

Next day I heard from Ken Staple, the airline's Secretary and Legal Adviser, that I had been selected and an offer was in the post. The following day he phoned again and said Donald Fish had resigned, with immediate effect, was in fact gone, and could I come at once. Again Dick Pim helped me and persuaded the Ministry of Home Affairs, now headed by Brian Faulkner, that the security function of the UK's flag-carrier airline was an important position and that an RUC Officer achieving success in it would reflect well on the Force. He had from the beginning been concerned about my pensionable position; pension "portability" was less common then, and certainly it was not unreasonable that a public service such as the RUC and a publicly-owned (Government) airline should have no difficulty in the NI Government handing over its and my contributions, and the airline in accepting these to give me the benefit of 15 years of previous pensionable service. My BOAC letter said this was acceptable and Dick was sure that the NI Government would also, so like the 20-year-old in the Prudential ad, I gave this pension issue little thought.

It was sad saying good-bye to so many friends and colleagues, and as the house we rented in Victoria Street would suit the Durkan family (Brendan Durkan, father of the SDLP's present Deputy First Minister, Mark Durkan, was to succeed me as District Inspector), Heather and the children moved out to Kilmore to a flat in the manor house, owned by our friends Richard and Lydia Graves-Johnston.

Chapter Eight

BOAC – CHIEF OF SECURITY

The job I was taking on was challenging. BOAC Security had staff in the United States and Canada, Pakistan and India, Hong Kong and Africa. There were about sixty uniformed staff at Heathrow, many of whom were ex-policemen and/or ex-servicemen. The senior officer was Douglas Buchanan, an ex-RAF Scot, against whom I had been warned by Fish, who disliked him intensely. This probably warmed me to Douglas, who took me under his wing and told me the whole story of the Fish regime, not all of which had, by any means, been unsuccessful. Fish had certainly achieved high co-operation from the Metropolitan Police. He was grudging in his praise of the efforts of his staff, highly suspicious of them and indeed of Directors and Managers all over the world. There was clearly much to be done to raise morale and achieve recognition and respect for the airline world-wide.

Buchanan's final revelation was that Donald Fish had negotiated the publication of a book *Zero One, The Airline Detective* and that TV rights had also been negotiated. Rather diminishingly it seemed as though it was not so much my arrival which had caused his departure, as the need to get the book and TV series on the market, which of course he could not do while still in office. If Douglas's information was right (and it usually was) the sum he was to get was huge, well into six figures.

Ken Staple, whose department I was part of, asked me to give him a report in eight weeks, outlining the plans I had to fulfill the outline objectives discussed at our first meeting. Fortunately my aunt Kitty Fraser at Hampton Court was happy for me to live there for a while, and another aunt at Walton-on-Thames, Marie Baynham (whose husband Hubert had served in the RIC with my father and had been very badly disabled by being shot by the IRA), was ready to have me when Kitty and her husband were away. This was one of the most testing times of my life.

One of the first jobs I had to do was to repair what was clearly some disaffection towards me from the Met. I wrote to Sir Joseph Simpson, the Commissioner, asking for an interview, and to my delight shortly got a letter inviting me to meet him at Scotland Yard. When I got there he had with him his deputy Sir Ranulph Bacon (whom I later knew as "Rasher") and the heads of the departments I would probably have dealings with, including the CID. They could not have been more welcoming and helpful, and when I left Joe Simpson said, "Any friend of Dick Pim's is a friend of mine", or words to that effect. Years later Dick told me that Simpson had phoned him to find out about this Irish interloper into London Metropolitan's bailiwick!

Within three weeks I embarked on a journey round the world by Comet, Boeing 707, Stratocruiser, DC7, to mention only some of the BOAC aircraft types. Douglas Buchanan came with me as far as Hong Kong and we spent a day each in Beirut and Bahrain, two days in Karachi and Delhi. Then Hong Kong and flying on my own to Hawaii, where I met my North American security chief, John Buckley, formerly of the New York City Police, travelling with him to New York, where I met his staff, all NYCP men and excellent, then back to London.

On this journey I met BOAC Managers, who were clearly glad to see a new man, though many of them were cautious about Buchanan (and seemed to me to have accepted too readily Fish's assessment of him), police chiefs, Ambassadors and High Commissioners, business leaders, such as Hong Kong "taipans" Hugh Barton (ex-Irish Guards) and Sir Michael Young-Harries, his successor at Jardine Matheson and the Hong Kong and Shanghai Bank. The outstanding man on my staff was John Dominic in Pakistan. Of good Christian stock, a devoted Catholic, John had been a Superintendent in the Indian Police before Independence. He was in the Punjab when the partition of the Indian sub-continent took place and the internecine massacres started. He described seeing trains arriving at the new border with Pakistan, filled with dead and dying men, women and children, Muslims trying to escape to save themselves from the Sikhs, the "Surdajis" as he called them (the turbaned ones), and how his appeals to his senior Indian Police Chiefs fell on deaf ears. Without a thought for his own career, this brave man climbed on one of these blood-soaked trains and left for Pakistan, penniless and jobless. It happened that Buchanan was in Karachi and when he met Dominic realized what an outstanding man he was and recruited him as a Security Officer. He was to play a major part in our lives.

John Buckley, whom I met for the first time in Honolulu, was an Irish-American, wise-cracking, benevolent-looking, but with an extraordinarily racist outlook. Italians were "guineas", blacks were "nig-nogs", Germans were "krauts". He was a talented policeman, who had retired early enough to begin a new career, and was popular with his staff and the North American management of the airline, which had just absorbed British South American Airways after crashes of the Tudor aircraft.

He clearly wanted to impress me and had booked me into a Penthouse Suite of the Reef Hotel on Waikiki Beach, and then took me to a Japanese restaurant – his chauvinism did not extend, it seemed, to the Japs. He ordered a meal from a menu totally incomprehensible to me. It started with shrimps, fried, continued with shrimps, boiled, then shrimps in sauce, followed by a shrimp salad; shrimps followed one after the other, in a flow which only ended when I suggested mildly that a cup of coffee would go down well. It must have been made of the water in which shrimps had been boiled, as it tasted strongly of shrimps.

When we returned to the Reef Hotel I inspected my suite and discovered that I had a laundry room with washing and drying, ironing and every sort of soap powder. Having been on the move for two weeks or more, I had a mass of shirts and decided to try my hand as a launderer. I washed them alright, but could not get the hang of the drying and automatic ironing machines. As I had a balcony to my 10th floor suite and there was a balmy breeze from the Pacific, I hung my ten shirts over the rail to dry and went to bed. Early next morning I was conscious of the wind getting up. My shirts had gone, but looking down the floors below me I could see them spread-eagled on many other balconies. The receptionist came with a hotel layout plan and we worked out which suites had one of my shirts. I rang the first bell and a rather angry-looking large man in a vest appeared. From noises we had heard as we waited at the door, it sounded as though the lady inside the apartment and he had been having a row. "I think a shirt of mine is here." "Wha-a-a-t – whatyamean- what were you doing here to leave your shirt?" The lady appeared, more shouting. The receptionist tried to cool it down, but the story about my shirt sounded shifty to say the least. Fortunately, the lady ran to their balcony where in the steady Pacific wind, a shirt was pressed against their rail, called her man to see, who saw some of the others too. A dangerous moment has passed. The receptionist and I used a more tactful approach at the other apartments, and got all, or most, of the shirts back.

John Buckley and I flew on to New York, where it had been snowing. My first impression of the Big Apple's skyline was that it looked elegant, especially in the snow, as thousands of pictures had shown me, but the underlying scene in the poorer, crowded, mostly black, parts of the city created a similarity in gardening terms of beautiful flowers springing from noisome dirt. Oddly the sudden snowfall had hidden this and the steam rising from manholes of the city's heating system gave an ethereal look to slums, which next day, when the snow had melted, looked worse than usual. John introduced me to the NYC Police Commissioner and many senior officers, and took me to meet the National Rifle Association chiefs. It was a revelation to learn of the obsession of law-abiding Americans with firearms. It was not just the hobby of rifle-range shooting as practised by the Ulster Special Constabulary which being subsidized by Government, gave a powerful incentive to join, but a manifestation of manhood, the possession of, and readiness to use, lethal weapons.

It had been a revelationary fortnight. I had got some understanding of the world-wide business, met key people, British and foreign, in many countries, and had begun to form some clear idea of a structure and role for my Department, which had some outstanding strengths and obvious weaknesses.

Well before my eight-week settling-in period was up, I gave a report to the Secretary and Legal Advisor. In it I recommended three Superintendents of Security should be appointed, Eastern Douglas Buchanan, Western John Buckley, and a third to cover Europe and Africa, to be recruited. I asked for a Security headquarters, in a small building opposite to the "Kremlin", as the main BOAC Headquarters block was called, and for my own office an Assistant, George Hogg, a Yorkshireman, reliable, intelligent and respected. The sixty uniformed staff needed a leader and I proposed to bring John Dominic from Pakistan to be their chief. There were proposals to draw up a Code of Conduct for Security and to ensure that everyone in the airline understood the role and functions of Security, which is so often blown up by its practitioners and rubbished by its critics. I suggested a small account for the payment for information at home and abroad. I had already had an invitation to join Interpol, from its President, now Sir Ranulph Bacon, and proposed to accept. The world's airline Security chiefs, about seventy strong, had been invited by Fish to hold the annual meeting of the International Airlines Security Conference in London the following month. I recommended that since I had only been in the job for just over a month it was premature for me to chair this important occasion. Finally I costed my recommendations and said that, to justify its existence, BOAC Security ought to earn an income and suggested how it might be done.

Mr Staple sent for me. He said he disagreed with only one of my recommendations. All the rest were accepted and I could go ahead with them with no further reference to him. The one he disagreed with was opting out of the International Conference chairmanship. He believed that if it took place as planned, (and he would help by himself and Basil Smallpeice playing a part), it would be a very good start to my international career.

The Conference delegates started to arrive from all parts of the world. There were several US men, all CIA, FBI or other American "spooks". There were a number of Middle East delegates, including Sheikh Mohammed Mubarak, a charming Druse, with his beautiful wife. There were Indian, Pakistani, Greek, Australian, South American and South African delegates, all with wives. Fish had been assiduous in booking hotels and arranging receptions and dinners, but his work programme was non-existent. "Rasher" Bacon, President of Interpol, opened the Conference; the Pan Am Chief followed with a fascinating account of the drugs problem which even then was becoming a US concern; "hijacking" was in its infancy, but the Middle East, Arab speakers, and a late arrival, the El Al, Israeli, Security Chief described the risks and the actions needed. I began to relax, realizing that as the Convenor of the Conference, its Chairman and host, I had done all that was needed. That evening we all dined at "The Talk of the Town", with Eartha Kitt singing. Heather joined us from Co. Armagh, looking as beautiful as ever.

As always euphoria was followed by letdown. Frank Wood, our Heathrow investigation officer, a little terrier in following up airline crime, told me that there had been a number of thefts from high security Post Office bags and that the Post Office were going to "raise hell" with the Board about this. These bags were identified by a coded tag, which required that they be given special attention. A Security Officer took delivery of them and stood sentry on them until they were loaded into the aircraft hold. The holds, those days, were quite cramped, and a loader had to be pretty athletic to squeeze into the recesses. Frank's view was that at destination exactly the same "squeeze" was required to get into the hold and that at destination the marked bags could be cut open, the likely saleable contents – diamonds, currency – slipped out, with the defence that this had happened at Heathrow (later entitled "Thiefrow"). There was an obvious solution – every loader must be searched after departure. When I put this to the London Airport Management, they were sympathetic, but said the Union (Transport and General Workers Union) would not stand for their members being searched. Nevertheless, with Ken Staple and Basil Smallpiece's approval, I instituted post-aircraft-departure loader searching. This was my first appreciation of the power of Unions. There was a total refusal, backed by the TGWU, to accept random searches by Security, with a threat of strike (which would have closed the airport) if we went ahead. The Commissioner pointed out that the Airport Police had power, with warrant, to do the searching, but only if there was indisputable evidence that the robberies were in London, not in Rome or Beirut, where most BOAC services transited on their way to the East or to Africa. I posted a Security Officer to Rome, a charming but non-assertive man, with orders to insist on a search of the hold of any BOAC flight about which we apprehended there had been a Royal Mail robbery. As it happened, I went to Rome, gave this nice man and his wife dinner and returned next morning early to London. I found a fuming Frank Wood, who told me that an informant had told him that the marked Royal Mail bags had been pilfered the night before, that he had told Rome and that our senior Security Officer had been unable to get the management and the Captain to agree to a delay while the bags were examined. Rome was a BEA station primarily, used by BOAC, but not operated by us. It brought home to me how important it was to integrate both airlines and how necessary to have security respected sufficiently to enable us to do our job.

Fortunately Frank Wood's informant knew where the valuables were and the Police obtained a warrant on Frank's affidavit, searched a loader's house and regained a consignment of diamonds worth many thousands of pounds.

The expected letter to the Board from the Postmaster-General arrived. It put the case for an inviolable Royal Mail most vehemently and warned BOAC that we were not the only airline flying international routes and might well lose this key market if we did not improve. It was a chastening time; things had gone almost too well to begin with for me, but clearly some initiative was required to make BOAC totally trustworthy as a carrier of really valuable property.

On my first long journey Queen's Messengers had been fellow-passengers on some flights. These were very senior retired Servicemen or Civil Servants, many of them titled, who travelled first class, with an empty seat beside them, on which reposed the Diplomatic Mail, destined for British Ambassadors all over the world. Britain's contracting Empire was putting the Commonwealth and Colonial Offices in a much larger role and it was an odd situation that the Ambassador to French Equatorial Africa had a monthly visit from a Queen's Messenger, but Nigeria did not. There was a system known as "By hand of Captain", which had been regarded in earlier days as adequate for the Diplomatic Mail to Commonwealth and Colonial countries. It seemed to me that the contrasting systems needed changing, especially when I heard BOAC Captains saying how tiresome they found a responsibility for which they got no reward, and which in multi-sector flights, could, and did, lead to a Captain forgetting to hand on the Diplomatic Mail to his successor Captain. There were cases when Captains unpacking their suitcase on returning home found a TOP SECRET letter addressed to a High Commissioner in India for example.

My "intelligence" background opened doors very easily, so I arranged meetings with Commonwealth and Colonial Office chiefs and suggested that BOAC would be happy to organize an "Economy Class" Messenger service, requiring very important and valuable consignments to be carried by BOAC Security Officers. The idea was accepted, indeed almost too enthusiastically. I have always found that if one's offer is seized on too quickly one has probably underpriced it!

The Economy Messenger Service involved Security Officers travelling not only on BOAC services, but, for example, continuing to Botswana and Swaziland from Johannesburg, to give mail to High Commissioners in those countries. Obviously some "trail-blazing" was needed, because the new service depended, to achieve its full potential, on Security Officers doing the journey, there and back, with no stopover. There was nothing for it but to route-prove the service myself. A journey to Singapore, then directly to Borneo, Labuan and Brunei, back to Singapore, thence to London, was tiring, especially as an important by-product of the Messenger Service was that one inspected the hold for interference with the Royal Mail. Not all our staff were either able, or willing, to take on this exhausting task, so we recruited, mostly from the Services, bright, personable and politely assertive young men, one of whom distinguished himself later. The presence of travelling Security Officers on flights, the emphasis on the integrity of the Royal Mail, the knowledge that we were in the business of prevention of crime as well as its detection, built up the image of the security operation.

In the RUC we were constantly dogged by the cost of our efforts. When we mounted an operation against the IRA there was always the worry about the bill. A call-out of the Special Constabulary in County Armagh cost £3000 per night. The fact that this was 3000 men, paid £1 for a night of 12 hours, was probably the cheapest security operation in the world, but when the IRA, due to good intelligence work and the combined efforts of Police and Army, were beaten, the Treasury was quick to demand a reduction of security cost. So it was with airline security. Everyone wanted it, no one wanted to pay for it. The Economy Messenger Service halved our cost because the charge to the Government earned £200,000 p.a. and provided us with an extra constant security "patrolling" of our routes. It also gave us a prodigious insight into what was happening round the world.

Chapter Nine

BOAC – ROYAL TOUR OF ASIA

I had been in the job two months when the Palace invited me to come to a meeting on the Royal Tour of the Indian sub-continent. The Queen's Private Secretary, Sir Michael (later Lord) Adeane, was in the chair. His Deputy, Sir Edward Ford, and my main interest, Sir Edward Fielden, Captain of the Queen's Flight, were also there. The detail in which this, the largest and longest Royal Tour, was planned left me breathless – dozens of air journeys, some by local airlines, some by train and car. Two large aircraft, Britannias, each with 120 seats, were commissioned. Every journey required a different combination of passengers and load, meals and ground transport arrangements.

Gold-smuggling by BOAC aircrew had given a bad reputation to our airline and we had been doing our best to raise confidence in our determination to stop it. Many of the officials in India and Pakistan, Police, Customs and Intelligence officers were to have duties in connection with the Royal Tour, and it seemed sensible to develop all these briefs on both levels. Gold-smuggling by British aircrew had resulted in over sixty of them being declared *persona non grata* by the Indian and Pakistani Governments. The background to this, which resulted in the dismissal of those so declared, was that the rampant inflation of the currency of the Indian sub-continent, plus the desire of Indian women to have an overt demonstration of affection by their husbands or father, made gold, with its stable value, a unique commodity. Another trip to Karachi and Delhi with Buchanan made it clear to me that nothing less than a "sting" would convince the Government of both countries and frighten the godfathers. As India was the most attractive destination then for illicit gold we designed a joint operation with Mr Shrivastrava of Customs Intelligence, which would involve a British Agent. He assented readily and Douglas and I set off home in a

Comet, with confidence that there was a good chance of breaking the syndicate operating the gold racket. As so often happened in those days, a technical problem resulted in the Comet having to divert to Karachi for what turned out to be a 24-hour delay. We had already intended to set up another "sting" in Pakistan, so the delay was useful and we saw the Customs Intelligence chiefs to outline our strategy. They welcomed us with the respect which we were accustomed to; we set up codes and communication systems which paralleled the ones we had designed for India, but we left with doubts about whether they had taken us seriously. This was worrying in view of what happened later.

We had settled on a young Security Officer, an Irishman as it happened, whose family had included several members of the Irish Guards. He had joined us from the Military Police very recently. He was personable, intelligent and had courage, we believed. So we asked him to resign from his job and to rejoin the airline as a steward, to go through the training, and to put himself in the way of being propositioned by the gold-smugglers. He was offered no inducements. It was an operation which offered great danger, no glory, no reward. There are people, I like to think many of them Irishmen, who are prepared to take frightful risks for aims they believe in. "Roddy", the code-name we gave him, was one of those. He agreed, resigned from the airline, applied for the job of steward and was accepted. During this time, because "Roddy" had to go through stewards' training which took several months, several more aircrew were declared *persona non grata* and dismissed.

He passed out as a steward and did his first flight to the East, which involved a stop at Beirut. With his fellow aircrew members, he went to the Golden Bar, a rather appropriately named watering hole for aircrew. He was propositioned, not homosexually, which, as stewards, they had to put up with, but by an Indian who asked him to smuggle some gold.

"Roddy" agreed and, as he was scheduled for another Beirut stop shortly, he went again to the Golden Bar. The smuggler took him to a tailor who measured him for a vest of linen, with long pockets to fit slim gold bars bent to conform to the shape of his upper body. The vest was ready next day and he telephoned using a code we had agreed to let us know that he was taking off on a flight to Karachi that night. We had not expected that the smugglers would have been able to get everything ready so quickly, and it had been our belief that Delhi was the most likely destination. There were rather frantic phone calls to the Pakistani Customs, with whom we had agreed a procedure which enabled "Roddy" to communicate with them, avoiding the Rest House phones which we believed were not secure. A small radio transmitter had been left at Karachi Customs, set to an agreed frequency, and "Roddy" had its duplicate. He went through Karachi Customs, his gold weighing him down, but with no trouble, went to his room in the BOAC rest house and telephoned the number he had been given by the gang in Beirut. He was told to take a taxi that night and to tell the driver of an address in a square in a poor part of the city. He was to make no more calls, as his phone was tapped. The radio link worked superbly and he gave the Customs chiefs the exact location and time. One can imagine his feelings when he got into the rickety taxi. He had never been to Karachi before, the gold, worth many thousands of pounds, compressing his chest, with no one to turn to if it all went wrong. He had taken our word for it that the Pakistani Customs people could be trusted, but how was he to know that they would be able to cope with a ruthless gang of gold-smugglers, possibly armed, who might well kill him, take the gold and vanish?

He got out of the taxi in the pitch dark. Out of the darkness appeared more than half-a-dozen men, who started to strip him of his gold. Floodlights suddenly illuminated the scene and so shocked the smugglers that they were arrested without a struggle. After making a statement to police and customs "Roddy" returned to the rest house and next day flew on.

This initiative, resulting in long terms of imprisonment for the eight smugglers caught in Karachi, and the loss of the gold had a dramatic effect not only on the smuggling cartels but also on BOAC's reputation. The authorities in the countries concerned, including Lebanon, were impressed by the determined way in which we had rid ourselves, and them, of this scourge. No longer were British aircrew targeted as "honest" smuggling agents and we were able to convince authorities in India and Pakistan that use of the *persona non grata* mechanism to ban named aircrew from their countries was no longer necessary.

It would be absurd to claim that never again was there smuggling by British aircrew. Indeed I visited one aircrew member caught smuggling gold into India and the conditions of his prison (which were no worse than that of any other inmate) were such as to be a powerful deterrent to his colleagues. We made sure aircrew knew about "Roddy" when the Karachi case, at which he gave evidence, was over and the culprits sentenced. He resigned from BOAC as a steward and, using his own name, now rejoined Security Branch, where he had a most successful career. The series of joining, resigning, joining, resigning and then joining again only to end up where he had begun gave me an idea as to how we might avoid recruiting known troublemakers, which we developed later.

Donald Fish's book *Airline Detective* was now on the market and was very successful. Some of his former security and police colleagues were critical, as he tended to take credit for others' ideas and work. He completed the deal with T.V. to have a series of fictional programmes with the title "Zero

One" produced, with him as Advisor. Nigel Patrick took the part of Donald Fish. A greater contrast could not be imagined. The saturnine, grumpy, rather petty Fish, with the ebullient, charming, and adventurous Patrick did me no harm at all, since, quite erroneously, I was typecast as a Patrick figure! Indeed my staff found the glamorous image they now presented as Economy Class Queen's Messengers and the fellow-officers of "Roddy", coupled with "Zero One", to be highly beneficial in doing their job, which depended very much on their acceptability by Corporation staff members.

By now the Gorman family was tired of separation. I knew we had a big problem ahead in finding a house and placing Angela, Johnny and Rosanagh in schools which would keep their good Northern Ireland educational progress on track. Justin, our fourth child, was one year old. Heather's sister, Jill Langdon-Down lived in Hildenborough, Kent, in a lovely house, Bassetts, the *Daily Mail* "House of the Year 1910". It made sense for us to find somewhere close to Bassetts and to send the children to the local schools at which Jill's children had started their education before going on to Eton and Westheath. We found a house to rent with the impressive name of The White House, Hildenborough, an extraordinary house in that it was most imposing, viewed from the front, but was only a room-length in depth. There was a pond full of little fish and a greenhouse. It was a joy to be together again, much as I had enjoyed being looked after by my Aunts Kitty and Marie, and, though I could not commute to Heathrow from Hildenborough, I was abroad so much that it did not seem so divisive to family life. The younger children seemed happy at their little school, Foxbush. Angela was doing very well at the Sacred Heart Convent in Armagh, where Seamus Mallon taught her history, and, keen as she was to join us, Heather and I felt she should finish her year there as a boarder. It was typical of her, and a great credit to the Convent, that she accepted being left in Armagh when the rest of us were in Kent.

The pressure was now on the Royal Tour of 1961. The combination of high profile, through Fish's book and "Zero One", "Roddy" and the total support of the Board, resulted in the Palace making me a member of "The Entourage". At least, that is, I believe, the reason for the extraordinarily positive position in which I found myself. There were thirty-one destinations on the programme, from 20 January to 6 March 1961. Each required its own careful programme.

The aircraft we were to use for the "core" part of the programme were Britannias, a 312, the latest model with more capacity, and a 102. They were Turboprop-engined, not fast, but reliable, quiet and comfortable. For shorter air journeys we had Herons, DC3s and helicopters. Meetings with the Palace, headed by the Commodore of the Queen's Flight, Air

Commodore Sir Edward Fielden, KCVO, soon developed into each problem of the ground arrangements being put to Security. Fortunately I had invited Douglas Buchanan to come to London to help me. He was invaluable. He knew all the people on the ground, both airline and local. His far-seeing approach to likely problems meant that there was much we could do ahead to ensure a smooth operation. He left dealing with the senior members of the Entourage to me, but early on he identified the Queen's Butler, Charles Candy, as a key person for him to liaise with. The Queen's Page, Mr Bennett, was another. He trusted me to keep in touch with Miss Macdonald, the Queen's Dresser. Bobo Macdonald became a good friend and a wonderful counsellor; through her we were able to anticipate, and plan for, things which might otherwise have been problems – for example, if the Queen was to wear a certain dress, that came off the aircraft first and into the first car. At each destination there was a first-aid station with blood from Britain. Malvern water was always brought with us and delivered to the Queen's apartments. She had been well advised that the water in India is the cause of many a stomach upset, and the belief that ice kills germs is one which often deludes the visitor.

When the Air Travel Arrangements for the State Visit to India, Pakistan, Nepal and Iran were reaching conclusions I sent "Buck", as I had come to call Douglas Buchanan, to reconnoitre the whole route. He returned with a complete analysis of what we might expect in all thirty-one destinations. He was particularly concerned at the fact that another aircraft, an old Stratocruiser, had been chartered by the media to travel with us. The prospect of up to 100 reporters, T.V. cameramen and freelance journalists spending eight weeks reporting on every aspect of this State Visit worried Buck immensely. Commander Colville, the Queen's Press Secretary, who had been at the Fielden-chaired meetings, was quite unperturbed. His view, which I respected, was that the more media coverage there was the better, and, although he did not know of their Stratocruiser charter, he was, on the whole, pleased rather than worried.

On a freezing January morning we assembled at Heathrow. I had said goodbye to Heather and the children and had told them that I thought I had found us the house of our dreams. Whether I could ever afford it was another matter, but to solace me on the long odyssey I had the plans and photos of a converted stables and shared these with Heather. The potential for disaster was clear. It was only six months since I had been a District Inspector in the RUC. I had had only one visit to Asia and was dependent on a man who had advised me and who was now out on the route giving last minute instructions to people, some of whom resented his authority to give them. Our first stop was Akrotiri airport in Cyprus – a warm night, a warm welcome. The Governor, with the Orthodox clergy, made us all, not just the Royals, feel welcome. As we took off it seemed that it would all work out. Then the arrival at Delhi. Now the Press, who had overflown Cyprus, were much in evidence. Pandit Nehru, his daughter Indira, a massive Indian Military Guard of Honour and Band, Sir Paul Gore-Booth, the High Commissioner, and an excited crowd were there to welcome us. At this stage the Press were respectful and enthusiastic. Many of them were Court correspondents and it was not in their interest to be critical of Royalty. Furthermore, in 1961 it was just not "the done thing". As the weeks went by we experienced a rather different attitude amongst *some* of the journalists.

The Independence Day Parade in New Delhi was a sight never to be forgotten. When we lived there later we saw this five times, but never in such circumstances as in 1961. Independence Day 1947, when Lord Louis Mountbatten had taken the last salute of the Indian Army and the Raj had ended, was an emotional moment in the history of India, and the Queen's presence fifteen years later was hardly less so. There is much nostalgia in India for the British period of government – 150 years of relationship, with the ups and downs represented by the success in bringing about a cohesive country, with dozens of States, over 100 languages and bitter religious schisms, but also the Indian Mutiny, the pro-Japanese Indian National Army, and finally, inspired by Gandhi, the comparatively painless transition to independence for India. Painless for the great majority of Hindus, less so for Muslims caught on the wrong side of the partition of India from West and East Pakistan.

"Buck" with his unerring instinct for finding the person who mattered, made friends with S.K. Anand, Indian Army Intelligence, and his information was invaluable to us throughout this part of the State Visit. S.K. travelled with the Royal Party throughout. A charming, alert, gentlemanly person, whose English was impeccable, he was able to give us a perspective from the host country's point of view. For example, some of our Press got hold of the idea that, because the Queen did not use the Indian gesture of greeting, "Namaste", with the palms of the hands pressed together while one bows, this was derogatory of an Indian custom. Anand's view was that this was as typical a politeness by Indians as the British handshake, that it had much to do with an Indian preference for a greeting gesture of a less physical sort. To abandon the western style would have seemed contrived and undignified. Whether this view, which I passed on to the Queen via Sir Michael Adeane, had the result of her continuing to use her friendly British handshake I do not know, but she did, and the Press dropped this story.

Visits to Udaipur, the Palace of white marble set in a lake which reflected it beauty, to Jodhpur, the great fortress on a rock, with the Maharajah's own soldiers on parade, and to Jaipur, whose Maharajah, an Indian Army

Officer with the title Captain Maharajkumar Singh, a star polo player, with his stunningly beautiful wife Gayathri Devi, took up most of our week, and integrating RAF Herons, Indian Army DC3s (Dakotas) with small numbers of the Royal party and their luggage was a challenge. There were many receptions and parades and I met the Chief of the Indian Army several times, General "Moochu" Chaudhuri, a Bengali Muslim. He had a fascinating tale to tell of his experience when he was Army Commander of New Delhi when Gandhi was murdered. First reports of this were that a Muslim fanatic had been the murderer. Pandit Nehru, suspecting a Hindu pogrom of Muslims, ordered that his Muslim General be put under house arrest. His Officers refused to carry out the order, while Chaudhuri had already sealed off Delhi with his troops and put thousands of soldiers on stand-by to deal with the expected rioting. After a few hours the murderer was identified as a Hindu. Years later we got to meet "Moochu", when he was the Indian High Commissioner to Canada, married a delightful Canadian woman, and later became Professor of Indian Military History at McGill University, Montreal. McGill was packed with Vietnam draft-dodgers from America, who put up a sign on a University tower, visible for miles, "Chaudhuri the warmonger must go". He rather enjoyed his high profile!

The Royal visit to Madras gave me a new perspective about British history in India. That, and the Governor of Bengal's Residence, once the Viceroy's, showed the Raj style. Those British rulers, probably pompous and self-important, imposed by military success on a population used to foreign domination as exercised for centuries by the Moguls from Persia, nevertheless had a public service ethos which dominated their lives. The climate, disease and danger of death from fanatics, their wives having to leave for the hills, especially if there were young children, the years of service required before the Port Out Starboard Home (POSH) sea trip back for six months in England, all were part of a dedicated uncorrupt lifestyle, which few of us would put up with now. A visit to the graveyard of St John's Anglican Church in Calcutta, with the headstones of young wives of British Civil Servants and soldiers and the number of little children buried there, brought it home to one how much we should respect our ancestors. My education at Kipling's old school had already prepared me for this; the evidence on the ground, and the reminiscences of Indians who had served the Raj confirmed it.

On the flight to Madras I was seated beside the Indian High Commissioner to the UK, Mr Baig. He told me of the connection between St Thomas the Apostle, and India, and especially Madras, where he was murdered. He took me to the church of St Thomas (a Portuguese Catholic foundation). Behind the altar is a rock with red slashes across it. It is here that Hindu Brahmins were said to have slain the Apostle. It was a nice, rather superstitious-sounding traditional belief, but slightly unconvincing. However, when he took me to Mount St Thomas, to meet the nuns of the Convent there, they showed me a headstone, covered in hieroglyphics. The story was that in the 19th century, the Convent (again a Portuguese foundation) wanted to extend itself to build a Chapel. During the excavation of the site the stone had been turned up. No one in India could decipher what it said. The headstone's writing was sent to the School of Asiatic Studies in London and the translation said "Here lies the body of St Thomas the Apostle, killed by Hindus in AD 30". There was further information, but the chief point was that Thomas had indeed on his missionary odyssey reached South India and was still remembered there.

Earlier in the Tour, a small Palace party consisting of Sir Edward Ford, Assistant Private Secretary, Lady Rose Baring (sister to the Earl of Antrim), Commander Colville and "Mouse" Fielden's Deputy, Group Captain Jimmy Wallace, had gone to Kathmandu to reconnoitre the visit to Nepal. They returned with a rather alarming account of matters there. King Mahendra, the ruler of this rather old-fashioned state, which had only recently begun to embrace democracy, had serious doubts about his Prime Minster and the Chiefs of his Army and Police and had put them under house arrest. The arrangements for receiving the Queen having been made by these men, it was questionable whether the visit should proceed without them in charge. The aircraft to be used had been intended to be the Herald, a modern uprated version of the Heron, but some doubts about its performance at high altitudes led to DC3s, the wartime Dakotas, being preferred by Fielden. The Dakota used in the war by Field Marshal Montgomery from Normandy on, which was in "mothballs" at Aldergrove, was reconditioned quickly by the RAF for carrying the Queen to Kathmandu.

Sir Michael Adeane and Sir Edward Fielden asked me to continue the BOAC air/ground work we had been doing. We were now in Lahore, Pakistan. I telephoned Kenneth Staple, my boss, who lived at Hampton Court, on a Saturday evening. There was a cocktail party going on and I spoke to one of the guests, who answered the phone, saying "This is John Gorman, telephoning from Lahore, Pakistan." I could hear a voice calling, "Kenneth, a whore from Pakistan wants you." Kenneth had no hesitation in agreeing to our taking on the Nepal visit, though it was not of direct BOAC concern, so I returned to Adeane and Fielden with this news when "Mouse" produced a revolver and said that they wanted me to guard the Queen's DC3 in Kathmandu in case there was a coup, which King Mahendra feared, and it was necessary to get the Queen out speedily.

We took off from Benares in the DC3 and I sat beside Lord Home, the

Foreign Secretary, who was completely relaxed about the whole Nepal programme and assured me that the only thing he worried about was the tiger-shoot which was in preparation in the Chitwan Forest, particularly because of the large Press group who were coming to Nepal, and the lack of "stories" which had resulted from the Royal Tour. He told me that, had the Queen herself not insisted on the Nepal visit going ahead, it would have been cancelled. He said that the Foreign Office was for cancellation, but he had left it to Royal decision, in the belief that she would feel it would be insulting to the Nepalese Gurkhas, soldiers of the Queen who awaited her eagerly, if she did not visit them. She decided to go.

Arrival at Kathmandu produced a parade of Gurkhas (the Nepalese, rather than British version, but just as smart) but no King Mahendra, who either through forgetfulness or fear of the coup, did not show up. We had to get used to this, as he was either late for, or did not come, to several of the journeys in Nepal!

When the Royal party had left the airport to the Palace I remained behind to supervise the guarding of the DC3. There was a circle of Gurkhas, bayonets fixed to their rifles, and their officer assured me that no one would get near this precious aircraft. It was very hot, the sun beating down on the soldiers. There seemed to be many Gurkha Majors walking past the Queen's aircraft. Each time a Major passes a soldier with a rifle, he is entitled to a "Present Arms", which involves the rifle being raised ceremoniously. With a bayonet fixed to the rifle, this ceremonial suddenly constituted a real menace because, as I watched the soldiers, they were imperceptibly shuffling back to get under the shade of the DC3's wings. As the wings were stretched linen over framework, a single bayonet penetration would have made the Queen's aircraft unserviceable. It was lucky, in the absence of their officer, that when I ordered the Gurkhas to "Unfix Bayonets", the sound of a military voice got them to do just that and the danger was over.

It was at night that I felt any coup might happen, and Mouse agreed that I should take my elderly Webley to the DC3 every night and sleep on board. The DC3 has a rather unusual mode on the ground. Its tail is lower than its cockpit, so it is not easy to find a comfortable sleeping position, especially if one rolls over a loaded revolver. I had been impressed by Mouse's dedication to his job as Commander of the Queen's Flight and noticed that he never had a drink, even though on all our journeys this was offered. I followed his example; the Nepal visit was too fraught to take chances.

The Royal Hotel, Kathmandu, a rather down-at-heel place owned by a Middle European aristocrat, was where the entourage and the Press were all housed. I did not see much of the goings-on at night time because of my tryst with the Queen's Dakota, but it was clear that the media were getting restive. The King's tiger shoot now came into their sights. He had sent great numbers of beaters into the Chitwan Forest to drive tigers from their lairs to the site of the shoot. They set off explosions, lit fires and even carried bolts of white cloth spread between beaters to scare tigers towards the shoot area. It did not take the media long to discover all this and to tell their masters in London. Commander Colville, who every evening braved a Press briefing, announced that as *The Field* had sent a former Indian Army tiger-shooting Colonel as their correspondent, and as it was obviously impossible to bring all the media men and women to the shoot at Megauli, he suggested that the Colonel should represent his colleagues, that a radio-link to the Megauli Camp be established and that the Colonel's account of the tiger shoot should be transmitted to the whole Press party gathered at the Royal Hotel. I was there when he announced this, to me, very sensible scheme, but I left for the airport before "Any questions", which, I learned later, were hostile. "Animal Rights" were represented on the party, and all of them wanted a story, preferably a scoop. They were not impressed with the likelihood that the Colonel would give them this.

The following afternoon I flew to Megauli on one of the numerous aircraft which were supplying the Camp. This was as close as I could imagine to the field at Agincourt before the battle – dozens of tents, all with washing facilities, a bedroom and sitting room, a bonfire at each with piles of wood, for the guests to sit around in the cooler evenings, and an army of bearers, a great marquee for dining, and an enclosure for a large herd of elephants. Tiger Tops, the famous Chitwan Forest Camp, with comfortable little houses high in trees, reached by ladder, was part of the Camp, and is still in operation, giving guests, 41 years later, a chance of seeing tigers in their natural state, and all the other animals, rhinoceroses, for example, for which Chitwan is famous. I flew back to Kathmandu and for a meal at the Royal Hotel. The evening Press briefing was taking place. The Colonel was on the loudspeaker to the radio from the Camp and gave a description of the preparations for the shoot, and quoting, what he had been told by the King's Head Beater, gave an optimistic forecast of the numbers of tigers which had been gathered in for the next day. He said that unfortunately Prince Philip had a whitlow on the forefinger of his right hand which would prevent him shooting, as it was his trigger finger. Again I had to leave for my night task, but heard afterwards that once again there was a sour Press reaction.

Early the following morning the Royal couple were, as usual, on time for the flight, and the King late. I noticed the Duke of Edinburgh had his right hand in a bandage, for the whitlow presumably, and the aircraft took off for the tiger shoot of the century.

At dusk that evening the Colonel came through to an excited Press

Corps, who had had a very boring day enlivened by some partying. His account of the shoot was of a total disaster. The whole effort had produced one small tiger (it became smaller as the Press described it). It rushed around the elephant ring and was shot at by British visitors, who all missed. It seemed lost and ran into the shooting area, where the Foreign Secretary, Lord Home, hit it, but did not kill it. It needed the *coup de grâce*; at last a story for the Press. They fought over the line to London and were still at it when I left. The whitlow was diplomatic, the Foreign Secretary a butcher, but not a competent one, the poor little cub . . . etc, etc. It was no wonder that the perceptive Foreign Secretary was worried about the tiger shoot.

Next day the Queen and Prince Philip went to Pokhara. The Gurkhas had been preparing for this for weeks. They are very poor and their ambitions to give a fairy-tale look to this rather unexciting little town had resulted in there being erected dozens of arches made of Oxfam milk containers. These were bucket-size, but rectangular and shiny. By putting a rope through the containers, about 200 of them a time, a shimmering arch resulted. From the Dakota we could see this wonderful example of ingenuity, turning the mendicancy for outside help to the pride of self-help.

The Queen walked along the ranks of Gurkhas, some very old, some who had walked for days from remote mountain fastnesses. Young or old they remained in their ranks, and the Gurkha Officers, many of them British, knew each man's name when the Queen stopped to talk to him. It was one of the most moving sights of my life. My pride in her, who had had every reason to cancel the visit, was immense. The Prince gave her the support which made it possible.

Then back to Delhi to start the homeward journey, with stops at Tehran for three days, and Istanbul.

When we arrived at Tehran the Shah and Queen Farah greeted the Queen and there was much media attention, which fascinated the airport ground staff who would not get on with the job of unloading the luggage on the lorry to take it to the Royal quarters. In modern management style I took it on myself to do the unloading, believing that the Iranian loaders would be shamed into doing it. Not a bit of it. They watched, grinning at the sweaty "Englishman" showing them their job, and when the tailgate of the lorry fell on my head, the applause was deafening. They took me to the First-Aid station, where the blood had been delivered, and I was given an heroic turban bandage to deal with the slice which the tailgate had taken out of my scalp. When I reached my hotel the entourage were on their way to the British Embassy reception, so I had a great deal of sympathy – more than I deserved – but mostly caused by this huge turban bandage. Later that evening I had a message from the Queen commiserating with me, and felt such a fraud that I got sticking plaster from Surgeon Captain Steele-

Perkins RN, the doctor of the trip, who patched up the "flap" and we threw away the turban. Isfahan next day was memorable because of the domes of the city, in colours of every shade of blue/purple. There were huge crowds. Queen Farah had made Isfahan a centre for her desire to emancipate women and give them a status which fundamental Islam denied them. We probably saw the last flowering of women's liberty in Iran, now sunk in traditional veiled-women servitude.

Next it was Shiraz, the airport for Persepolis. The Persian domination of the world in the 13th century and later is epitomized by Persepolis. Here, literally, the rulers of the world had their palaces. The Moguls who had conquered the Indian sub-continent saw Persepolis as their home. Darius, their emperor, had defeated local Asian armies by his generalship and the quality of his soldiers. Art, architecture, including drainage (hitherto unrecognized as important) were all Mogul skills. Persia (now Iran) was then the world's leader, just as Britain was in the 19th century.

On both sectors to Isfahan and Shiraz the Shah had asked to visit the flight-deck. Captain Johnny Maher (of Irish descent) offered him his seat and to my untutored eye he showed he knew what he was doing. Prince Philip certainly confirmed this. The Shah was doomed, as we know now. I wonder if American support could have saved him.

Next day we set off for London with a call at Istanbul. Before leaving India I had bought a Kashmiri wooden carved screen to take home. Obviously I could not use the Royal paid-for hold, but asked the Queen's Private Secretary if he would get her permission to put it into the space between the Queen's four wardrobes and the curvature of the Britannia body, which had exactly enough space. He told me it was OK.

Istanbul was to have been a transit stop, with no problems as we were not leaving the airport. The Head of State, General Gursel, a dictator, wanted to show the democratic world the liberalism of Turkey and there was no control whatsoever of the Press, Turkish this time. They swarmed on to the steps of the Britannia. The Queen stood at the door. Prince Philip and all able-bodied passengers drove a phalanx down the steps and, with the Queen at the heart of this scrum, got to the airport building where the smirking Gursel was waiting. I think he was unaware of the disgraceful behaviour of the pressmen. It was a very short transit stop and we could not wait to get on to London and home.

I was relaxing beside Mouse when the Chief Steward said the Queen wanted me to visit her up front. When I got there she was standing with a medal and said that she had been so grateful for the work of the Security staff on the whole trip. She told me that Buck was also to be decorated. She put the medal round my neck and gave me a photograph of her family at Balmoral. Prince Philip talked to me about my time in the Irish Guards, but I was in such a state of surprised euphoria that I left the cabin without much recollection of the conversation. I went back to my seat to a grinning Mouse. "Do you know what you have got?" "No," I said. "Look." It was the Order of Commander of the Royal Victorian Order. Originated in 1884, there had only been 1874 recipients since.

When we landed at Heathrow the Chairman, Sir Matthew Slattery, and Managing Director, Basil Smallpeice, were there and full of congratulations, which increased when I showed them the CVO. It will sound "apple-polishing", but before we left Tehran, the Shah's Security Chief gave me six tins of Imperial Caviare, which I had in my hand, so I gave them one each.

When I got home to Heather and the children it was after 10 p.m., so the little ones were sleeping, but the others were delighted to see me and all terribly impressed by the great Order. Not so the caviare. Heather does not like it, and at that hour I was not hungry. My brother-in-law, Tony Langdon-Down, was thrilled, and we did justice to Iran's best over several weekends.

Before I left for the Royal Tour we had seen a house at Crawley Down which we thought was exactly what we wanted. It was close to the Benedictine school Worth Abbey and we had visited the Headmaster, Dom Dominic Gaisford, brother of "Tigger" Gaisford, a brother-officer of the Irish Guards. He accepted Johnny as a dayboy at the Junior School.

Angela and Rosanagh were accepted by the Notre Dame Convent at Crawley and we would soon be looking at schools for Justin. We were at last in a house of our own, a converted stable-block, with tiny rooms, former horse stalls, but a big garden with high walls, and a greenhouse. The only problem was the distance from Crawley Down to Heathrow, over 60 miles, for me to commute. Once again my aunts at Hampton Court and Walton gave me a bed when needed, but it was certainly a long day, driving round the outskirts of London a journey of unpredictable length, though I experimented with many routes. The M25 would have been invaluable then! We were only 20 miles away from Hildenborough, so were able to see Heather's mother, Ethel Caruth, and Jill and Tony Langdon-Down frequently. Ethel, with whom I now got on well but getting quite old, had sold her little house at Kesh and gone into a cottage at Bassetts, from which she later moved into a flat adapted for her in the big house, where she died.

Chapter Ten

BOAC – ROYAL TOUR OF AUSTRALASIA

Now began the objective which I had been set, of curbing the influence of the Communist party in the airline. Lest it be thought that this was a McCarthy-type project (Senator McCarthy, the fanatical anti-Communist, was about his abhorrent activities in the States), it is worth considering the Communist scene in the United Kingdom in the early '60s. The Cold War was hot. Russia had suppressed Hungary brutally, many European countries had governments, which if not precisely Communist, were by no means anti-Communist. Our horror of the Nazi regime, and its concentration camps, was transferred to the Gulag Archipelago. There was real fear that, pretending to be orthodox trade-unionists, Communists were seizing power over workers, some at least of whom still thought of Stalin as "Uncle Joe".

I decided to tackle the problem of left-wing unions and their staff travel on two fronts. One was to discover the names of activists who had already demonstrated by their behaviour that they were more concerned with disruption than with workers' rights. The other was to find a means of giving workers another vision than the Soviet one which they had from articulate and persuasive people purporting to be their advocates.

The first task, keeping a watch on recruitment, was not too difficult. The Metropolitan Police were very helpful, and our own efforts (and MI5 sources) made clear that we must have a security input to the vetting of candidates for employment in BOAC. After all, Britain's flag-carrier around the world was not helped if it had employees who wanted to bring down democratic government in our country and abroad. With the co-operation of Freddie Chesterton, the head of selection, training and development, it was comparatively simple for security to have an input into the antecedents of applicants, whereby a number of individuals were kept out.

That was the easier bit. Creating an ethos in the workplace which made Communism less attractive was more difficult, but Sir Matthew Slattery, the Chairman, formerly Chairman of Harland and Wolff, came across an organization linked to the Catholic Church, which specialized in creating such a spirit in the workforce. It was in Engineering that our problems were greatest, and one of the areas in which we needed to create this healthier climate was among the apprentices. These youngsters, our future technicians, were a critical segment. Industrial disputes involving technical staff were disastrous, as an increasing number of functions were specialist, requiring special skills, equipment and tools. A strike by even a small group of such specialists could ground the airline, as had happened.

An elderly man, an Irishman as it happened, would invite these youngsters to informal evening meetings to give them information about the Communist threat to the free world, and how legitimate trade union activity was being perverted for political ends, in the service of communism. Once the youngsters realized what the dangers were, they were keen to do something about the problems.

There was a highly technical function entrusted to a specialist engineering unit. A "red" shop steward called an emergency meeting of the unit's staff and told them that another unit had designs on their work and were planning to take it away from them. As evidence of this, he claimed that a highly sophisticated, essential tool had been removed from the kit needed, and he proposed that they should stage a walk-out on the issue of potential job-loss. He claimed that this was all a management plot and that the strike should continue until a management declaration was obtained that the unit would *always* have the function. The shop steward knew very well that no management can bind itself for ever to continue a function which might well, over time, become redundant. He had one of the unit inspect the tool kit, who reported that indeed the tool was missing. A show of hands was imminent when a young apprentice asked to speak. "I saw you put that tool in your dungarees," he said. "They are hanging on your hook outside." "Rubbish," said the shop steward. "If anyone believes me capable of doing such a thing I will resign." The youth brought in the dungarees and produced the tool. The shop steward, showing some honour at last, did resign.

News of this plucky action spread among the workers and must have played some part in reducing overtly political activity, which was not to say that there was not still a radical attitude in the engineering workplace.

Our first summer in my new job made it possible for us to sample the joy of family travel. We had a Dutch au pair girl, whose parents owned a house in Majorca and were prepared to let it to us for a couple of weeks. It was close to the beach at Magaluf. All six of us set off, joined by Helen Style, our niece, and it was one of the best, if not *the* best, of all the many Gorman holidays. The children ranged from Angela, now 14, Johnny 12, Rosanagh 10, to Justin 5. We had for the first time water which was not "b-b-b-boiling" as in Ireland, and wonderful sandy beaches with no violent tides, and the music and colour of Spain. I got into snorkelling and, with a fearsome trident, went after octopus with much success, though I seemed to be the only one who liked eating them; the rest only saw the menacing tentacles and the beating of the dead octopus on rocks to rid them of their "ink".

Swimming in Magaluf Bay, with little to show for my octopus fishing, I saw a largish sailing-boat with a Red Ensign sail into the bay and drop anchor, after lowering its sails. After some time I ended up close to the boat and hung on to its steps to catch my breath. A furious face appeared in my goggles. "Get off my steps. Go away." The sound was so authentically British Army that I pulled off my goggles and started to speak. Another voice, "Keith don't be so hard on the poor man. He is probably just trying to feed his starving family." An American lady, obviously. By now I had regained my breath and my mask was off, so I introduced myself.

The boat owner was Colonel Keith Robinson, the lady was the charterer of Keith's boat. Keith was to achieve fame with *Islands of Blue Water* and other books. I was invited aboard and that night we had the boat party to dinner. Keith has been a dear friend ever since, now married to Barbara. They live in Majorca all the year round now. In his book Keith reminisces about an island in the Aegean called Skiathos and the name remained in Heather's and my minds, because it sounded so idyllic.

By now the Security Branch was doing very well: the Royal Tour had been much praised, the Economy Queen's Messengers were covering all of the Colonial and Commonwealth territories which now relied on BOAC Messengers for their high security mail; the mailbag robberies were at an end and, though pilferage from passenger baggage had not been totally eradicated, some well-publicized arrests (by the police on our information) had been a deterrent.

I suppose I was becoming a bit complacent. One Sunday at lunch, when I was carving a pheasant I had shot at my brother-in-law Tony Langdon-Down's shoot, there was a call from Control. "There has been a murder at Lima, Peru, and a BOAC First Officer has been arrested." There was nothing for it but to pack a bag and drive to Heathrow, from whence a 707 was departing shortly via the Caribbean to Caracas, Bogota and Lima.

When we landed at Lima, the British Ambassador, Sir Berkeley Gage, was there to meet me. His Rolls-Royce took us to the Embassy, where he gave me a "Pisco Sour", a formidable Tequila concoction with a deceptively mild taste. "Gorman, this is very serious. Peru is going through an anti-British phase and the behaviour of your man, First Officer Elliott, is appalling. You must get this matter under control. The reputation of the UK in the whole of South America is at stake. Look at the leading paper in Lima today." He produced it. My Spanish was good enough to read that *Un piloto Inglese* had been arrested for murder. There was a photograph of a Boeing 707, which had the words "Air France" not very well obliterated. When I pointed this out to Sir Berkeley, his reply was, "We don't want to be too explicit just yet, do we?"

Berkeley Gage was a remarkable man. In the War he had been Consul-General in Chicago, the heart of isolationism, and he had the apparently impossible task of turning the leading Mid-West newspaper baron, Colonel McCormick, from being the arch-advocate of "Keep the US out of the War" to a sympathizer with Britain's lonely position as the only enemy of Hitler still standing. When I got to know him better, he confided in me that McCormick's Irish ancestors had come to the States during the Famine with a deep hatred of the English and that gradually he, an educated man, was persuaded of the absurdity of blaming England for Ireland's food disaster, though he had reason for antipathy to the Corn Laws, which had been maintained (producing impossibly high grain prices) when millions in Ireland were starving. Gage was seen as having turned this anti-Brit into, if not an ally, at least not an enemy. It helped me that a neighbour in Crawley Down, Dorothy Akers-Douglas, was his sister.

After this briefing I went to Lima Prison. First Officer Elliott was in a cage with a motley crowd of arrestees. He looked awful, the left side of his face had three deep scratches starting on his brow and going down the cheek. With some difficulty I persuaded the warders to let me see him on his own. He was in great fear. The police had been very threatening and he had had no one to consult. On his arrest he had denied any knowledge of the death of the girl found in a brothel not far away, although it was clear that the police knew who they were looking for when they arrested him. He had refused to answer questions.

I told him that he must tell me the truth and that this would help us to help him. Hesitatingly he described how he had gone with his Captain and the other members of the 707 crew to a night-club and had danced with a very pretty girl. Despite his Captain's warnings, he had agreed to go home with the girl and they had checked in to this "hotel". He had never been in Peru before and was unsure of the currency. When she told him that the price was 200 solas, he believed he had a note of this value and, after they had had sex, he handed her the note, which was only for 20 solas. At this she flew into a passionate rage; he could not understand why and she started to claw at his face with long fingernails, thus the three wounds. He pushed her away pretty violently and she fell against the metal end of the bed and lay still. He realized that she was dead and panicked, rushing out of the brothel.

The Ambassador sent for a lawyer who he described as the best in Lima. He listened to the story, but was not optimistic about Elliott's chances. He made it clear that, to the Peruvian public, a British pilot was a rich capitalist, used to treating the poor badly; that Elliott, by running away, had lost any chance of sympathy because the girl's life might have been saved if he had called for medical help, that his lies to the police were unhelpful and that he stood a good chance of the death penalty. The Ambassador asked him, after this gloomy analysis, what he suggested should be done. The lawyer, after thought, reminded us that Peru, like many countries of European colonization, had the Code Napoleon as its basis of criminal law and that the Code provided for a visit to the scene of a crime by an examining magistrate, in the presence of the accused, for a re-enactment of what was alleged to have occurred. The lawyer told us that very occasionally an accused confronted by the evidence at the scene of a crime will, under skilled interrogation by the magistrate, break down and confess. In this case the recommendation of the magistrate is material in the trial of the accused person. The lawyer gave as his considered advice that Elliott should say nothing to the police, and that he, the lawyer, would press for a quick "scene of the crime" hearing.

When I told Elliott this he found it pretty depressing, because he was going to have to continue in the dreadful conditions of prison, but finally he entrusted himself to the lawyer whom Berkeley Gage had found.

A few months later we learned from the Embassy that the "confrontation" had taken place, that there was scientific evidence that the prostitute had an unnaturally thin skull, which would break easily, and that Elliott had broken down under interrogation, admitted all and pointed to the similarity of the 20 and 200 sol notes. He had been released by the Court and was on his way home. A very lucky man, thanks to British Ambassadorial prestige. He was dismissed from BOAC, but found a job with another airline, as he was a good pilot.

More Royal flights, to West Africa, where growing disenchantment with Nkrumah in Accra, Ghana, where a statue of Queen Victoria was bombed, leading to calls for the Queen to cancel the visit which found her as determined as ever to go. To the funeral of President Kennedy, where Prince Philip represented the Queen. It was an eerie sensation when I arrived at our hotel to see on television the murder of Lee Harvey Oswald. Later the funeral procession with John Kennedy's horse, his riding boots reversed in the stirrups, and his little son saluting the coffin. It was a time of great insecurity; there was a sense of vulnerability of all the foundations of civilization. At such, fortunately rare, times the permanence and reliability of Monarchy is a solid reassurance to us British.

Another ambitious Royal Flight was in the planning stage, with Security more involved than ever because of the 1961 success. This time it was a major visit to Australasia, with BOAC taking the Royal Party to Fiji, where the Royal Yacht *Britannia* would be anchored, to take the Queen and Prince Philip across the Pacific. After a lengthy tour of New Zealand and Australia, BOAC would then take them back from Perth, Western Australia, via Sydney, Fiji, Honolulu and Vancouver to London.

The Boeing 707 was proving a world-beater. It was reliable, comfortable and economic. Its range was increasing all the time. There was a strong body of opinion that non-stop Europe – US West Coast flights were safe, practical and profitable. The Operations Control staff, headed by Duggie Newham, were not convinced that a direct flight London – Vancouver was 100% practical. There was never any question of there being any safety risk, but there was the unpredictability of Pacific weather on the West Coast, the Rockies and the unblemished record of BOAC and its predecessor airlines of never being even a minute out in Royal Flights. The Flight Operations pilots were unanimous in their belief that a direct 707 London–Vancouver flight was totally within its range, would benefit the Royal party as it would avoid a Canadian stop which would require a programme. It was a decision in the end which was left to Mouse. He opted for the direct flight to Vancouver. He did not take this decision lightly and anxious research was done into the factors which could interfere with the "long-hop", over 3,500 miles. Every study showed that even the most adverse wind conditions would not make it impossible to reach Vancouver. The only risk was that a hurricane-type weather system could strike the North American West Coast. The odds of this happening over the 500 miles between Vancouver, Portland and Seattle, all "alternatives", were astronomical. Even Duggie Newham, the wisest of the wise in the control of world-wide operations, found it impossible to believe that all three airports could be closed at the same time.

The configuration of the Boeing gave a little "cabin" for the Captain of the Queen's Flight, Sir Edward Fielden, and me behind the Flight Deck. Behind us was the Royal cabin and sleeping compartments, beds on either side of a corridor, curtained. Behind was the main cabin with the Entourage, and staff, in normal First and Economy seating.

All went smoothly. The Captain, Tom Nisbet, one of the many ex-RAF "stars" of the airline, not by any means given to panic, told me of some distant problems over the Pacific, but that there was no reason to suppose Vancouver could be affected. We were now over Ontario. There was a lot of dialogue over the air and Tom gave me a headphone. American air-traffic controllers were now beginning to talk of a "hurricane"-force wind blowing east, which was affecting Honolulu. The messages came thick and fast. Honolulu was closing down for landings and take-offs, the hurricane was intensifying and moving eastwards fast. Portland and Seattle both came up with forecasts of the storm hitting all the north-western seaboard. Mouse was by now very much in the picture. The inconceivable was happening. Fifty years of "on the button" Royal flights were to come to an end. We could only land at Vancouver if risks were taken. It was a dramatic moment, but the decision was the Captain's and Mouse's, much as he must have wished that some miracle could keep the schedule, made no effort to affect Tom Nisbet's verdict. "We are turning back," he said. "Edmonton, back across the Rockies is where I am going. We shall land there in an hour."

By now the Royal couple were in bed and asleep, so it was a delicate question as to how the diversion was to be conveyed. Mouse suggested that Bobo Macdonald would be the right person to wake Her Majesty and tell her, so I tiptoed through the Royal sleeping cabin to where Bobo was sleeping. She woke instantly, told me not to worry and we both went forward, she to wake the Queen, I to rejoin Mouse.

The next hour was hectic. There was a heavy snow storm in Alberta, and Edmonton, though shielded by the Rockies from the hurricane, had great drifts of snow on the runway. It was cleared and the Mayor of Edmonton and the civic dignitaries were invited to meet the Queen at the airport. As dawn was breaking we landed.

Given the short notice, it was a credit to the loyal citizens of Alberta that there were so many there, wives in best hats, all so delighted at our unexpected arrival. It meant us getting the crew from Vancouver, Captain James Percy in command, to Edmonton to fly the next leg to Honolulu. The storm abated somewhat and Air Canada got them to us. Edmonton was not a 707 airport so there were technical difficulties in doing all the checks. Fortunately, as one of the products of the many planning meetings, it had been decided to take a very highly qualified Ground Engineer as a passenger on the flight. He was a one-legged man who had lost the other in the War.

Captain Percy was all set for take-off, and started his engines. One would not fire. A ladder arrived quickly and the Ground Engineer started work. This required him to delve ever deeper into the recesses of the Rolls-Royce engine and he fell off the ladder into the engine, with his artificial leg sticking up to heaven. All of us in the 707 were watching and worrying about him; indeed the Queen was kneeling on her seat, rather criticizing the ribald laughter at the bizarre sight of this heavenward leg. The Engineer got his leg under control and, the engine fixed, came down his ladder. The engine started perfectly.

So off again. This time to Honolulu, where the hurricane had passed over, and Governor Burns, a widower with a disabled daughter, who had expected us to arrive earlier in the day after a night stop in Vancouver was now given a new arrival time. The British Ambassador, Sir David Ormsby-Gore, later Lord Harlech, was also given the new arrival time. Captain Percy was one of the airline's great pilots, whose Commercial Pilot's licence was one of the first to be issued in the 1920s, number 29. The 2,000-mile flight from Edmonton to Honolulu was into the setting sun, and Mouse and I were beginning to believe that our troubles were over. James Percy, urbane and authoritative as ever, came back to our little "cabin". "The wind has turned by 180 degrees and we are going to have to land an hour earlier than scheduled." Irritating but not disastrous, we felt, and beyond letting the Royal staff know, there seemed to be nothing to be done.

"There is now a full-scale hurricane in Honolulu," said the Captain. "Aircraft are being blown upside down on the tarmac. I have been refused permission to land and am diverting to Vancouver." The Queen was in her bunk getting some sleep in advance of the heavy schedule she faced. I got Bobo to wake her again. She came, in her dressing-gown, to our "cabin", where Percy was explaining the situation to Mouse. "Captain Percy," she said, "can you tell me where exactly we are going now?" No fuss, no criticism. A perfect example of the self-discipline which has marked her life.

The journey back over the Pacific required a huge effort by all the Royal staff. Not only were we arriving on a different day, at the wrong time, but the main hotel, the Hotel Vancouver, having had no business the night before, when we had cancelled their rooms, were now faced with emptying the hotel of guests and a security sweep of all the building. The airport arrangements, stood down the previous night all had to be reinstated. The protocols of a Royal visit to British Colombia had all to be revived within a couple of hours. This was in the days before global telephone networks existed and it said much for the coolness of Percy and his crew that they were able to do their job and also to deal with the incoming and outgoing messages. The hotel cleared out its visitors and we wondered how many citizens of other countries would have stood for such treatment.

We carried a considerable amount of the Royal jewels on these journeys. The Queen would have seemed less real if her jewellery was not worn. In the security business it is always a matter of acting unpredictably; routine is the enemy. The jewel pouch was therefore carried by various trusted people such as Mr Bennett, her page, and this time I gave him the task of carrying it from the aircraft. The cars which took away the Royal party, eleven in all, had a twelfth car, a Rolls-Royce, and as I had asked for a special car for Mr Bennett, I took it that this was the one I had ordered. He took the pouch and got into the Rolls. I slept the few remaining hours in the 707 and at dawn the first of the passengers came aboard. One of the first was Mr Bennett. "You really gave me VIP treatment," he said, "Mr Garfield Weston was my host and he could not have been more welcoming. I was so comfortable carrying the Crown Jewels with him." It turned out that Garfield Weston, the illustrious biscuit king had prevailed on the airport authorities to let him join the queue of cars. Security is all about acting unpredictably. Terrorism is about observing routine. Still I was rather shaken by the biscuit man's role.

It was too late to leave Vancouver Airport when we finally got the Royal party and entourage away, so I, having spent the night on the Boeing, probably did not present a very well-turned out appearance at dawn, when the passengers began to arrive. At least the 707 was not as uncomfortable as the DC3 in Kathmandu.

One of the first arrivals was James Percy, the Captain. He was worried about the weather in Hawaii, and thence in Fiji. The quite extreme conditions of the previous day could, he believed, be repeated, and the optimistic weather forecasts which had been coming in all night did not reassure him. We took off at 0800, the time agreed with Mouse Fielden, and Percy in his own words "put his foot down". About an hour later, over the Pacific, he came back to report that a totally contrary weather pattern was now emerging. High winds were now carrying the Boeing forward and we were going to land in Hawaii far earlier than planned. He could "hang about" for a while, but was reluctant to do this in the volatile weather. We had to tell the Queen of this further anxiety and once again she took the news with composure. Given the BOAC reputation for "on the minute" departures and arrivals she would have been entitled to show at least some irritation, but there was not the slightest sign of this.

The following gale-force wind drove us further and faster, and it seemed no time at all before we had Hawaii in sight. A pass over Honolulu Airport showed a Pan Am aircraft on "our" stand, so Jim Percy did some circles of the islands until it took off. When we landed it was clear that the early arrival of the Royal Flight had confused everyone. After all we were arriving on a different day, at a different time. Sir David Ormsby-Gore was there, but not the Governor of Hawaii, Mr Burns, and his invalid daughter, who had been there the day before. The Royal party were taken towards the VIP suite and for some reason I was included in this group. We got into a lift and it quickly became clear that the lift operator did not really know how to operate it, as he stopped the lift in the attic and the Queen stepped out into a dusty room with cardboard boxes and rubbish. The CIA man was apologetic and crestfallen, and, helped by some pithy comments from Prince Philip, managed to get us to the VIP suite. There were numerous Hawaiian officials there, but no Governor. The Ambassador did all he could, but it was not one of the most convivial of occasions, and it was my job to support Mouse in pressing for a speedy departure for Fiji.

To my horror, as the Royal party approached the Boeing I could see that the aircraft steps were filled with garbage cans, the crew believing that they still had time to prepare the Royal Flight for the next leg. It was not the most elegant or graceful of departures. For the first time Her Majesty showed some disappointment. She told me that she had been looking forward to the "Lei" ceremony (flower garlands for visitors) and had been told by her father of the unique flag of Hawaii, which has the Union Jack in one corner, in honour of Captain Cook, who discovered it. There was no flag on show.

Rather naively in retrospect, I ran to the airport shop and bought a Lei for her. This was observed by the Ambassadorial staff and caused quite a stir, the theory being that my action had indicated Royal displeasure with the welcome to the Queen. Quite a reasonable point and, while she thanked me for the rather beautiful Lei of hibiscus and other flowers, she did not put it on!

The flight to Nandi, Fiji, was uneventful. We arrived at this airport, over 100 miles from the capital, Suva, on time. There was a ceremony, a band, and we, the airline staff, relaxed when the Royal party left in Rolls-Royces. Mouse Fielden who had taken responsibility to the Queen, for all the problems, and who had never, in dozens of Royal flights, ever experienced anything like this one, for once, at dinner with me, accepted a glass of port, Penfolds, as I remember. Maybe he had two. I had never known him to have a drop of alcohol when organizing and carrying out his duties as Commodore of the Queen's Flight.

Early next morning I was called by the Hotel Manager to say that Sir Edward Fielden had had a heart attack, that the local doctor insisted that no one should visit him and that he must be flown to Suva at once. The Governor's staff were very good and before long a Short Sunderland sea plane landed in the bay. The invalid was brought out on a stretcher. It was clear that the "heart attack" had not silenced him. I could hear phrases like "Bloody nonsense" as the stretcher was put on a boat to take him to the Sunderland. It was my first sea take-off and, dramatic it was, the doubt that the aircraft will ever rise over the waves is quite different from the increasing feeling of airborne-ness on a runway.

At Suva the Governor was there to meet us, with doctors, an ambulance and police escort. An official asked me to explain who I was and what was I doing there. I got the impression that I was interfering in some way, in official view. Having got Mouse into the ambulance, I checked into a guest-house and visited him early next day. He was extremely agitated about the "fuss", as he called it, and particularly about the doom-laden messages about him sent to the Royal Yacht *Britannia*, now steaming to Sydney. It was clear to me that he had had no heart attack, that a couple of glasses of port, to someone who had forsworn alcohol, could have given some such symptoms, but that we should get on our way as soon as possible.

This I was able to organize quickly and realized that, leaving Fiji early in the morning, catching flights to Honolulu and Los Angeles, we could be in London in the early evening of the same day. In my couple of days' unexpected sojourn in Fiji I had seen orchid plants growing in profusion in the forest, parasites on trees, thriving in the heat and humidity of the island. Tony Hedley, a Grenadier Major whom I had known in the Guards Armoured Division, had invited us to dinner on the same night and so it was possible to present our hosts with a present of orchid plants, collected on the same day in Fiji. It made a good talking point, and Tony told me later that they had thrived.

Six weeks later BOAC flew to Perth, Western Australia, to fly the Queen home. Mouse was in his usual good health, cheerful and efficient, and the return via Honolulu was triumphant – Hawaiian flags with Cook's Union Jack, leis in profusion. The island chiefs each had a band and dancers to perform the dances special to their tribe. The return journey in the Boeing 707 was in total contrast to the unhappy outward one. The Queen sent for me and said, "We were so worried to get the Governor's message about Mouse, and the only thing I could do was to ask who was with him. When I heard it was you, we felt he was in good hands." The undeserved credit for looking after a friend touched me deeply – especially when she drew out of her handbag a little case containing cuff-links with the Royal cipher inscribed. I wear them all the time. Heather swears that if pyjamas had cuff-link holes I would wear them in bed!

Chapter Eleven

BOAC – FROM SECURITY TO PERSONNEL

1962 was a good year for us. Basil Smallpeice promoted me to report to him directly. The Economy Queen's Messengers were established and earning praise as well as income, the "Thiefrow" reputation of Heathrow was dwindling, the Communist control of some Unions was clearly declining and our Irish Chairman, Sir Matthew Slattery, was being seen as a remarkable leader internationally, resulting in him becoming President of IATA, the International Air Transport Association.

He asked me to suggest how the control of airline fares could be achieved. I was rather surprised to find myself in this new Security area, security because we knew that, internationally, money was laundered through Air Travel Agents. My gold experience had demonstrated how it was possible to carry out illegal deals, using gold as the pay-off, and there was a strong belief that small airlines were economizing on maintenance of their aircraft and hiring cheaper pilots, and that the maintenance of IATA fare levels was necessary. The Director-General, Major Ronald McCrindle, had been persuaded that methods used in Northern Ireland, the Middle East, and indeed, later, in Africa, could be employed in the IATA drive for "no cheating" by the airlines of the world.

McCrindle invited me to meet him at the Hotel George V in Paris and we had, for me, the most illuminating meeting of my life on the past, present and future of the world aviation. He was extraordinarily communicative. After all I was only an airline Security Officer, commended by fellow-Irishman Slattery, but the role he was suggesting to me was breathtaking. IATA had an Enforcement body, commanded by a nice Swiss gentleman, whom I met later. He had achieved this position by accident – he just happened to be there – when IATA was looking for an Enforcement Chief. His methods were naive and many of his staff corruptible. IATA's fare system was a disaster. The 105 member airlines proposed fares which were fair, economic and promotional. The smaller airlines (some British) opposed them on the grounds of being too cheap. On a majority vote, the Pan Ams, TWAs, BOACs, Air Frances were voted down, and the small carriers got a majority for *higher* fares. They cheated then, because the public's perception was of big airlines being greedy, and they, the smaller carriers, of trying to give the hugely-growing market what it wanted.

Ronald McCrindle, who had the Churchillian fashion of spending mornings in his dressing-gown, gave me this proposition. "Would you take on the enforcement role of IATA, without being part of its Official Enforcement?" Impetuous as ever, I agreed. He told me that costs would be cleared by him, with Matthew Slattery's co-signature, and I could spend what I liked to get "cheating" out of the system.

The philosophy of this worried me. Surely some other system could give the ordinary traveller the benefits of the Boeing 707 or Douglas DC8? Why should smaller airlines with indifferent aircraft sabotage the investment of the airline leaders which had pioneered world travel? Once again the system was easily available. Honest, brave agents, prepared to risk their lives and reputation in a good cause, like Northern Ireland, or gold-smuggling, was what was needed.

I told the Director-General of IATA that there would be huge press attacks on a BOAC activity to stop IATA cheating, and how would he see Sir Matthew surviving this. His answer was quick, "Slattery is known as the most honest of the airline men. Don't worry."

So the system started. In the Security Branch by now there were Indians, Africans, South Americans, who all had a background of faithfulness in service. John Dominic, now my Chief Officer in BOAC Security, had chosen the team.

It was an operation which made Northern Ireland seem amateur. We had to have operatives who could be vouched for, who were not corruptible and were brave. In India we would use Pakistanis, in England Irishmen, in France Germans, in South Africa black men. The system was that a telephone call would make a travel deal (illegal), the agent would promise to pay in cash, would be searched to prove he (or she, as we had female operatives) had no money on them other than the agreed sum, representing an airfare. For months case after case was built up, towards the Presidential address of the President of IATA, Sir Matthew Slattery.

Sir Matthew, a distinguished Naval aviator much decorated for his wartime achievements, had brought Shorts/Harland, as it was then, into profitability. He had initiated the Harrier Jump-Jet, a victor later in the Falklands, he had come to BOAC to promote its market, and to reduce its cost. He was dogged by the debate about the VC10. This handsome aircraft, with four jet engines on its tail and lovely lines, was the last British chance to be a serious competitor to Boeing. He wanted to support it, he wanted to keep the British skills of innovation and design afloat, but his Board, particularly the Managing Director, Basil Smallpeice, were determined to make a proper and defensible bid for the best aircraft on international offer, the Boeing 707, they believed. The Board was badly split, at a time of change when a new Minister of Aviation, Julian Amery, was appointed. He decided that BOAC should not have acted patriotically, but commercially, should not have backed the Vickers VC10 so significantly and should be "set free" to behave commercially, rather than as a British Nationalized Industry. Sir Matthew, at the end of a difficult press conference to announce the rather lacklustre figures of the previous year, was shutting his briefcase when a pushy BBC reporter pushed a microphone at him and asked, "What are your views about the Government relationship with BOAC?" Answer: "A bloody crazy way to run an airline". A furious Minister denounced this and that led quickly to the dismissal of Sir Matthew Slattery and Sir Basil Smallpeice, "The Knight Shift" as described by the Trade Unions.

Slattery, an un-Irish Irishman, rather dry with not much sense of humour, had been responsible for getting me into the high politics of IATA; by now there had been scores of "cases" in which my Security staff, of several nationalities, had bought tickets at below the IATA rate all over the world. As IATA's President, Sir Matthew made a sensational speech at the IATA AGM, in which he named the offending airlines, some of them the world leaders. Uproar followed; vehement denials, backed by Government Ministers, protested the sanctity of Air France, Sabena, Pan Am, TWA, Aer Lingus and a dozen others. At a following press conference, Sir Matthew, backed by Major McCrindle, named names and put down a paper giving the facts (which I had prepared). Another IATA summit was called, where every Chairman or President was required to swear a solemn oath that his airline would not cheat on fares ever again.

I was proud of my staff who gave evidence about their success in getting discounts, sometimes as high as 50% on IATA airlines. Invariably the defence would be a denial, with allegations of impropriety by my "Agents Provocateurs". In every case the Security Officer concerned was believed. A great clean-up of the fare-cheating took place, which led to BOAC inventing the cheap fare, APEX as it was called, requiring advance payment, non-refundable, for a particular flight. This tapped a huge market and is now the basis of the long-haul aviation business.

This international success did not, however, cool Julian Amery's determination to get rid of Slattery. I thought it unjust, and even more unjust that Basil Smallpiece should be sacked too.

Some years later the Slatterys stayed with us in Montreal because of a flight cancellation. He was still rather bitter about his "summary execution". Lady Slattery was revealing. She said that when he was appointed to BOAC's Chairmanship she had been quite amused by the Press catchphrase "Slattery will get you nowhere". She was *not* so amused by another press ribaldry describing him as "Lady Slattery's lover"!

Julian Amery wanted to do something dynamic about Aviation, as had many Aviation Ministers before. They wanted to have an obedient nationalized industry. They wanted to have it use British aircraft. They wanted to have the Empire (not just the Commonwealth) dominant in world aviation because of the huge spread of British connection worldwide. But they also required that the state airline should be profitable. BEA was easy. The Minister could set tariff levels and, by going along with European airlines, could ensure profit. World competition was another matter and, despite its outstanding trail-blazing, Imperial Airways and BOAC had not succeeded in profit terms.

The Amery plan was to go for profit and having sacked the two Knights, he brought in a Baronet, Sir Giles Guthrie DSC, the Deputy Chairman of BEA. Guthrie, the Eton-educated son of Sir Connop Guthrie, the British Intelligence Chief in the United States, was the Managing Director of Brown Shipley, a Fleet Air Arm pilot in the War and a test pilot. BOAC was apprehensive about him. The feeling was that he was too much of a BEA man, would want to play safe and would be hooked on British aircraft, never mind how uncompetitive. Furthermore that he was a devoted admirer of David Craig, one of BEA's stars, who had made a name for himself as the BEA Italy Manager with the British Ambassador's wife. Shades of Nelson and Lady Hamilton.

Guthrie arrived the day after the departure of the Knights. On his first day he visited my little set-up. He was clearly well briefed by his two predecessors (he was Chairman/Chief Executive), and told me how much he wanted to support all the security initiatives.

Charm is an overworked word, but Giles Guthrie had it "in spades". Hours after he took us over, he had every one of the key directors on his side. It was not just that they wanted to secure their jobs. They saw him as a younger, vigorous and approachable man, who would be close to them in their responsibilities and who would have the independence from Government "Diktat" which would help us internationally. Not only was he a Baronet but also a millionaire.

A few days after his visit I was invited to his office. Without any preliminaries he said, "Will you accept the post of Director of Personnel and join the Board of Management?" To my eternal shame I replied, "Chairman, I am Gorman, your Security man". Irritated, he said, "You don't have to tell me my job – do you accept the job?" I did, and left his office in a daze.

The background I had obtained from my Army and RUC experiences had been invaluable in the Security job, but to be in world-wide charge of the administration, training and industrial relations of 24,000 people, as their Personnel Director, was a greater challenge then ever before. Family stability was essential. By now we were living at Crawley Down, Johnny a dayboy at Worth Junior School, Angela and Rosanagh boarding in Devon and Justin at school in Copthorne. My business experience was minimal. The previous Personnel Director was the former Chief Medical Officer of BOAC, so there was a certain precedent in appointing a non-professional Personnel Chief, though it has to be said that he had not been regarded as a success in the post, having fallen foul of BOAC's Personnel Chiefs. He was to revert to being Director of Medical Services, which was why the post was available for me. The infighting between BOAC and BEA was a whole new and unexpected problem, compounded by the fact that my new Chairman (and Managing Director as Guthrie was combining the posts) was ex-BEA, as was David Craig who had the title Senior General Manager for his rather new role in BOAC.

A few days after my meeting with Giles Guthrie I got into a lift at the "Kremlin" to find a very depressed Public Relations Director, Alan Ponsford, with a draft of the *BOAC News*. In it was a scathing attack on the previous Management of the airline, describing it as inefficient, over-manned, uncompetitive and not a patch on BEA. The ramifications of this going out in the name of the new Chairman were horrendous and would bring into the open the appalling disunity between the two national airlines. The announcement that the Chief of Security was to become Personnel Director would be taken as meaning that I was to be the hatchet-man, to cull BOAC of its Managers, replacing them by BEA staff. So I insisted on joining Alan Ponsford when he entered the Chairman's office. He had with him Keith Granville, Deputy Chairman, and the new Senior General Manager, David Craig. I apologized for butting in to a meeting, which was to discuss BOAC's future, but said that if the Board wanted me to join it as Personnel Director I saw it as my duty to consider the effect *on the people* in BOAC of this crucial statement. I gave them a little homily on leader-ship, and said that I was already having second thoughts about the new job. While I thought I could cope with it, it was my contribution to the Board of Management which I feared would be inadequate, because of my lack of commercial knowledge. There was a long silence, interrupted by Giles Guthrie, "Thank you, John. Goodbye."

My feeling on leaving the room was rather similar to that at Cagny. Had I through impetuousness thrown away the hopes of the others – a wife and four children – with no pension, as the Stormont Government in a final piece of malice had pronounced that my and their contributions to my pension, were not transferable. So 15 years of service were wiped out. Where could I go now, having turned down this key job? As always, Heather supported me and was sure that the Security job would not be withdrawn, although a BEA-dominated BOAC might not put so much emphasis on the function. BEA did not have a comparable post.

There was an anxious 24 hours in the Gorman family. As expected, the Chairman sent for me, this time with only Keith Granville present. "John, you made me even more confident in you by your outburst yesterday. We are not making the pejorative statement. Keith and I want to thank you, but in case you are blaming David Craig for the statement, he has reminded me of what you said about your lack of commercial/financial/business experience, and he had booked you on the Harvard University Advanced Management Programme. So – are you willing to take this on?" I stammered, "Yes", thanked him and left to call Heather, who typically said, "I knew you would get Guthrie's support. He is like you, acts first, thinks later".

The first thing to do, of course, was to meet my new team, the second to find a new Chief of Security. There were three top figures in Personnel, Oliver Hinch, a Catholic, whose wisdom and compassion made him beloved by staff all over the world, Leonard (Jim) Atherton, the Industrial Relations chief, who was the butt of BEA's antipathy, and Alex Cameron, whom I had met in the Freddie Chesterton days of Selection, Training and Development, and who was clearly destined to succeed Freddie.

It was a surprisingly cordial meeting. I suppose if any of the trio had been chosen to succeed the rather devalued Dr Bergin it would have been less so, but all three gave me their support. I asked them to set out what they believed were priorities for the "people" of BOAC.

Oliver Hinch said, "To get harmony and pride in our great company."

Jim Atherton said, "To bind in Trade Unions to *commercial* success in a savagely competitive world."

Alex Cameron said, "To achieve selection, training and staff development standards of the highest quality in the aviation world."

Meeting them separately, I offered Oliver Hinch the job of General Manager Personnel Administration, responsible for every detail of policy which affected "people" in the airline; Jim Atherton the job of General Manager Industrial Relations, to carry out his own ambition of getting the Trades Unions bound into commercial success; and Alex Cameron Selection, Training and Staff Development.

They all accepted, obviously happy to have a "neutral" boss! One problem which Jim Atherton had flagged up was the pilots. Himself RAF, he warned me that American pilots were braced for a battle with the big US airlines and might well win on the basis that pilots were "special and different". The first "Airport" programmes were being filmed. Jim Atherton was convinced that nothing other than a combined European attitude could stop this rot. Pilots were looking for $100,000 dollars a year. Managers were getting $50,000. The Managers ran the airline. Why should the "operators" be paid twice as much as their Managers?

It was clear that a huge problem faced us. The majority of our Captains were heroes of the Battle of Britain or ex-bomber pilots. It was up to me to find a solution. I talked to the Board. Eminent men, Lord Normanton for example, said, "You can't believe that pilots with DFCs will really strike?" My reply was, "Yes". The Board was flabbergasted. The idea that gentlemen, many of them wartime heroes, could strike was astounding.

Then the Government changed. Harold Wilson introduced the Prices and Incomes Policy and Giles and I were sent for to meet George Brown. He was wonderfully persuasive, well briefed as to BOAC's ambitions, and it seemed to us that he could use the same arguments with the Unions as effectively as with us. Jim Atherton rubbished this idea and again said that this would cut no ice with the Pilots. To make matters worse, the British Airlines Pilots Association chief, Captain Norman Tebbitt, of BOAC, resigned to pursue his political career. Tebbitt was my last hope. He had kept the frustrations of our pilots under control, reminded them that they were not "special and different", that there was no such thing as an international pay-rate for pilots, and that what had happened in the US would lead eventually to airline collapse. (The demise of Pan Am, Eastern, and TWA (almost) bore out his prediction.)

By now my three General Managers were in position with clear terms of reference. One of the initiatives which I had told the Unions about was my intention to make myself the spokesman for, and the consulter with, the Senior Staff list. This was a key group in BOAC; here were the Management brains, where ideas and attitudes were formed. It seemed to me that a Personnel Director who was not in touch with them was not going to give his Board good advice.

The invitation to the top 400 managers went out to them, signed personally, and I adopted a tactic, which was useful later, of saying that I would be alone on the platform. Almost all 400 accepted and I had excellent briefing from Winston Bray, the Planning Director, from Jim Atherton, my General Manager Industrial Relations and from Oliver Hinch, the senior of my trio, GM Personnel Administration. Best of all was Giles Guthrie's personal involvement in giving me details about his proposals, made by now to Government, to bring BOAC into profit and world leadership.

It was another "Cagny" in a sense, but this time I felt that there was a good chance of getting this key group onside, especially as I was going to detail the "golden handshake", which would be offered to those whose applications for it were accepted, but better still, the security and confidence in themselves which a refusal to "let go" one of their number would engender.

My predecessor had got into the habit of sending anonymous letters to politicians and influential people, like the Editor of *The Times*. These were sent to some of the 400, in which he described me as an Irishman of limited intelligence but unlimited charm. Several of the furious speakers quoted this (which is probably a true diagnosis as to the first part, and quite untrue as to the second). When the uproar died down and I was able to reveal the G1 Plan, there was a different atmosphere. G1 was Guthrie's first plan. It involved cutting out unprofitable routes, majoring on those which gave a good return, but essentially competing ruthlessly with the world's airlines which saw the decline of Empire as a signal to dismember the British airline overseas. There was generous approbation at my effort to reveal G1 and the terms of staff contraction. BOAC had about 24,000 staff world-wide. To get our costs down we needed to reduce this to 20,000. When a company says it wants to reduce costs, get higher productivity and efficiency what is meant is that people must go. "Staff are too expensive to have." The severance terms were the best in the UK, but more was needed. The airline had a very proper need to ensure quality control and safety of aircraft operation was paramount. The tradition had been "That wherever two or three shall be gathered together there shall be a Supervisor". There were layers of Supervisors/Management, which had emerged from wartime problems, well set out in Winston Bray's book *The History of BOAC*. It was a culture which had to be changed if the dynamic of the airline was to come through.

By now Guthrie had been to every nook and cranny of BOAC world-wide, had been heartened with the morale and enterprise of the staff, particularly overseas, and had recalled his pre-war time in Poland as BOAC's Manager before 1939.

People hate to have someone else telling them what they should be doing. The SSL (Senior Staff List) had now accepted that there had to be a "culling", but my fellow directors saw this as an attack on them for having presided over manning extravagance. I started a Monthly Manpower Planning Group, which ostensibly was to do with the future, but was very much to do with the present. These meetings were difficult; the Commercial, Engineering, Flight Operations, Airport Directors, etc, could hardly be blamed for resenting this jumped-up Security Officer telling *them* what should be their manning levels. Fortunately, the SSL had by now been suggesting how the severance scheme could get some expensive, but under-employed (or inefficient), people out of the system. The staff numbers started to go down and the Government and media made much of this, as it coincided with a world aviation upturn, and Giles Guthrie's success in getting HMG to accept that he would always act commercially, unless Government had given him a direction *in writing* "in the National Interest" was a huge strength.

But the slow numbers descent was not as dramatic as was planned. It was almost a test of our masculinity to get 24,000 staff down to less than 20,000. I knew it could, and should, be done, but at a Manpower Planning meeting I was attacked by the Engineering, Commercial and Flight Operations Directors on the grounds that I was a large employer myself. What was I going to do about it?

The Personnel, Industrial Relations, Staff and Training Administration under my aegis had nearly 1,000 staff, 500 of these employed in Staff Catering, Staff Rest Houses (Karachi, Khartoum, Santiago), even an expensive restaurant in Central London. They were marvellous, loyal and efficient people, who did not deserve the chop, especially as we would have to provide the service they gave by sub-contracting to, say, Forte's. Yet to keep 500 people on our payroll, many of whose jobs were only peripherally to do with aviation, made no sense and made me, the staff executioner, look rather foolish: "Do what I say, don't do what I do."

Giles and his Deputy Chairman, Charles Hardie, had in 1939 funded Charles Forte to open his ice-cream parlour in Piccadilly. I went to Giles and suggested that :

Forte should take over staff catering and rest-houses.

We should form a joint company. I suggested BOFORT, amalgam of BOAC and Forte; that this should be a progenitor of privatization, as BOAC staff would now be employed by BOFORT.

That staff travel privileges be maintained for the staff transferring, but not their successors.

A "golden handshake" for all transferring.

BOFORT should become the BOAC consultant on hotel enterprises world-wide. It was obvious that hotel unavailability was inhibiting traffic growth.

Giles said "Snap. You will be the first Chairman of BOFORT, but we must ensure that Sir Charles Forte is happy."

We went to the Cafe Royal, the Forte power-house. Charles Forte met us and took us to his offices, where Lowry paintings dominated the scene. He had Jack Hollingshead to support him. Giles outlined the BOFORT plan, Charles Forte bought it at once, on condition that I would become the first Chairman of the new Company.

The staff in the UK, Asia, Africa and South America were surprisingly receptive to the plan. They had felt very insecure when the staff reduction world-wide had been announced and many had concluded that we would simply contract out this non-core activity. At our first BOFORT Board meeting, I outlined the hotel objectives, which were:

carry out feasibility studies at places where hotel accommodation would provide a passenger service and Aircrew lay-over facilities;

use a minimum of BOAC capital by obtaining partners, preferably locally;

have standards which were adequately comfortable, but not super-luxurious, at an affordable price;

franchise the staffing of the hotels, employing the minimum of in-house supervisory and quality control management.

David Craig, the Senior General Manager, and Jack Hollingshead carried out the first feasibility studies. It was a lesson to me that capital, partners and franchises are readily available for a demonstrably marketable product or service.

There was little Union resistance. The TGWU had some token ideological distaste for the transaction, but the general feeling was that getting staff numbers down so painlessly by 500 had been a good move. The word "privatization" was studiously avoided, though Giles and I saw in this non-controversial event a good omen for the total privatization which was our objective.

The next foray into quasi-privatization was in Wales. At Treforest, near Cardiff, the BOAC Engine Overhaul operations was located. Treforest had been developed in wartime to overhaul the engines of the whole fleet, over 200 aircraft of seventeen types. The management and staff were true professionals and our facilities in overhaul were much admired by our competitors. The M4 motorway, passing Heathrow on the way to Bristol, meant that engines could be at Treforest in five or six hours and back ready for service in a few days. The Engineering Director, Charles Abell, was not enthusiastic, but his senior, the Technical Director, Beverly Shenstone, who had come from BEA as one of Giles's "support", was. I went to Treforest and explained to the Managers and staff that the same principles would apply as had been accepted by BOFORT, and in addition the "hived-off" operation would now be marketed to the whole airline industry, which would be much easier to do credibly if the new company BEOL, British Engine Overhaul Limited, was no longer simply part of the BOAC Engineering Division. It would have its own Board, though, as the main shareholder, the Chairman would be from BOAC. I proposed that one of the Board should be Clive Jenkins, the Welsh General Secretary of ASSET, now ASTMS.

The British airlines had a National Joint Council for Civil Aviation. This post-war body was the forum for pay and conditions negotiations for all staff, except senior management; it gave opportunity for dialogue with Unions and did its best to keep a sense of fairness and equity between the many grades of worker on the ground and in the air, and between employers, some as big as BOAC and BEA, some small feeder airlines and charter companies. On the whole it worked well, though the more aggressive Unions, particularly the pilots' one, BALPA, and the Engineering Unions generally, looked on the NJC as a useful industrial relations weapon to use in support of strikes, go-slows and demarcation. The Union side was quick to perceive any crack in the employer side's unanimity and this was particularly worrying in the BOAC/BEA relationship. BOAC's Industrial Relations General Manager, Jim Atherton, a persuasive and quick-witted man, full of ingenuity and initiative, was heartily disliked by the pedestrian BEA Industrial Relations senior staff and it became a tedious chore for the two Chairmen, Guthrie of BOAC and Anthony Milward of BEA, to listen to the opposing views which my opposite BEA Personnel Director, Cyril Herring, and I were expressing. As Giles almost always supported me, the outcome was usually a victory for Atherton, to the fury of Herring and his people. BEA had no real incentive to reduce numbers and to get its costs down. It had no competition then in the UK (no British Midland then) and its European routes were run in parallel with airlines such as Air France, Alitalia and Sabena, who were only too happy with the cosy cartel which such routes as London-Paris constituted. The cost per mile of airfares in Europe was then three times that in North America, a searing indictment of the European Union's inability to curb this "anti-trust rip-off" of the customer.

When the NJC Union side realized what we had in mind for Treforest, a great storm of protest ensued. The BOFORT precedent was given high profile and, with a Labour Government now in power, the "creeping privatization" which we were seen to be carrying out was "politically incorrect". BOFORT became BOAC Restaurants Limited, BRL, and the Treforest plan was postponed.

After a few months I was accepted by the Harvard Business School for the Advanced Management Program. This rather stressful thirteen week experience has 160 participants, eighty Americans, eighty foreigners. The 160 are divided into twenty "Cans" of eight men (no women then), and work starts six days a week at 8 am, ending as late at night as one can stay awake. The Case Study is the method used for teaching. Every day a detailed real live "Case" researched by the School is presented for study. Discussion in Can Group gatherings, preliminary to full debate in the School amphitheatres, required the students to make presentations, analyse options, accepting and responding to criticism from professors and fellow-students. American "AMPs" were much more self-assured and "verbalized" uninhibitedly, but as time went on the "foreigners" came into their stride. It was good training in marshalling and presenting one's thoughts and opinions and accepting a challenge. Many of one's fellow AMPs became real friends, and we keep in touch with James Van Sant of St. Louis, Missouri, Mubarak Kanoo of Bahrein and M.V. Arunachalam of India. We were given subjects for research and a team to assist. Mine was "leadership". My team included several military men from US and European countries. It was my task to present our findings to the 160-strong class. A quotation from T S Eliot, mentioned later, with which I ended the presentation, seemed to sum up this amorphous subject.

The final week was "Wives' Week" when Heather joined me for a series of lectures and exercises (Case Studies) especially designed for the senior executives' wives. We gave a "brunch" party of Hot Dogs and American champagne on the last day. It was with horror that we heard in the course of the party that an aircraft bringing two of our guests from New York had crashed, killing one and permanently crippling the other. Looking back on Harvard I feel it was one of the most productive episodes of my life. I had passed Trinity Entrance (Trinity College Dublin) before joining the Army in 1941, but the Cadetship in the RUC had ruled out University after the War. It was a generous and I hope worthwhile experiment to send one of the Guthrie Board of Management away "to be educated", and typical of him. Oliver Hinch, again, held the fort with distinction.

Every week one of the class was required by the Faculty to find a distinguished speaker to address the class. When the task fell to me I had great difficulty in finding a suitable person. The British Ambassador would have fitted the bill, but he was not available. One evening in a Boston bar I met two Doctors who had been members of the Kennedy Commission studying "The Causal Relationship between Cigarette Smoking and Cancer", who accepted my invitation to address the class. With film slides and a polished presentation, they did a superb job of frightening their 160 audience. At that time the smoking/cancer link was not fully accepted, but anyone seeing and hearing what these two had to tell had to be convinced.

When, to tumultuous applause, they finished, I realized I had to thank them and walked to the front of the auditorium stage. Pulling out of my pocket what was in fact my very last packet of English cigarettes (I dislike American) I threw this at the wastepaper basket in the well of the auditorium saying, "I shall never smoke again". The packet flew up into the spotlights and fell neatly into the basket. Later that night I searched the basket. It was full of scraps of paper, pencil shavings and detritus, but the cigarettes had gone! The hand of God, or a friend who knew my pledge was bravado? I shall never know, but I have not smoked since.

On return to London, the drive for productivity and profitability was now getting into its stride. It was my job to hold regular meetings with all the Divisions and to encourage them to examine every one of the functions for which they were responsible, using specialist Work Study and Organization and Methods staff to help. This was painful work. Many of the people whose jobs were threatened had had long and valuable careers in BOAC and were often close friends of the management. The volatile nature of the airline business, with its peaks and troughs of demand, the intensity of competition particularly in aircraft, the interdependence of functions, the great strength of the Unions in those days of "beer and sandwiches at No 10" made it difficult for Directors, all of whom had served for many years more than me, to accept my urging to be ruthless so far as manpower was concerned.

George Brown was Chancellor of the Exchequer and came out with his Prices and Incomes Policy. He invited the Chairmen of Nationalized Industries to come and see him and so Giles Guthrie and I found ourselves again being given a dissertation on the benefits to the country of his plan. I had met my opposite number in British Rail who had been through the same experience shortly before and had put to the Chancellor his and his Chairman's plan to cut staff in British Rail by closing unprofitable lines, the so-called "Beeching Plan". Dr Beeching had told George Brown of the golden handshake system used in the City to obtain voluntary severance of senior management and asked for permission to use this to remove very senior Rail management surplus to his plans. Brown had agreed to this, to the apparent surprise of his officials present. Giles and I, knowing of this breakthrough, made a strong case to him for extending the system of golden handshakes down the line, pointing out that to make a real impression on staff numbers, without creating serious industrial unrest, severance must be voluntary. Enforced redundancy would result in strikes, with catastrophic consequences to the airline, which was at last getting into profit. Brown thought for some time and on this occasion asked us to leave him while he discussed the idea with his officials. We did not get an answer that day, but we had told the Chancellor of our intentions and in the absence of prohibition we took it that we could go ahead, and did.

My staff drew up a schedule of severance pay, related to years of service, final salary, and pensions availability. We called a meeting with the seventeen Unions covering staff in the UK and outlined in detail our proposals to reduce staff world-wide from 24,000 to 20,000 over the next couple of years. Then we showed them the severance pay schedule. All seemed impressed and I thought that we were going to get co-operation from the Unions for what we believed to be a workmanlike and compassionate scheme. Then Clive Jenkins started to denounce it. His fiery rhetoric and scathing criticism of my "amateur" effort was bad enough, but he then demolished the credentials of Giles Guthrie whom he credited with the most unworthy and unpleasant motives for staff reduction. It was a *tour de force* which galvanised his colleagues and it was clear that they would rubbish our plans publicly. Unwisely I asked him to join me in my office and, quoting some of his criticisms expressed so pungently, asked him to justify them, particularly those directed at Giles. He refused to do so and made to walk out, so I stood with my back to the door until he gave some explanation, which was when I realized that some of the 400 senior staff had joined his Union, and so he had prior knowledge of management's plans, and in particular believed that much of the "down-sizing" would effect that senior group, probably many of those he had recruited for his Union. Next day I had a letter from a lawyer representing ASSET, his Union, to the effect that I had "imprisoned" him in my office against his will and he was suing me. Ron Smith, a Board Member and head of the Postal Union, went to see him and the three of us had a convivial lunch together, when I saw and heard the other side of this brilliant and entertaining man, who, when I got to know him better, I came to like and respect.

The episode gave me concern and I discussed with Oliver Hinch and Jim Atherton what the implications were of the top-level staff being unionized, and particularly the conflict of interest which was inherent in them doing so. We concluded that this must be met head-on, and that I should put myself forward as the person with their interests at heart and who they should consult about their problems.

I called the first of many meetings with the senior staff to convey this message, when, to my chagrin, David Craig persuaded the Board that senior staff should have their first-class travel entitlement removed from them. It so happened that I was not present at the board meeting at which this was decided and so was not able to countermand the decision. It had always been accepted as a perk supplementing pay rates, which were by no means excessive, that senior managers would fly first-class, *if a seat was available*, and frequently there would not be an empty seat and the senior man, or woman, would perfectly happily travel Economy (no Business or Club Class then). The result of being ejected from a first-class cabin, with seats available, was too much. The meeting with the 400 was stormy to say the least. I had to defend what seemed to me indefensible, and my hopes of finding "hearts and minds" in common cause with the 400 almost absurd. Fortunately Giles heard about my session in the pillory and got the Board to agree to drop the decision, so the senior staff meetings became much more cordial and constructive and indeed many of them took me up on the offer to see them individually. Much of the follow-up to such individual problems fell to Oliver Hinch, who did his usual wonderful job in calming, or at least ameliorating, them.

Job insecurity is sometimes seen as a modern phenomenon arising from technological advances and the removal of levels of management, empowering more junior staff to take decisions formerly reserved to their seniors. A manifestation of this insecurity was the large number of senior staff who applied for severance terms. Very many of these were key personnel who could not be spared and would be extremely difficult to replace. They were relieved and pleased when we turned down their applications and told them how much they were needed.

Severance terms applied to pilots and many availed themselves of them. We introduced a maximum age for pilots of 55, and some of these very senior and high-quality men took the terms and went to other airlines for another five years flying. One who did this was our dear friend Captain James Percy, who had joined Imperial Airlines in the 1920s as a boy apprentice. He was Senior Captain in BOAC, had pioneered the Empire Mail scheme to Australia and flown the first direct civil aircraft to Russia after Germany invaded. He and I had seen a lot of each other on Royal flights and Heather and Pat Percy had become good friends. They were to come back into our lives again years later.

To return to the Pilots Union, BALPA (British Airline Pilots Association). Norman Tebbitt's moderating influence had been removed and many pilots came to believe that special and different terms and conditions of service should apply to them. Their model was ALPA, the American Union, which had through a series of crippling strikes come to dominate the Union scene in the US, where the "one for all, all for one" National Joint Council system did not exist. Companies gave in, one by one, to enormous pay demands from their pilots, whose salaries far outweighed any other staff remuneration. Admittedly they flew more hours and had more flexible rostering systems, but in effect they held the US airline industry to ransom and their demands were met. The disappearance of such world airline names as Pan American, Eastern and Continental Airlines can be credibly put at the door of this crazy phase in airline pay. British pilots came to believe in the American slogan "An international pay rate for an international top job". This had no justification in economic or parity terms. No salary level can ignore national levels of pay, taxation, cost of living and social expenditure on health and welfare. It was Jim Percy, Master of the Guild of Air Pilots and Navigators, who alerted me to the strength of opinion among his fellows, particularly the more senior ones, who looked forward to the sort of pension enjoyed by their American peers.

Taking this very seriously I persuaded the Director of Flight Operations, Captain Frank Walton, and his Deputy, Captain Tom Nisbet, to join me in a presentation to the full Board giving warning of the danger, indeed the likelihood, of an all-out pilot strike. The Board were not persuaded. Many of them were ex-service and could not believe that "Officers and Gentlemen" could seriously consider bringing the airline to a halt. The BEA attitude was patronizing, "Our pilots are loyal, unlike your BOAC rebels. They will never strike". Session after session of the Airline Chairman's Committee, Guthrie and Milward, produced no real understanding of the imminence of a disastrous pilot strike. Furthermore, the Prices and Incomes Policy, so beloved of George Brown and Harold Wilson, lulled the BOAC Board into complacency. Giles, a distinguished former pilot himself, who made a point of joining the pilots on the flight deck and chatting to them, was on my side, and on that of Walton and Nisbet, but the imminence of delivery of our first Jumbo Jet, the Boeing 747, was yet another temptation to euphoria. Clearly a new pay rate for the big aircrafts' pilots would be justifiable and this would satisfy the "International Pilots Pay" brigade.

At Harvard I had heard much about Staff Attitude Surveying. This management technique had proved itself in the States as a means of discovering what was really uppermost in the minds and aspirations of staff, and, by going directly and anonymously to each employee, cut out the false optimism of line managers, eager to show how highly they had motivated their workforce, and equally discounted the doom-laden predictions of Unions, always eager to intimidate management to achieve pay and conditions breakthroughs. The leading exponent of Staff Attitude Surveying was the University of Chicago, so I went there with Jim Atherton and met Professor Jack Stanek who had headed the Faculty.

The technique was to divide staff into discrete units whose tasks and objectives were broadly common, and to devise a questionnaire which would cover not only pay and conditions, but much deeper questions. They had to consider Board policy, their own management, their Unions, manning levels, adequacy of supervision, empowerment of fairly junior staff to take decisions within their competence, training, promotion and recruitment. The questionnaires were devised by Stanek and his team in consultation with the line management, who were to be responsible for disclosing, directly to their employees at all levels, what the findings of the Attitude Survey were. At one of my Senior Staff meetings I authorized the scheme, then only a proposal and not yet approved by the Board.

After each weekly Board of Management meeting I would brief my three General Managers, and after the full monthly Board, all the Personnel Managers of the Divisions and Regions, about thirty in all. These were valuable occasions and enabled Personnel Management to be at the right hand of their bosses to ensure that the human side of all decisions was taken into account, and that the company's objectives and values were understood world-wide. The Attitude Surveying process, which had started as a rather desperate stratagem on my part to warn Board and Government of what I believed to be in store for BOAC, took on a wider significance when applied right across the airline all over the world, pervading even the smallest and most remote units. As it would be administered by Personnel Managers it was important that they supported the policy, explained it persuasively and took a leading part in dealing with the results, however unpalatable in some cases these might be.

With the enthusiastic backing of the Chairman (who was also Chief Executive), the Board of Management then endorsed the plan, and with some hesitations the full Board agreed it. I believe my clinching argument, supported by Flight Operations, was that at last we would know what *each pilot* believed, since all would be interviewed, and would in privacy and anonymity fill up the carefully prepared Pilots' questionnaire.

No International airline had ever embarked on such a scheme world-wide and Unions were dead against it, as became understandable when the results started to come in. Several key ones were as follows:

Pilots were overwhelmingly in favour of massively higher pay and wanted to leave the National Joint Council, using the "Special and Different" argument, and the fact that Senior Management was not, ostensibly, unionized.

The 747 introduction, which had justified enormously larger remuneration to US and Air France pilots, for example, should take precedence over UK Prices and Incomes Policy.

Many Managers were seen to be weak and vacillating, the staff tolerating rather than respecting them. One common theme was that they were never seen by their juniors and communicated with them via Shop Stewards.

While many Union members, the majority in fact, were loyal to their Unions, and hesitated to criticize them, many were appalled at Management's capitulation, as it was perceived in, for example, the Union strike at the time of the VC10 inaugural to New York in 1964, giving the Boeing 747 Pan Am inaugural next day the glory; the Rooks v Barnard case in which Rooks, a conscientious objector to Unions, would not join one, and was sacked; and the electrician's strike of June 1961 over new supervision which spread throughout Engineering and cost £3m in revenue.

Industrial Relations in the US was in crisis. The airline industry there, intensely competitive and heavily overspent on new large aircraft such as the Boeing 747, Douglas DC9 and Lockheed Tristar, and having bowed to their Pilots' Union demands, were totally unable to visualize standing up to strikes, and one by one were picked off by the main Union, the International Association of Machinists. Again it was salutary for the Board to be alerted to the imminent danger.

A host of small deficiencies in control, deployment, leadership and communications, mostly easily correctable, but representing in sum a major burden to the airline, were revealed.

A major exercise in dialogue directly with the Management and staff then took place. A heavy load fell on Personnel Managers to assist their bosses in dealing, often for the first time, with criticism of them personally and the administration of their units. I took on myself the job of addressing the twenty or so panels, part of the NJC machinery, which covered all the main staff groupings. A combination of the staff reduction scheme, the Prices and Incomes Policy, and the deficiencies revealed by the Attitude Survey made for some fiery meetings, and, while permanent Union officials were not allowed to appear, their lay representatives had been well briefed to challenge me. After many difficult confrontations, I had what looked as though it would be an easy one, with the Stewardesses. A roomful of beautiful and charming young women listened to my homily, by now well practised, about the need for harmonious relationships between staff of all "trades". We must see ourselves, I said, as part of a great family, dedicated to customer service, and for management's part we were determined through our Personnel policies, to planning through selection of new employees, the training and development of all, to give to the human side of business the same strategic commitment as we gave to route and equipment, commercial and financial planning. In a word, said I, we must introduce Family Planning into BOAC. The tale of this hyperbolic rhetoric spread through the airline and every Stewardess I met on my travels seemed to have heard the story, which, since I was a Catholic, lent a further quirk to it!

Now began the painful work of staff reduction. A combination of the Severance Pay scheme, the inefficiencies and inadequacies revealed in the Survey, and the new drive towards profitability spearheaded by Guthrie produced a large crop of applications for severance, sometimes by people seeking reassurance that they were essential and valued, but one of the conditions of the scheme was that only in very exceptional circumstances were vacancies created by a "golden handshake" departure to be filled. So those who wanted to get the terms had to devise ways of having their function carried out in some other manner. This led to quite fundamental changes in working practice, for example:-

"Empowerment" of more junior staff.

Demarcation being blurred so that additional duties hitherto requiring a single specialist could now be taken on as an addition by a qualified and competent peer.

The British habit, which I described in the phrase "Wherever two or three are gathered together, there shall be a supervisor", was questioned.

Gradually numbers started to drop, productivity to rise and the staff cost element in our budgets ceased to inflate. Staff total in 1962, 21,664 and in 1965, 18,845.

A series of landmark agreements with groups of staff at home and abroad came to pass and the threatened US strike was short-lived when BOAC stood firm against the IAM.

One part of our network which was worrying was India. BOAC had had services to India from the early days of Imperial Airways. Karachi, New Delhi, Bombay and Calcutta had quite large numbers of people who had served the Airline loyally and well for generations, and whose chances of employment elsewhere were not good. Calcutta was a particularly hard case. From being a main destination and transit point, it was now reduced to a couple of services a week, with East Bengal now served directly to Dacca, East Pakistan. Basil Bamflyde, Eastern Routes General Manager, and Donald Erskine, General Manager India, made a plea for Calcutta to be retained on the network, which I supported. This decision had implications for my future which I could not have anticipated.

The third of my General Managers was Alex Cameron, General Manager Staff Development. His career in this field had been outstanding as the Deputy to Freddie Chesterton, when they had introduced manpower planning to BOAC in the early 60s. In my Security role, we had worked closely together not only to weed out criminals and Marxists from our applicants, but also to provide training of high quality directly in the case of Supervisory and Management training, but indirectly in influencing training in specialist sections.

Staff Development had been a special interest at Harvard and, under Alex Cameron, systems were devised along the lines I had observed in America, which set firm objectives to individual employees, appraised their performance formally each year and gave constant attention to training requirements.

In any large organization there is the danger of "typecasting" people. "An engineer is an engineer is an engineer." The individual may have superb qualities such as leadership, communication skills or innovatory talent, but often such attributes are not recognized when an appointment, particularly at senior management, has to be made, and the firm goes outside for the filling of a vacancy.

As my own translation from the military/police/security niche to Personnel was an example of cross-fertilization, I was particularly keen about Succession planning and groups of very senior management were set up to analyse and record in-house potential "stars", who could be considered for posts outside their specialism. These individuals should know that they had been spotted and special training and posting should be given to them. Thus the inevitable and unpredictable need to fill key vacancies did not necessarily involve advertising outside or employing head-hunters.

BEA had a Management Training building at Burnham Beeches. BOAC had another at Dormy House, Sunningdale, but this served the double purpose of being also an Aircrew Resthouse, and the mixture was not satisfactory as inevitably clashes occurred over availability of accommodation. Whilst mixing aircrew with managers under training had some benefits, these were less significant than having managers from all over BOAC getting to know each other. Furthermore numerous hotels were going up in the Heathrow area, all hungry for custom and Dormy House costs could not compete.

It was therefore a good example of BOAC/BEA collaboration to suggest that Management Training should now be merged at Burnham Beeches, which, with some expansion and more intensive utilization, could accommodate it. Much of the training programme was common to both airlines and a element of competitiveness was healthy.

After my initial clash with Clive Jenkins, I got to know and like the employees' representatives on the National Joint Council. They were professionals whose job was to improve the position of their members and if this meant playing one airline against another or quoting foreign pay and conditions to me, this was fair game.

What we set out to do was to concentrate on the common interest we all had in making BOAC profitable, extending its market and serving that market excellently. I devised a scheme which I named LUCRE, Lower Unit Costs and Related Earnings (acronyms were coming into fashion then!), and by concentrating on cost reduction, in which staff numbers played such a major part, and output and revenue per employee, we were able to get all the unions, even the Pilots Union, BALPA, to accept three-year contracts from January 1965. All were roughly comparable, so there was a sense of fairness, and the NJC thus proved itself as a body ready to accept the economic facts of international airline competition. Furthermore the Prices and Incomes Board, now under Anthony Crosland, President of the Board of Trade, accepted our LUCRE deals as falling within the Prices and Incomes Policy.

Ron Smith, General Secretary of the Post Office Union, was on the BOAC Board, as a non-executive Director. He was particularly helpful to me and gave support at times when the Board was unconvinced by my arguments, for example in my gloomy portents about the pilots, and the need for staff attitude surveying. He was positively lyrical about the LUCRE three-year agreements and suggested that the General Secretaries of all the main Unions should be invited to a weekend "jolly" to celebrate it. The Chairman was enthusiastic. I was not, as the national figures, most of them

Knights, were far removed from the NJC interface, had played little or no part in the three-year deals and were so hostile to Clive Jenkins, for example, whose comparatively small Union (in membership, but not in importance) was not to be included, that it seemed to me rather insulting to fête these figureheads. As always Giles was sympathetic to my views and we made a deal that this weekend, which was to be spent in the West of Ireland, was to be the curtain-raiser to a series of visits by the airline's union chiefs, to the States, Australia, Hong Kong and Scandinavia, to study aviation personnel practice, and the operations of competitors, aircraft manufacturers, and management/union relationships. BALPA did not accept.

Over the next year the Management/Union team visited all these parts of the world, with significant benefit. For example:

BOAC, which was used for all flights other than BEA to Scandinavia, greatly impressed the group, and they were conscious of our high standing in the world.

Spending upwards of a week together created understanding, leading to consensus of what was needed to face *international* competition.

The dead hand of overmanning, not just on the airline's unit costs, but on the chances of improvement in the lives of highly trained and motivated "professionals", was made clear to us all, especially in the States.

Particularly in the States, but to a considerable degree in Europe, the consequences of capitulation to excessive demands from pilots were emphasized again and again by our hosts. We understood why BALPA had refused our invitation!

There were about 1,500 pilots and, as we were well aware because of the Attitude Survey, they felt frustrated at being lumped with other staff for pay and conditions, especially as they were only too conscious of the capitulation of American and European airlines to pilots' demands. Early in 1966 complaints that the pilots' three-year deal was ungenerous, and needed topping-up, were referred to Conciliation, but with no immediate salary rises; the discontent erupted in April 1967 when BALPA gave six months' notice of resignation from the NJC. This was later amended to June 1967, significantly as a new round of LUCRE negotiations was due to start then, towards a second three-year agreement, covering all staff. There was great pressure on BALPA to withdraw its resignation from employers, employees and Government; a Ministers' Inquiry under Mr A J Scamp found for the employers and exhorted BALPA to stay in the NJC. It refused and from November 1967 imposed a "work-to-rule", euphemistically described as "Restriction of Co-operation". Five weeks later it called a strike of pilots from 8 December, which would ground BOAC world-wide. I informed every pilot that "BOAC has neither the freedom nor the desire to concede that separate negotiations should take place outside the National Joint Council". I added that we were ready to negotiate an improved pay/productivity agreement directly, within the NJC constitution. The strike lasted until 10 December, when the Minister of Labour appointed another Court of Inquiry under Lord Pearson "to consider how the Air Corporations could carry out their obligations under the Act of 1967, having regard to the dissatisfaction of BALPA with the existing negotiating machinery in the industry". Lord Pearson's Inquiry required BALPA to rejoin the NJC, but steps should be taken to remove pilot dissatisfaction about access to decision levels, about status and about consultation. BALPA rejoined NJC on 7 March 1968 and negotiations began next day. At the end of April an agreed proposal was put to the Department of Employment and Productivity, the new name for the Ministry of Labour, which it could not immediately approve under the Prices and Incomes Policy. Another ROC campaign started on 17 May, which affected the airline badly and on 12 June formal notice of an all-out strike from midnight on 15 June was given. A last-minute intervention by Barbara Castle could not stop it and from 16 June to 3 July the airline was grounded. The strike cost £10 million. A large sum then, but with long-term additional penalties, not least the refusal of pilots to fly the 747s, which were now being delivered and which sat on the tarmac for a year, unflown.

A new Inquiry under Professor Wood of Sheffield University was set up leading to agreement on service conditions being reached on 1 November 1968. Agreement was not reached on pay. A complicated system called "Bid-line" had been agreed in principle. The objective was to use pilot seniority to govern bids for flying route patterns, some of which, because of their duration, would attract more pay than others. It was not expected that this new complicated system could be implemented before autumn 1969. The relationship between BOAC and its pilots remained difficult long after Sir Giles Guthrie and I had left the scene, and it constituted a failure on our part, which I often wonder might have been prevented.

It was a time of severe stress for me. I had fellow-feeling and admiration for the pilots. After all I was perhaps still alive because of the daring co-operation of the rocket-firing Typhoons which helped us cope with superior German armour. The RAF pilots then were essentially the same men who piloted BOAC.

Why did Giles and I and the excellent Flight Operations Directors not succeed? I think it was for these reasons:

Salaries on the "international" level were totally ruled out.

BALPA Management was uninspired, and reactive rather than positively active.

The way in which a Conservative Government had set up BOAC and

BEA resulted in a joint approach to pay and conditions, not only through employer solidarity, but also in making it impossible for a maverick Union to "scoop the pool".

While very senior Management's pay was not Union-negotiated, and thus outside the NJC, I wondered and worried about how this exception might be extended even to Captains. Had it been, there might at least have been a solid core of senior pilots whose loyalties might have been with Management. The Deputy Chairman, Keith Granville, and I were invited to dinner by the Chairman and Deputy Chairman of BALPA, one a senior Captain, the other a senior First Officer. Hints about how the very senior staff were non-NJC and there could be a possible breakthrough there were dashed when the First Officer declared that BALPA had already considered this but rejected it out of hand. His line was that if senior BOAC Directors and Managers were content with their miserable remuneration, BALPA members would not be. The prospect of us making common cause with militant pilots was not inviting.

Our PR was dreadful. There was sympathy for the pilots, and the feeling abroad that we were not aware of their special, difficult and pivotal role, that we were too responsive to militant ground staff, and did not pay enough attention to pilot grievances and suggestions. After an all-night session at St James's Square, the Conciliation headquarters of Government, Giles was buttonholed by a mob of reporters and said, "The headlines did not do anything for pilot feelings towards us."

The Prices and Incomes Policy made it virtually impossible to make the quantum leap in pilot remuneration which could have bought peace, but at a price of putting all other staff and Unions who had played so positive a part in LUCRE at odds with us and each other.

So, from 1966 until I left London for Montreal in 1969, this huge problem dogged me. How Heather and the family put up with me at times I don't know. I am eternally grateful to them. In November 1968 an old friend, Professor Renato Taguiri of Harvard, came to stay with us at Crawley Down in Sussex, and my car and driver came early to pick us up to get him to a flight from Heathrow. On the way a patch of ice caused Ron Fox, my driver, to lose control of my Ford and it skidded headlong into a lorry. The engine was driven through the dashboard, ending in the front passenger seat, where fortunately no one was sitting as Renato and I chose to sit together on the back seat. I had a fearful blow to the back of the head, but after a short period of unconsciousness was able to get out with Renato, who was unhurt, to pull Fox through the windscreen, which was shattered. A couple of weeks in hospital and repair to the skull, which was fractured, seemed to indicate complete recovery, but I was disorientated, forgetful and depressed, and somehow the pilot problem became the focus of my unhappiness. I had a plan to take on the presentation of BOAC's case at the Wood Inquiry, and possibly further such hearings, which might, I flatter myself, have helped to assuage pilot dissatisfaction that they were not given special status, but there was no question of my being well enough, and in the event Jim Atherton did his usual thorough and professional job of not only presenting the BOAC case but standing up to questioning by a leading QC, who represented BALPA, and the penetrating and often critical questions and observations of the Professor.

Through the thoughtfulness of Henry Marking, Managing Director of BEA, Heather and I had a week in Malta for me to recuperate. Gradually my depression started to lift and life seemed worth living again.

Chapter Twelve

BOAC – CANADA

During 1969 Giles Guthrie had several interviews with me. He told me that I was someone who would be considered for Chief Executive if I had Commercial/Marketing experience, and that he intended to post me, if I wished, to the job of Manager USA for a year or two. He clearly thought of himself then as continuing as Chairman for another five years. Discussing it with Heather proved yet again how brave and adventurous she is, as the United States was, after the UK, the most important part of the BOAC network, with more problems and opportunities than anywhere else. The announcement was to have been made in October, but some weeks beforehand it leaked. BALPA had got hold of the story and saw it as a victory for them, that their main opponent was being sent off the field. We had to do something, so Keith Granville, who had now succeeded Giles as Chairman, and I, in consultation with Ross Stainton, issued a denial of the story, having confirmed that the Manager Canada, Ossie Cochrane, was ready to step into my putative shoes.

Once again a major family upheaval was to take place. Johnny was still at Worth Abbey and Angela and Rosanagh at Stoodley Knowle Convent in Devon, doing well, and both bright achievers. Worth Abbey's Preparatory School was now closed because Worth had decided to become a Public School, in competition with Downside, for which it had been its main supplier of pupils. Justin was a dayboy at Copthorne Preparatory School, only a mile or so from our home, and would become a boarder there, before going on to Worth Abbey. We were living in Montreal by this time and the school holidays were particularly happy times, with skiing in the winter and summer weekends in an old stone house on the Ottawa River, ideal for sailing and water-skiing. Justin did a basic training course with the Irish Guards when he left school, but decided that his talents lay elsewhere, going on to qualify as a tree surgeon at Merrist Wood, and setting up his own company in Northern Ireland, where Heather and I were by now living. He now runs a successful furnishing artefacts company, Dove Cottage Industries, is married to Mimi with two daughters, and, happily for us, lives not far away.

Returning to our Canadian venture. My first action was to visit Ossie Cochrane who had had a very successful sojourn in Canada and gave me a thorough briefing on the Canadian scene. He and his wife Pat lived in an apartment high on the mountain which gives Montreal its name. His friend and neighbour was Stanley Haggett, the founder and Chairman of General Aviation Services. The Marketing Manager Canada was Jim Harris, later to become Marketing Director of BOAC and, with his wife Angela, a close friend of ours.

My first problem, having digested the comprehensive briefing I had been given by Ossie, Jim and Stan, was to find a house. BOAC was very generous in giving me carte blanche in this. There was a bewildering choice. Close to the downtown office in the prestigious Place Ville Marie, thirty stories up, there were apartments of every sort, with facilities such as basement swimming pools, restaurants and underground parking. Most of the houses were for sale only. At the very top of Mount Royal was Redpath Crescent, a "millionaires' row", with graceful granite family homes, far too big for us, and certainly unlikely to be on the market for rent, and infrequently for sale. A new building was almost complete of five small houses in a group modelled on Cheyne Walk in London. They were larger than they looked, with four bedrooms, two bathrooms, basement garage and playroom, a small garden each, and steps up to the Park, summit of the Mountain, the haunt of joggers, squirrels. chipmunks, courting couples and scenery viewers, as the whole City and the St Lawrence River were stretched out below. I fell in love with one of the houses, now ready for sale and occupation and went to see Mr Gameroff the developer. It took some persuasion for him to agree, but finally he did so. The rent was substantial but fair, and BOAC approved. We put our house on the market and sold it quickly. Heather had been out to Montreal to vet our new house and was enthusiastic about it, so we packed our furniture, ordered some more from Bentalls, Kingston-on-Thames, and set off for our new life. Unfortunately for us there was a UK – Canada freight boom, and as the company rule is, quite rightly, that staff and their furniture can only be accommodated if space is available, it was only possible to squeeze in a minimum of essentials, a bed, some folding chairs and table, and a few cooking utensils. The "camping-out" period was protracted, but finally a huge consignment of our things was delivered and we were able to live a more civilized life. We had charming neighbours who showed us great hospitality in those early days and later, particularly the MacDougals and Crosses who also lived on Redpath Crescent. Jasper Cross was the British Trade Commissioner for Quebec, about whom later.

I had about 400 staff, predominantly in Montreal and Toronto, with sales staff from Newfoundland to Vancouver, so it was a great experience to travel 3000 miles over BOAC territory, seldom more than 200 miles deep, but with the same area as the United States.

The Province of Quebec was still in a rather euphoric state in 1969. Having hosted Expo '67 and the Olympic Games in 1968, its international status was much greater than the now dour image of French Canada. I found rather the same contrast as between the Republic of Ireland and Northern Ireland. But trouble was on the way. President De Gaulle of France from a balcony on Redpath Crescent had declared "*Vive le Quebec, vive le Quebec libre*". This irresponsible remark had become the war-cry of the Parti Quebecois, led by René Levesque, and the FLQ, the equivalent of the IRA in Canada, which demanded the independence of the French-speaking Province from the rest of English-speaking Canada. Already some businesses were covertly moving their centre of gravity to Toronto, and there were cartoons of Brinks (equivalent of Securicor) vans racing, heavily laden with the assets of international firms, to Ontario. In the opinion of the British Canadians, the future of Quebec was one of French provincialism, with no place in it for British-descended Canadians. Education, culture and business were French-dominated, they felt, and would be increasingly so in the future. The position of Irish-descent Canadians in Quebec was interesting. Many of the Irish famine refugees landed in Canada and obtained land on the banks of the St Lawrence. One was struck by the O'Donnells, the Moriartys and the Murphys, names on the post-boxes in which mail was deposited. Frequently the owners of these small farms would be French-speaking and have little or no English. All spoke the patois of Quebec called "Joual". The Catholic Church in Quebec was split between the English-speaking and French-speaking congregations and it was apparent that this double identity was the cause of some friction. Both sides tended to accuse each other of capitulation to the materialism of the age, and the dominance of the Church was nothing like as great as I had experienced in Ireland.

Our neighbour Jasper Cross became a great friend. He came from Tipperary and, after Trinity College, joined the Diplomatic Corps. He and I and our wives had lots in common, of interest to us Irish and Ulster people. Very often we would walk to our offices in the Place Ville Marie or, in bad weather, share a car. On one such day Heather offered to drive me to the Place Ville Marie and we stopped briefly outside the Cross house, as was our wont, to see if Jasper would come out of his front door. Little did we realize that a terrified Barbara was watching us from behind a curtain in an upstairs room, having been warned by the kidnappers of the British Trade Commissioner that he would be killed if she gave the alarm.

In a few hours news of the kidnapping spread over the world. The High Commissioner, Sir Peter Heyman, announced that any concessions demanded by the FLQ as the price for return of Cross would not be met, and in this he was supported by the Prime Minister of Canada, Pierre Trudeau, and the Quebec Premier Bourassa. The FLQ demand was the usual one of release from Canadian imprisonment of their comrades in the "armed struggle". An FLQ deadline passed with speculation that Cross had in fact been murdered. This grim possibility was made more probable by the kidnapping and murder of a Quebec Government Minister in the most brutal of circumstances. It was a great relief therefore when a message from Cross was received in his handwriting, clearly under duress, saying that he was well, but asking that the demands be met. He appealed for what he described as his "medicaments", meaning pills which he took for blood pressure. A reporter who had heard the statement called me and asked whether "medicaments" was a term which Cross would be accustomed to using. My response that it was not a particularly idiomatic English word, and not one which I had ever heard him use, resulted in a piece in the *Montreal Star* suggesting that Cross was using code to bring rescuers to an address in Montreal. This piece of journalistic irresponsibility was a lesson to me of the danger of press interviews.

After nearly two months a message from the High Commissioner asking me to be on an island in the St Lawrence where there was a small airport resulted in my meeting Jasper Cross, with gaunt appearance and haunted look, one hour after he had been exchanged by the terrorists, five in all, where they were flown from the same little airport, en route to Cuba.

Jasper said that he had been kept in a sort of cowl, preventing him from seeing his captors, all those terrifying days and nights. They took it in turns to interrogate him about French-Canadian politics and were intrigued at the thought of an Irishman from Tipperary being a British diplomat. Surely the British had been driven out of Ireland, which had achieved the sovereign independence which was what the FLQ were fighting for? Cross was sure that it was the apparent paradox of an Irishman achieving high position in the British Foreign Office which turned the FLQ 's minds away from murdering him. That and the resolute attitude of the Governments against bargaining their diplomats' lives against surrender to kidnap demands. The granting by Cuba of asylum to the gang could hardly been seen as much of a bargain to them, as reports later showed that they were employed as normal labourers in Havana and had no status there.

The new challenge of marketing and administering BOAC in Canada was an enthralling one. I was blessed by having Jim Harris as my Marketing Manager, and later Zachary Clark, who moved to Air Canada after I left. Both men had consummate skill and inspired ideas for making BOAC the favourite of the dozen foreign airlines serving Canada, and indeed the choice of many Canadians in preference to Air Canada or Canadian Pacific. It was at this time that Charter airlines were coming into their own, and great numbers of people who had never considered travel abroad were doing so. The effect on scheduled carriers was pretty damaging, to begin with. The fact that a passenger could claim to be part of a group, and thus qualify for airfares, was not lost on the business community, and rules such as having an accommodation element in the ticket price, or being a member of a community group organization, were very easily circumvented. An aircraft seat is a highly perishable commodity. It is seldom, no matter how heavily booked a plane may be, that there are not a few seats empty at the close-out time. People are late, lose their way, change their minds or are sick. A myriad reasons can leave this expensive product unsaleable. Some airlines overbook purposely, but nowadays an airline which does this can be forced to pay "Denied Booking Compensation", as well as having to provide alternative travel later, and provide hotel accommodation.

BOAC, which was becoming British Airways by this time, the merger with BEA having started, was, as always, a leader in devising ingenious fare structures. These were then put to the International Air Transport Association, meeting annually somewhere on the globe. In 1973 the IATA AGM was in Montreal and this was the launch pad for BA's Advanced Purchased Excursion Fare. Essentially this had two new features:

The APEX ticket was not changeable. You booked firmly for a given flight, and its return sector. No show, no refund.

Payment had to be made in advance, sometimes quite far in advance, sometimes as little as two weeks before flight.

Given these firm conditions the airline had a guaranteed load as a basis for future sales of standard, business and first-class passengers, "leakage" to charter companies was stemmed, and the scheduled airlines were now able to market holiday travel robustly.

IATA in those days was divided into the big international carriers and the "predators". The Pan Ams, Air Frances, Lufthansas and BOACs were frustrated by the predators insisting on keeping fare levels up, including cargo rates, so that they could illegally undercut by offering bargains. The IATA enforcement mechanism, whilst effective if applied severely and professionally, had an unpopular aspect of "restraint of trade". The US Anti-Trust laws were in effect suspended.

Predictably, the industry failed to approve APEX at Montreal and the soaring fuel costs arising from the OPEC Middle Eastern agreements began a long period of airline losses, which were magnified by the new Jumbo aircraft coming into service. 747s, DC10s, Lockheed Tristars and later the Airbus produced millions of empty seats on routes which had previously been the mainstay of international air transport. The demise of such famous companies as Pan Am, Eastern and Braniff in the States should have led to many more closures, but Governments in almost all other countries were reluctant to lose their national carrier, even if it lost money, and countries such as France simply continued to pick up the bill, which extended the slump. Many charter companies, Laker Airlines among them, went to the wall.

Gradually, however, the efficiently run companies such as British Airways, which had continued its cost-cutting effort, brought about a modified form of APEX, and the growing demand for holidays abroad led to higher loads and a genuinely competitive market.

All this was of great interest to us in Canada, where the shape of the airlines' future was first outlined, and we were quick to introduce holiday packages, particularly to the UK, which provided accommodation, leisure activity and inclusive airfares, at a price which was half of previous such holidays, paid for item by item.

One of our first offerings was the London Show Tour. This provided seats at theatres, concerts, ballet, rooms and meals in good quality hotels, and firm seats on our 747s. To promote it we engaged the Gore Hotel, which specialized in Medieval Feasts, to fly a team of serving-maids, musicians (lute players particularly), serving-dishes, tankards and mead to Canada, on an itinerary covering nearly every Province, starting at St John's, Newfoundland. We concentrated on travel agents and media representatives. While the show was a great artistic success with the serving-wenches in their busty costumes and the Lord of the Feast selected from the audience, in one case the High Commissioner himself, the hard-drinking Travel and Media people were highly dismissive of mead and many were the comparisons to other yellow liquids. Fortunately Zachary Clark showed his usual flair by lacing the rather innocuous honey liquid with vodka. As the Show Tour promotion moved across Canada, from Halifax to Quebec City, to Montreal, to London, Ontario, to Toronto, Winnipeg, Alberta and British Columbia, it achieved more and more enthusiastic reviews, and the travel agents, whose endorsement of a travel product was usually as effective, or more so, than the airline's own efforts, filled all the available seats on aircraft, beds in hotels and theatre bookings.

The British-Canadian Trade Association (BCTA), with several thousand members, was engaged in encouraging trade in both directions. Britain's entry into the European Economic Community in 1972 was not well-received by Canadians of British descent. The disappearance of

Commonwealth Preference by the UK in Customs and Excise and the preoccupation with Europe shown by many British companies which had hitherto wooed the Canadian market was deeply resented by many Canadians.

BA had always taken a leading part in BCTA and I was elected to its Council, in place of my predecessor Ossie Cochrane (a fellow Ulsterman). BCTA's headquarters was in Toronto, its MD Bob Bleasby, a hardworking and likeable Englishman, and there were offices in Montreal and Vancouver. It worked closely with the Trade Commissioners in the main cities, and organized trade missions, individual visitor's business itineraries and sales promotions, and encouraged in every way possible growth of British-Canadian Trade. Although member firms paid a sizeable fee for membership, the UK Government, which had subsidized BCTA over many years, decided that Non-Official Trade Organizations, NOTOs, as they were rather negatively named, must in future be self-sufficient and rely only on locally-raised funding. This was a major challenge, for not only were Canadian companies to pay import duties on their goods sold to the UK, but also they were to pay more for British encouragement to continue doing so. In less than two years I found myself elected President of BCTA, with the daunting target of increasing membership and finding the income to replace the subvention from HMG. BA were very supportive. After all trade between our two countries produced the highest-yielding passenger traffic – businessmen and women. Air Cargo was growing and not only were the 747s able to accommodate much larger loads, but we were modifying 707s to all-cargo and taking advantage of the decline in shipping across the Atlantic. Working with our partners, Air Canada, with whom we had a traffic-sharing agreement which benefited the customer as well as us, in that we were able to provide a more frequent and multi-destinational air service, we were able to promote this to the Canadians through BCTA.

As President it was up to me to devise strategies in collaboration with my Council and the excellent Bob Bleasby which not only kept the trade links but also quietened the anxieties about the EEC, whilst doing this on a sharply declining budget. We settled on a series of seminars to attract the leaders of industry, explaining the benefits of our EEC membership to Canada, reassuring businessmen of our continued interest in them and encouraging contact through tourism in both directions.

The first of these seminars, in Toronto, I organized with the help of William Rees-Mogg, Editor of *The Times*, who got his Chairman Roy Thompson, himself a Canadian, to make the keynote speech. Nearly 500 came and the occasion was a great success, not only in promotional terms, but also financially. BCTA set a high price on entry and it was clear that people were quite happy to pay for a worthwhile event. Other speakers covered specific sectors of the subject and there were lively question and answer sessions, with groups of specialists reporting back to the main body in plenary sessions. Terence O'Neill, later Lord O'Neill of the Maine, former Premier of Northern Ireland, and brother officer in the 2nd Bn Irish Guards, now a Director of a London Bank, David Howell, later Minster for Energy in the Thatcher Government, who spoke on North Sea Oil, and Geoffrey Knight, salesman for Concorde, now applying for flying rights over Canada, were other keynote speakers. Geoffrey and I were interviewed in Vancouver on TV by Wasserman, the David Frost of Canada. "How does it feel to be the world's chief salesman of the world's biggest double disaster economically and ecologically, the Concorde?" asked Wasserman. "I see you have a chip on both your shoulders," replied Geoffrey.

By now both our daughters were at McGill University Montreal and enjoying the change from the strict regime of Les Filles de le Croix Convent, Torquay, where they had been for four years getting good University entrances. Johnny had been commissioned in the Irish Guards at 18, and Justin was at preparatory school in Sussex, as a boarder, prior to going on to Worth Abbey. A rather interesting sideline to Worth was that both Johnny and Justin were taught French by Andrew Bertie, now Sovereign of the Knights of Malta, the oldest Order of Chivalry in the world, and who welcomed me to the Knighthood in 1997.

Our first winter in Montreal was a revelation to us, used to the milder climes of the British Isles. Temperatures going down to -30 degrees, with sometimes the meretricious sun shining to give an impression of warmth, made it easy to be misled into thinking that the Montrealers were "soft", muffled up in their furs, galoshes and mittens. An Irish friend of ours, thinking this, went out boldly on a very cold sunny but windy day (the chill factor) and was frost-bitten on both his ears.

We took up skiing and had many happy weekends in the Mountains and Eastern Townships. The children, particularly Justin, became good skiers and Heather and I were able to negotiate easier runs pretty safely and enjoyably. That is until we went to one of the Township resorts close to the US Border on a particularly cold day. Justin and I were on a ski chairlift, with Heather and Rosanagh on the chair first in front of us. Reaching the top of the slope, Heather got off on to a dangerously icy patch and fell over quite gracefully and slowly, but her skis did not disengage. She lay there obviously in pain, but the first-aid team were there in quick time to bind her into a ski-stretcher and take her to the aid post where a fracture of her left leg was diagnosed. On the way back to Montreal to take her to hospital, we hit a whiteout. This is a terrifying experience. I was driving at speed when we ran into a solid wall of snow which completely blanketed us giving only a few yards of visibility. The Ford Estate started to skid and we were conscious of rotating past other cars on the motorway, halted in all sorts of attitudes, but which by the grace of God we had not struck. Eventually we came to a standstill and, hugging the verge, emerged.

One of the reasons for the remarkably good results from BOAC's Canadian operation was the fact that our ground handling at Canadian airports was carried out by a subcontractor, General Aviation Services. This company, headed by a remarkable Englishman, Stanley Haggett (incidentally a brilliant skier), had hit on the idea of offering all airlines using a particular airport a comprehensive service providing engineering, re-fuelling, cleaning, check-in and all the multifarious activities which routinely have otherwise to be provided by the airline itself, at great expense and unproductively, as the arrival and departure of its aircraft have gaps in time when staff have little or nothing to do. By offering this comprehensive service, GAS were able to move their teams from airline to airline throughout the day and night and do this for less than half the cost to each customer than 'do it yourself' would have been. Naturally airline staff disliked this. It led to redundancies, while the pace of work of GAS and the higher supervisory challenge to the airline made the older senior staff uneasy. But the economics of the operation and the customer service provided by GAS were far superior to our own and BOAC led the way in engaging GAS, and the IAM, the Ground Union, accepted this, though unhappily to begin with. Some years later, when I was in India, Stanley Haggett sold his idea to the British Airports Authority and there was vehement Union resistance to it. I contacted my friend Clive Jenkins to help Stanley to put his case that, while to start with airline direct employment would decrease, eventually the economics of the GAS system would create more and better jobs, with unionized employees working infinitely more productively in a more challenging environment. Despite Clive's advocacy, the British Unions at Heathrow, through strikes and 'work-to-rule', forced BAA to withdraw the GAS contract. Mrs Thatcher had not yet appeared on the scene.

Summer in Canada is a glorious time – twenty weeks from snow to snow, May to September. We made friends with Kevin Clarke, a charming and gregarious Irishman and his wife Kay, who lived near us in Redpath Place, and had a house near Cushing, on the Ottawa River 50 miles away. Several weekends there convinced us that we should find a weekend house of our own.

The leading resident of the little village was a Miss Mildred Douglas, who lived in a converted Anglican Church surrounded by priceless pictures and *objets d'art*. She was fond of Irish people and explained to us why. She had been born on a small farm at Carillon in the Ottawa Valley, nearby. Their farming neighbours were called Kelly, Irish immigrants. When the Yukon goldrush of 1900 started, her father and Mr Kelly decided they would look for gold in the Yukon and set out on the trail over Chilcoot Pass, part of the Rockies, to reach the gold-fields. They succeeded not only in crossing the Pass, where many were to die in the attempt, but in finding a large quantity of gold. This they then carried to the Alaskan coast and embarked by ship to Vancouver. The ship struck a rock and was sinking. Both men ran to their cabin to fetch the gold, each taking half of the load. The ship sunk and Douglas was drowned.

Mildred Douglas remembered Kelly's return. He came to her mother to break the news of her husband's death and spread out on the kitchen table his, Kelly's, half of the gold. Then he divided it and gave half to Mrs Douglas. With his own half, Kelly went to Vancouver and started Canada's first supermarket chain, which is named Kelly-Douglas, which spread right across Canada and in which Mrs Douglas invested and prospered. This fine example of Protestant-Catholic trust and co-operation gave her much satisfaction and we were even more impressed when Miss Douglas took us to her old home, the Carillon farmhouse, which she had had transported bodily from the Carillon Valley in the 30s, when the Carillon Dam had inundated the valley. This pretty two-storey house with a longish garden had never been lived in and she offered it to us as a weekend cottage. We were overwhelmed and accepted at once. She had made a hobby of restoring it exactly as she had remembered it from her childhood. The furniture, curtains and pictures were all in place, the only difference being that the electricity from the Carillon Dam now enabled her to put in heat, light and every electrical convenience possible. This was to have a dire consequence later. In the meantime we enjoyed the glorious summer days, tending our garden, swimming in the Clarkes' pool and sailing a little boat on the Ottawa River which later developed into water-skiing behind an ancient fibreglass boat with a more powerful and heavier 40 hp outboard engine than it was designed for. Every time there was a heavy rainstorm and wind which raised waves the boat would sink to the bottom of the small harbour where it was moored in 3 or 4 feet of water. It was only necessary to release the Evinrude engine, dry the plug and bail out the boat to get the vessel on the river again, going splendidly. A week or so of total immersion seemed to improve the Evinrude performance.

The BCTA, thanks to the pro-European campaign which we were leading, was now gaining in reputation and respect and I was honoured to be invited to become a member of the British Overseas Trade Board which had a North American Group, chaired by Sir Martin Redmayne and meeting regularly in London. NAG, the BOTB North American Group, had a dynamic membership of Brits who had much influence on British-Canadian as well as British-American trade. Outstanding of these was

David Garnock, who later became the Earl of Lindsay. He had been working in Canada earlier in his life, as an engine driver in Canadian Pacific Railways at one time, and was an engaging, articulate and entrepreneurial Scot with whom I felt an immediate rapport. We suggested to Martin Redmayne that, as BCTA was engaged in its pro-Europe tour of Canada which was doing well in persuading Canadian business to see the benefits of Britain's membership of EEC, which was to be achieved in 1972, it would make sense to mount a rather similar exercise in Great Britain to persuade British business of the benefits of trading with Canada, maintaining old links and forging new ones. Sir Martin, later Lord, Redmayne was enthusiastic and about twenty of us, including the Trade Commissioners of Quebec, Ontario and British Columbia set out on a tour of England, Scotland and Wales, meeting business and commercial leaders, holding seminars and organizing visits to Canada by individuals and trade groups, just as the Canadian tour had done in the reverse direction. Each of us had to organize our own presentation, which in my case was essentially to do with the BCTA, the aviation developments between Canada and the UK, and the Canadian perception of the EEC, including its Common Agricultural Policy, CAP. An amusing poem in the *Toronto Star*, a leading Ontarian paper, entitled 'Farmers make a fortune NOT raising hogs' which set out an early version of 'set-aside' whereby pig-farmers were subsidised to reduce their output, thereby raising prices, saving feed, gaining leisure and reducing manure mountains, was a popular part of my presentation. It was always good for a laugh during what was sometimes rather heavy debate. Years later, in London for a housing event, I met David Lindsay coming out of the Ritz. He said he had just been making a speech at a business gathering and pulled out of his pocket his script which included the 'NOT raising Hogs' poem. There and then he accepted my invitation to holiday with us in Greece that summer and Pempy, his wife, and he joined us at our villa for a week.

My posting to Canada was in a sense a step down from Personnel Director and Board of Management Member of the whole airline, and it was difficult for those who had been my juniors now to find themselves my seniors. It took sensitivity on both sides and I know I failed in this sometimes. For example, having had considerable experience of Public Relations at Board level, I found much to criticize in this in Canada and made this clear to my PR Manager, an excellent man called John Dawe, now a leading media figure in Canada. This greatly incensed Alan Ponsford, the PR Director for the whole airline. Quite rightly, the Commercial Director, Dick Hilary, a charming and great ally on the Board, sent for me to chastise me for failing to consult the Policy Director, Ponsford, in my PR strategy as given to Dawe. I thought I had made sufficient apology as the head of the operation in Canada, reserving policy to my former Board member colleagues, but it had clearly not been enough.

Shortly afterwards I was invited to London again to be told that the Board had had a confidential communication from the Chairman of Air Canada, our Pool Partners, recommending that, in view of the anti-Britishness which existed in Quebec, BOAC should remove its Canadian Headquarters to Toronto, leaving Air Canada, whose new Chairman, M Yves Prat, was a Quebecois, to represent BOAC in French Canada. The Cross kidnapping was quoted as an example of French dislike of the British. I was outraged that the Board had come to the conclusion that we should concentrate our efforts on English-speaking Canada and that I had not been consulted earlier, as I was strongly of the view that the exodus of many Anglophone companies from Montreal to Toronto, apprehending Quebec separating from the Dominion of Canada, was a great mistake and that the threat to separate was bluff, intended to blackmail concessions from English-speaking Canada. It is ironical that over a quarter of a century later Quebec is still a Province of Canada and is still threatening to separate!

Anyway, there were deep apologies for taking so seriously the confidential request from Air Canada, and much respect, it was claimed, would be given to my contrary opinion. It was clear, however, that something more was needed to reinforce my view, which at my request was backed by Sir Peter Heyman. I had written out a comprehensive analysis of the thinking of my Canadian Managers and myself in opposition to the Board's view, when it occurred to me that a personal commitment to reinforce my view was needed. I went to our landlord, Mr Gameroff, and said I would like to buy our Redpath Crescent house, not on behalf of BOAC, but on my own. He was astonished and reminded me that the exodus to Toronto had caused such a market slump that no one was buying houses in Montreal and that he himself had several houses which he could not sell. He had not built the Crescent cluster of five for sale but for rent. In the end he agreed and I asked him to tell me what the house had cost him. He told me 60,000 Canadian dollars. Next I went to the Royal Bank of Canada, the owners of the BOAC office building, the Place Ville Marie. When I went to the RBC Manager's office there was a delay as he had a visitor still with him. It turned out to be Earl McLoughlin, Chairman of the Royal Bank, and also Chairman of the Federated Appeal of Greater Montreal, of which I had just been elected Vice-Chairman. Coming out of the manager's office and seeing me he said "John, what do you what from us?" "A lot of money," I replied. "Give him whatever he wants, Yves," said Earl as he departed.

When the Manager heard of my proposition he was as astonished as Gameroff and when I told him that I wanted a loan of all the purchase price, on my own guarantee, not one from BOAC, he said he would have to go higher for approval. Later that day he asked me to visit him, and said, "You have had me and my wife as your guests, so I know what a lovely position your house has, and my Chairman knows it well too, so here is a cheque for 60,000 dollars." Next day Mr Gameroff and I completed the transaction and the last sentence of my report to the Board read as follows:

"I am so confident that the view of BOAC Canadian Management is the correct one, and that the Chairman of Air Canada, Yves Prat, is wrong, that I have purchased the house you rent for me on Redpath Crescent and will thereby save the company the rent you are now paying for it."

The decision to leave Montreal was cancelled, and the staff, who had been under great stress because of the risk to their jobs, particularly in sales, reservations and operations, were now safe. The great majority of the 100 or so such staff were French-Canadian, fluently bilingual. More loyal and efficient people it would be impossible to find. They had performed outstandingly in the switch from the standard reservations systems to the new real-time computer BOADICEA, later BABS, pioneered by BOAC world-wide. This used satellites and transcontinental telephones in such a way as to enable instant acceptance of reservations world-wide, no matter from what part of the globe the request came. Our Reservations Manager came to us after the threat of the move to Toronto and said that he had consulted all his staff with an idea that our growing operation in Western Canada, Vancouver, Calgary, Edmonton and Winnipeg could be linked to BOADICEA by direct telephone so that a local call to any sales office in those cities could be handled instantly by Montreal. The fact that there was a five-hour time change from East to West would require that a 24-hour shift system would have to be introduced, but he was certain that this could be worked and would cost infinitely less than separate reservations offices, although the large Toronto office would not be affected. It took no time to fit 'dedicated' lines to the Western Canada reservations, all now getting instant response from BOAC, though the call was being handled up to 3000 miles away. Sometimes in Vancouver or the other Western cities (except Winnipeg with a high French population) people would say, "What courteous and efficient reservations staff you have here. They all seem to have French accents." I found no need to tell them why!

A worried call from my father early on a Saturday morning gave me the news that my mother had suffered a serious stroke, was paralysed and unable to speak. To get to Co Down, to my parents' house, by the shortest route was by Aer Lingus to Shannon and with an Aer Lingus connection to Aldergrove. I had not flown by Aer Lingus from Montreal before and was very impressed by their cabin service. The stewardesses made allies of the passengers, asking them to help them in small ways, which customers like doing. Their care of the old was outstanding and they seemed to relate warmly with small children. My theory is that family life in Ireland is closer and thus girls are more used to looking after children and old people. It may have been that my worry about my mother made me more sensitive to caring cabin service, but certainly the recruitment of Irish stewardesses by BOAC increased.

On the Shannon-Belfast flight I found myself beside Lord Antrim, Chairman of Ulster TV. He told me of the riot on Craigavon Bridge the previous day, Saturday, and how for the first time TV cameras had filmed the whole event. He believed that this new ability to show the public such sights would revolutionize the way the authorities handled public order. How right he was. How many times have we seen a furious RUC Officer brandishing his blackthorn stick over the head of a rioter who had knocked his hat off.

Arriving in Belfast that Sunday morning early I hired a car and went straight to the Dundonald Hospital. My mother was unconscious, there was nothing I could do, other than go to Mass at Ballyhackamore to pray for her. Coming out of church, I met Jamie Flanagan and his wife Florence, who took me to their house for coffee. Jamie, who had been recruited to the RUC by my father and served as his Staff Officer in Greece, was rather vague about the Derry bridge trouble of the previous day, as evidently was Tony Peacocke, the Deputy Inspector General, who telephoned asking what had happened. It seemed that the Inspector General, Albert Kennedy was out of the country. In view of the fact that the start of "the troubles" is dated from that day in 1968, it is perhaps a commentary on both the inadequacy of RUC communications then and the effect on public opinion of TV coverage.

After the award of the CBE in the Birthday Honours of 1972 I had a congratulatory message from Captain James Percy, pilot of the eventful 707 for the Queen in 1963. He had retired from BOAC when we brought in the Pilots' Severance Scheme in the 60s at the age of 55; so now this world-famous pilot was available to continue his career to 60 and was recruited by Olympic Airlines, the Greek national carrier. His first job was to reconnoitre the Greek Islands to develop landing-fields for tourism. He told me that he had discovered one, Skiathos, which had a reasonably flat piece of land between two hills, which could make a short airfield, and, because it could be constructed uphill, might make possible landing by larger aircraft, such as the Boeing 737, given suitable winds. This meant international routes to Skiathos, such as from the UK. Jimmy and his wife Pat were so taken with the little island (only 8 miles wide by 4 deep) that they had built a villa there and were eager for us to join them. We spent a few days with them and were instantly bewitched. The scenery and history of Skiathos (in English "In the shade of Athos", the holy mountain, to be seen on a clear day), its significance in the German occupation when thousands of Allied soldiers were rescued with the help of the Greek Resistance, all lent a glamour to an unspoilt treasure, with some of the most lovely beaches in the Mediterranean. We selected a site, found an excellent builder, Nikos Andritsoupolis, and even went so far as to choose bathroom tiles. Sadly the Mayor fell foul of the Greek Colonels' Government and our hope of building on a site approved by him was dashed.

On return to Canada I was invited to take up a new post as Regional Manager Southern Africa for BOAC. This was when apartheid was in control in South Africa, Rhodesia was still in British possession and such states as Angola, Mozambique and Tanganyika were colonialist dominated. The post would require strong relationships with white rulers in all this large area, who were resisting change adamantly. Having seen the effect of this in my own country, Northern Ireland, I could not see myself having sympathy with such people and declined the post, but was treated with great understanding. Shortly afterwards I was offered the post of Manager India, Bangladesh and Sri Lanka – all of South Asia except Pakistan, in fact. Yet another major move, this time with the added problem of selling our Montreal home. This succeeded splendidly and left us with a handsome profit, as the Separatist campaign had fizzled out and business was returning to the Province of Quebec.

Before we left Canada our son Johnny, a Second-Lieutenant in the Irish Guards, then based in Hong Kong had been awarded the George Medal – the first to be gained in the Regiment. His citation read that after prolonged rains a Chinese apartment block on the Peak had collapsed, crushing and killing over sixty residents. His Platoon was ordered to assist in recovering bodies. After some time at this grisly task Johnny heard what he believed was a call for help from the collapsed building, a mountain of mud and debris. Grabbing a small spade, he started to dig into the site and was joined by a Chinese fire officer. As they continued this tunnel oxygen was fed into them, and in the words of the citation: "They were in imminent danger of entombment for 16 hours, reaching over 30 feet into the ruins". Johnny found the body of a Chinese woman and, hearing some sounds, he continued his tunnel until he found an Englishman trapped in the remains of a door-frame which had saved him from being crushed. He got the man out.

Both Johnny and the fire officer were awarded the George Medal. We went to Buckingham Palace to see him being presented with it by the Queen, followed by a big family party at the Guards Club. Subsequently he joined the Sultan of Oman's army to fight in the Djebel against Communist invaders of that country which saved the neck of the Gulf, from where the world oil trade was supplied. During this three-year posting he came to India to spend holidays with us. We knew the Indian Army President's bodyguard, who had the best Polo team, and Johnny was invited to take part in the Kadir Cup Pig-sticking Annual Competition, for the cup presented by the Viceroy in the 1870s. Although he had never taken part in this dangerous and skilful sport he won the Cup – the first European to do so since 1947. The original is still in the Cavalry and Guards Club in London, but a replica was presented by the Chief of the Indian Army, General Malhatra, at our house in Delhi. Another great party, despite Mrs Gandhi's prohibition on alcohol.

Chapter Thirteen

BOAC – INDIA, BANGLADESH & SRI LANKA

Heather and I went straight to New Delhi, which was to be my headquarters for the airline, now British Airways, and took over our new home at Aurangzeb Road, a 'bungalow', as the Lutyens-designed homes for senior Raj civil servants were called. It was a palatial place in two acres of garden, with nine servants and set in a tree-lined suburb. The BOAC chief had been provided with this fine house since before the War when Imperial Airways had pioneered its Australia route, via India. On our first day I was showing Heather her new home and went to the "In" entrance which had an elegant gate. As we surveyed the scene at our gate, a respectable-looking Sikh with turban cycled slowly past and, seeing us, wheeled his cycle towards us, saying "You must be the new Sahib and Memsahib for the British. Welcome." He then brought out a leather-bound book and told us that there had always been a contribution to a Sikh charity from the Sahib. He suggested about 10 rupees. I had only a hundred rupee note. Taking it from me, he told us that he would get change at Claridge's Hotel opposite. We watched him cycling majestically to the hotel entrance. He never returned! This gave us a lesson in the need to check the authenticity of charitable requests. We found our staff the best judges.

The job was very challenging. Competition in the international air business was intense and the IATA rules were falling apart as the reign of Sir William Hildred, the Director-General, was coming to an end and the US was leading the way to deregulation of fare-fixing, which ironically led to the demise of famous airlines such as Pan Am, Eastern and Continental. The same dire formula based on smaller, less competitive lines insisting, with their Government's help, in setting fares high so that they could undercut them, made cheats of most, so that the British carriers, as well as the American, were forced to find ways of competing, often by charging such low rates that they made no profit, although carrying huge loads. "Profitless Growth" was the order of the day.

The national carrier in India, Air India, set up the "Board of Airline Representatives" and to my surprise I found myself elected its Chairman. Our chief objective was to stop the fare-cheating, and to a considerable degree we succeeded. The main reason, I believe, was that air travel was growing in the subcontinent so quickly that there was in fact enough demand for airlines to realize that "profitless growth" was stupid and that there was enough business for everyone.

We had maintained quite a large number of staff at Calcutta, although our business there had reduced greatly from the heady days of Imperial Airways. The loyalty of the staff, and their poverty and poor living conditions, led to my wanting to meet their families at their homes. It was a rather exhausting day, very hot and dusty, but what impressed me was the dignity and cleanliness of family living, even in the poorest homes, (some even lived in 8-foot sewer pipes which were awaiting installation). Hindus and Muslims have a fierce devotion to personal cleanliness and even the poorest wash all over every day.

When I returned to the Great Eastern Hotel I found a copy of *The Times* which had an article about the "Dirty Protest" by IRA Maze prisoners being visited by Cardinal O'Faich, who described their conditions as reminding him of the living conditions of the "poor in Calcutta". I was so incensed that I wrote that night to *The Times*. On my return home to Delhi there was a message from *The Times* saying that my letter was too controversial to publish. Instead I sent it to the *Belfast Newsletter*, which did. This was to influence future events.

With British managers in the main Indian cities, Bombay, Delhi, Calcutta and Madras, and in Dacca, Bangladesh, and Colombo, Sri Lanka, it was important that we did not behave as "Colonialists", but brought in locals who were more appropriate to the political and commercial environment of former British possessions, now independent. I was lucky with my personal staff: a charming Anglo-Indian Secretary, Sunita Andrews, and her father, a former RAF officer, Das Dang, who was also an old-time stalwart of Imperial Airways and a man of ingenious talent with ability in many languages and unselfish devotion to the British Airways cause. He was elected Secretary of BAR (Board of Airline Representatives) and was responsible for ensuring that the fare-cheating problem was tackled in conjunction with Governments in our territories. Dilip Mitra was my Marketing Manager and Harish Malik my Personnel Manager, who had the difficult task of according pay and conditions of technical staff in the subcontinent to the runaway improvements of conditions in the UK for technicians whose Unions were intent on trying to force the "international terms" which had taken so much toll in our Pilots Negotiations.

Air Cargo had become very important, with the 747 capacity enabling airlines to carry vastly more. I suggested to BAR that an International Cargo Conference would benefit us all in Asia, and undertook to get the Prime Minister of India, Morarji Desai, to take part. I had already met him several times and found him both charming and interested in aviation. Desai had succeeded Indira Gandhi whose regime had latterly been unpopular because of her son Sanjay, who had offended the European community by encouraging her to abolish the sale and use of alcohol, and enforced sterilization of Indian men.

Desai agreed at once to open the Conference and we had the Chairmen of several airlines, including Keith Granville of BOAC, the Director-General of IATA, Knut Hammersholt, and David Coltman, Cargo Director of BOAC. On the evening before the Conference we invited J R D Tata, the founder of Air India, to a big occasion when Sir Keith Granville presented him with a silver rosebowl. He was clearly touched, especially as Granville had been BOAC's Eastern Chief many years before and had encouraged Air India's route extension to the United States, which at the time had been an enormous breakthrough. The UK up to that time had been very restrictive and only a few European carriers had traffic rights to fly there from London.

The next day many hundreds of government and airline senior representatives gathered at the Ashoka Hotel, Delhi's largest meeting place. I introduced the Prime Minister in Hindi, having been carefully coached by Sunita Andrews, which went down well with Mr Desai and the Conference proceeded splendidly, especially when the Indian Government announced several import tariff reductions, making exports to the subcontinent much more attractive and thus helping the airlines. Air Cargo rates were reduced, but because only the bigger carriers had Jumbos they were honoured, without cheating!

A lot of my job involved travelling to the countries I had visited on the Royal Tour of 1961 and it was nostalgic to find so many people who remembered. The British High Commissioners and their staff were especially helpful and welcoming, and we had a special rapport with Sir John Thomson in India, who later became the UK Ambassador to the United Nations. I introduced him to golf and we played early in the morning, 5 am, at Delhi Golf Club, before the heat made this unbearable. We had sons of the same age, who were both home on holiday, and he and his wife Elizabeth invited Heather, myself and Justin to join them on a railway journey to Rajisthan for two weeks and we delightedly accepted. This was a majestic occasion. A special train was brought out of retirement, known as the Rajasthan Special. Its carriages and bedrooms were sumptuous, and we each produced cooks and bearers who had a special carriage. We went to each of the Princely States, Jodhpur, Jaipur, Udaipur, Jesselmer, and several smaller ones. At each the ruler would meet us with a Guard of Honour and entertain us in his Palace. We would visit factories and farms, and be shown dancing, horsemanship and pageants of all kinds. Several times the High Commissioner would have to give press interviews which invariably concentrated on the actions of Indira Gandhi who was being her vindictive self towards the Princely States. Mrs Gandhi was carrying out excavations for gold in Jaipur, the home of the Maharajah of Jaipur's mother, the Rajmatur Gayathri Devi. This beautiful woman, who had dazzled us all on the Royal visit to Delhi, where the Maharajah's father had played polo with Prince Philip, had been jailed.

Months later Heather and I were invited to dinner by Indian friends and here was Gayathri Devi, released from prison that day. I told her that I was flying to London later that night and she left the table to return with letters to Buckingham Palace and the Chairman of Reuters to tell of her release and experiences. There was heavy censorship then in the Gandhi regime, and we depended very much on the BBC World Service and copies of London papers recovered as trash from BOAC services transiting India. The Indira Gandhi prohibition on alcohol I got over by importing wine-making kits from London and made carboys full of rather odd-tasting liquid which had at least the appearance of wine. I kept these in my bathroom until one which I had corked too tightly exploded. The resultant sticky mess led to the end of my vintner experience.

Chapter Fourteen

NIHE – DEPUTY CHAIRMAN AND CHIEF EXECUTIVE

When a new aircraft comes on stream the owners send it out on so-called Inaugural Flights, with passengers of importance whose views on its performance are valuable. So when the new Lockheed Tristar was being tested I was delighted to see the names of Kenneth and Elizabeth Bloomfield on the passenger list for a London-Bombay Tristar Inaugural and went to Bombay to meet them. The Tristar was not due to return for several days so we entertained them at our home in Delhi and talked nostalgically about Ulster. We found them great company and we had much in common. It was months later that I had a note from Ken enclosing an application form for the post of Deputy Chairman and Chief Executive of the Housing Executive, about which he had told me in India. It was a complete surprise. I knew nothing about housing, although I had been aware of allegations of bias towards fellow party-members in allocation, and had read of Austin Currie's "squatter" exploit in Caledon, Co Tyrone, when the Dungannon Council preferred the application of a Protestant single mother-to-be, to a Catholic family with several children, which led to the Nationalist politician being evicted and prosecuted. This was just one of the events which created a world-wide impression of injustice, which was later compounded by the police action against Civil Rights protesters on Craigavon Bridge in Londonderry, later to become Derry, when a Nationalist majority on the Londonderry Council demanded it.

Heather, who had hoped for another posting abroad, nonetheless supported me in my desire to try a new career and I sent off the application, without much belief that nearly twenty years away from Northern Ireland would make me a likely choice.

When the invitation to appear for interview came I was flattered and, as it was in the name of the Secretary of State, Roy Mason, whom I had met in Canada and also in London, when he was President of the Board of Trade, it looked a bit more hopeful. So Heather and I set off and spent the night before with my father, and sister Geraldine, who had returned from Australia to look after our mother after her stroke. A guest at dinner that night was Sir Jamie Flanagan, who had a fascinating, but pessimistic, tale to tell of Ulster's political situation and the growth of Republican strength and ruthlessness. He claimed that, had I remained in the RUC, I would have succeeded him, who had been the first Catholic Inspector-General.

The Housing interview was chaired by Ken Bloomfield, with Charles Brett, the newly appointed Chairman of the NIHE. It went very well, I thought, and I was particularly impressed by Charlie Brett's emphasis on quality and 'customer service' in Europe's largest public housing body. Surprisingly, neither man seemed to be too worried about my taking over 4000 staff, over 200,000 houses or a budget of £240m, although there were some dark references to a judicial report which was in progress.

After the interview Heather and I were taken off for lunch at the Strangford Arms Hotel in Newtownards. This took a lot longer than we had anticipated and when I returned to Stormont there was some perturbation because the Secretary of State, Roy Mason, had been unable to wait and had asked one of his Ministers, Ray Carter, to see me. This was a less satisfactory event. Carter had clearly been somewhat put out by being given this task at short notice and was convinced that my experience, or lack of it, in housing matters made me inadequate. In particular my response when he asked me about "The Right to Buy", which the Conservative Opposition was promoting, clearly upset him, as I gave enthusiastic approbation to it. As so often in life, however, the sincere rather than diplomatic reply turns out to be the best. When we returned to India there was a message saying that I had been appointed.

I had told Ross Stainton, who had succeeded Granville, of my application and he was supportive. Frankly I believe that, having been a possible Managing Director, had Giles Guthrie's plans for me worked out (particularly through his own desire to continue as Chairman), I was not exactly an embarrassment, but certainly was not going to be very welcome on return to the Board where my Personnel function had been seen as ruthlessly manpower-reducing. It was clear that the rather promiscuous growth in staff thereafter had failed to bring the profits needed to justify merger. The later King/Marshall robust measures cut staff world wide in such a way as to justify the new slogan "The World's Favourite Airline", at least in the minds of those who saw profitable operation as fundamental. Not only that but the PPF programme, "Putting People First", had had the effect which the Staff Attitude Survey had had, and the greater leadership, the Staff

Incentive scheme and the world-wide reputation for good service had won.

Our farewell from the BA family was emotive. Staff from my old Personnel function, now headed by Oliver Hinch, my loyal and efficient Deputy, (now Personnel Director,) from Canada and India had all come to say goodbye. We were presented with a marvellous picnic basket (it gave me the opportunity to get a laugh describing how inappropriate the word 'picnic' applied to Northern Ireland!) and three days after leaving India we arrived at Aldergrove, to be welcomed by our old friends Sandy and Pat Sandford. It was she who had given Heather strong support to the Ulster move and had organized a house for us at Rademon, Osborne King's estate. Pat had been a schoolmate of Heather's and was her closest friend. They had both been in the WAAF (Women's Auxiliary Air Force) and when Pat got multiple sclerosis had kept in touch for all nineteen years of our absence. She was a wonderful person who exuded happiness. We met them at our flat in London after she had been diagnosed as having MS. It was a happy evening. She insisted that we should not be sad and she never budged from this brave attitude. Sandy and she made our return to the Province a very happy one.

Because of our arrival before a house was available (odd, because I was the landlord of over 200,000 houses in NIHE) Pat Sandford arranged for us to stay at Old Court, the Maxwells' house at Strangford, while they were sailing. This had been built to replace the 16th century house of the De Ros's who had had their castle there destroyed by the IRA in the '20s. The De Ros family, the oldest Barony in England, descended through the female line, had devolved on Gina Maxwell, wife of David Maxwell, a Commander RN, with a distinguished career. We therefore made a very happy change from a Lutyens house to the distinguished Old Court, designed in its replacement by Robert McKinstry, the leading Northern Ireland Architect.

Meeting my new Directors was a major occasion; I knew none of them. The Director of Development (whom later I sent to Harvard Business School) was an architect, Donal Crawley, and senior to the others. Utterly honest, refusing to give me an opinion on his fellows, he conveyed his admiration for Chairman Brett, but showed some natural hesitance at Charlie's claim to be Architectural Chief and arbiter of "quality".

John Murray, Senior Civil Servant, seconded to the NIHE in the wake of the Rowland Report which had been published on 1 July 1979, my first day, was the outstanding member. He was a big, jolly figure, with no hang-ups or desire to support the several factions within the outfit. He recommended a decentralization which would involve my accepting that there would be six Regional Directors, effectively six County Chiefs, with authority over housing provision, fair allocation and staff. As it happened, this was exactly the mode I had developed in my Personnel Policy in Canadian and Indian management, so I was an enthusiast for it. Within two weeks the Regional Controllers became Directors, the role of the centre, mine, became one of helping the Regional Directors to become self-sufficient, and of promoting, within guidelines, the autonomy, personnel-wise, of the Regional Director.

Sadly the Personnel Director found this policy unappealing. His Deputy, Oliver Kearney, did his best to support him, as did Colm McGarry, but increasingly it became clear that devolution to the Regional Directors and no firm and acceptable Personnel policy were leading to serious problems with the staff and their Union, the PSA (Public Service Alliance), and we were heading for a strike.

I had had problems with the PSA. On my first Christmas in 1979, I had decided to speak to every one of my staff of nearly 4,000. My first meeting was at Coleraine before Christmas. It was a happy event and there was nothing but cordiality in the dialogue between me and the fifty or so staff. Next day, the *Sunday News* had a headline "Gorman softening-up NIHE for massive redundancies". I rang up my old friend Bill Henderson, former Captain Irish Guards, and owner of the *Belfast Newsletter* and *Sunday News*. He said "I allow full editorial freedom to the Editor. I am not prepared to criticize his article and headline". I could see that I was beaten, but added, "There is another piece in the *Sunday News* which says 'Prudish Catholic Gorman upbraids braless girl'." It claimed that I had ordered home a staff member who had a tight jersey and no bra. Bill gave the same very proper proprietorial reply. My response was "Sack the Sub-Editor, who should have used the headline 'Gorman boobs again'!"

On 1 July 1979 the Rowland Report was issued. It was a damning indictment of NIHE. No wonder at my interview it had been mentioned as a "ticking bomb". It described many areas of maleficence by senior NIHE Managers and how money had been, if not stolen, at least wasted. Fortunately for me, some of those most indicted had resigned, but there were still "bit players" on our staff. A lot of the problem was to do with poor control of contracts, "cronyism" in disposing with large sums of public money and, particularly in Londonderry, a perception of pro-Nationalist bias.

Clearly I had been appointed to clean up and my first solution was devolution, my second a much more transparent media "image". Here I was lucky. Brum Henderson, Chairman of UTV, and his brother Bill, Chairman of *Belfast Newsletter*, gave me every opportunity to describe the changes I was making in NIHE, and in particular the new attitude to home ownership.

Before my arrival, the Government had changed. Mrs Thatcher was the new Prime Minister, a believer in the Right to Buy policy. NIHE had, on the inspiration of the former Chairman of the NI Labour Party, Charlie Brett, developed a policy of selling houses in areas where housing *need* no longer existed to tenants at a discount.

The NIO Governmental procedure was then based on Orders in Council, which go through "on the nod" in the small hours at Westminster. This "Right to Buy" Order had gone through the year before Mrs Thatcher made it a big plan in the Tory Manifesto, so when the Conservatives got in we were able to start at once selling our stock.

The first eighteen months of Tory rule at Westminster were spent in acrimonious combat with the Labour opposition on this, but we in the NIHE were able to sell to avid buyers at a better discount than before and were earning millions thereby.

At one of my early meetings I met an Abbey National Manager, Bill Biggs, with all the seventeen Building Society chiefs in NI. After a good lunch, he told me of his success in Portsmouth of selling the mortgage idea to sailors, and told me of his abhorrence of the "Red Lining" of the Societies in Northern Ireland. This meant nothing to me so I asked him to explain. He said, "In West Belfast, on the West Bank of the Foyle [Londonderry] and in Newry, the Building Societies have a Red Line policy. They do not give mortgages in these places."

Next day, at home at Rademon, I was doing my weekly chore of clearing and laying the fireplace; as I was crumpling the *Daily Telegraph*, I saw the name "Oliver Chesterton", whom I remembered coming to the Irish Guards Mess in Norfolk. He was now Chairman of the Woolwich Building Society. I rang Sir Oliver, who kindly remembered me and told him of the Biggs conversation of the previous day. "How outrageous," he said, "I shall make damn sure the Woolwich is not involved in this bigotry." He returned my call next day to say that there was indeed a concordat which was not so much to do with sectarianism, but the fact that property prices in Catholic areas were volatile because of the IRA activity. I asked him to help me gather the Chairmen of the seventeen Building Societies trading in Northern Ireland at the Ulster Office, in Berkeley Street, London, and he agreed.

Charlie Brett and I, with the superb assistance of Brian Henderson, our PR Director, put on a show there which astonished these city figures, not so much as to the morality of excluding Catholic areas from mortgages, but more so the business which they were missing thereby. It turned out that, just as the NI Building Society Managers had found it safer to "Red Line", their seniors had found it expedient to limit their allocation of funds to Northern Ireland.

The Societies went into competition with each other to service a

Northern Ireland Mortgage Market and provided funds not only to NIHE because of their enormous take-up of mortgages, but also in supporting Housing Action Areas which brought whole estates into high quality and thus were more desirable houses.

This was all heady stuff and we had euphoric dreams of making Northern Ireland the housing example to the world, but the acrimonious debate in Parliament was lumbering on and there had been no answer to the question of how the proceeds of house sales should be distributed. In England the Government view was that Councils, having obtained about 50% of their funding for public housing from Government, should at the most be entitled to 50% of the proceeds, but even then, to curb left-wing councils which were prone to spend any money they got, these sums should be kept in the Treasury to be released on application, only for substantial causes.

The Northern Ireland Office had a brilliant Permanent Secretary of Finance, George Quigley, with whom I had a brief meeting. I told him of the problem, outlined the sales prognosis and explained how in my view the Government had the chance of seeing the NIHE as "special and different" from Local Authorities, in that, because of the reasons for setting it up, it was by definition not a local authority. He pointed out that of course the Treasury could say that because NIHE was not a local authority, its funding having been totally the Government's, all sales proceeds should go to Government, but he said he would try his best.

He succeeded and from 1980-90 the NIHE entered a phase of building and rehabilitation which made it one of the outstanding housing bodies in the world. The credit for these standards owes most to Sir Charles Brett and Donal Crawley, the Development Director, and a fine architect, and after my time to Victor Blease, who succeeded me as Chief Executive, and John McEvoy, who took my Deputy Chairman's place and later succeeded Norman Ferguson, Brett's successor.

Sadly, the Housing Executive has now fallen on difficult times. The Northern Ireland Office took the easy expedient of depriving it of the role of new housing provider, because of the marked distaste by the Tories of local authorities which were deprived of new housing provision, which was given to Housing Associations. It was a major mistake by the Northern Ireland Office to abandon its almost unique success, the Housing Executive, in favour of a totally different political stance adopted in England, and to reduce NIHE to an administrative entity, with a promise that "allocations" would be controlled to avoid Currie-type scandals. Five years after "allocation" was to be given statutory power to NIHE, nothing has been done. It is only a matter of time before a Caledon-type scandal puts housing back on the controversial scene, after so many years of its removal from the acrimonious, discriminatory allegations of yesteryear.

Furthermore, the interest and promotion of Building Societies and Banks in the political, economic and social success of NIHE has diminished, despite the efforts of a Board well led by Syd McDowell and Paddy McIntyre and a staff now denied the heady successes of housing provision. It was a tragedy that the Department of the Environment showed such pusillanimity about a body which took Housing out of politics.

An outstanding figure among my Directors was John Murray, a senior Civil Servant (later Permanent Secretary for Agriculture) who had been seconded to assist in the decentralization of the Executive and the empowerment of the Regions. With his help, many of the personnel problems were anticipated and dealt with, including the switch to computers throughout the organization, reducing paperwork, speeding up customer service, creating accessible and instant records and sourcing staff time for more productive work.

NIHE employed an in-house labour force of 1,500 staff whose role was carrying out repairs, dealing with housing emergencies such as IRA bombing of estates and town centres, and carrying out these tasks in competition with outside contractors. Inevitably there were peaks and troughs in the utilization of this force and indeed there were times when they were underemployed.

It was a sad necessity that I had to reduce the Direct Labour Unit, which had done a first-rate job, and eventually it was wound up. Because many of them came into public observation when they were doing work after bombing incidents, and because many had jobs as part-time RUC or Army, there was a steady casualty rate and a dozen were killed or seriously maimed by the IRA.

Sinn Fein, the IRA's political wing, did all it could to create disaffection amongst our tenants, many of whom lived in multi-storey flat blocks, such as Divis, West Belfast, and Rossville in Derry. I decided that we should raise our profile and attempt to get co-operation from tenants, many if not most of whom were unemployed and could do much to improve their admittedly unsatisfactory living conditions. These were 1950s high-rise "castles in the sky", favoured by local authorities as a way of getting rid of slums and still containing the dense voting areas so beloved of Ulster politicians.

Divis had about 1000 flats in half-a-dozen blocks and I recruited a Catholic Curate, Father Pat Buckley, to help us in painting all the front doors bright colours to spruce up the grim corridors. The sight of us both acting as painters made good TV and encouraged the tenants to join us. Pat Buckley was promoted to Larne as Parish Priest, but perhaps the taste for publicity led him to appoint himself a Bishop, to leave the Roman Catholic establishment and to carry out single-sex "marriages" and generally to challenge his church's teaching. He is not well-regarded in official church circles, but all I can say is that he was a good door-painter at one time!

With the full support of my Regional Directors, I embarked on a big programme of tenant consultation. There were very large meetings all over the Province and they gave tenants the chance of raising their problems and feeling a sense of ownership of their houses.

One meeting, in a large school hall, part of the Divis complex, was packed by tenants when the Belfast Regional Director, Billy Cameron, and I arrived. It was noticeable that the last seat of each row was turned inwards at 90% so that a Sinn Fein/IRA member could see along the row and note who was raising matters. A perennial grievance was the presence of rats in the complex, partly at least caused by rubbish being thrown from the flats above to the ground, partly through blockage in rubbish chutes. Billy and I were at a table in front of the audience when the rat problem was raised. At this moment the large doors at the end of the hall were flung upon and a man dressed all in white, holding a tray in the manner of a waiter, walked slowly into the room. The tray was completely covered by a white cloth. Suddenly there was movement under the cloth. "Rats" screamed a woman and there was instant panic, people standing on chairs, hysterically shouting as the white-coated man continued his menacing procession down the centre aisle. He reached the table and as he turned to face the audience Billy Cameron threw himself across the table, snatched the white cloth and revealed that through a hole in the tray the fingers of the man, with small sticks tied to them, had made the "rat movement". The man ran from the hall. Billy and I were then listened to more attentively as we outlined our plans for Divis, which has now been almost completely demolished, with many residents now in excellent houses there or at Poleglass, one of NIHE's finest estates, comprising 1,500 homes.

This development, high on the hill west of Belfast, but in the Lisburn Council area, was chosen to relieve the pressure on sites in Belfast. It was strenuously resisted by the Unionist-dominated Lisburn Council and Colin James, in whose Region Lisburn fell, had a hard time persuading the Council to support it. Appeals to consider West Belfast congestion fell on deaf ears, largely because an earlier estate, Twinbrook, not far from Poleglass, had a strong Republican element and had been the scene of troubles. A Government Planning Report recommended that the Belfast boundaries should be extended in several places, including Poleglass, so work on this new estate started, with McAleer and Rushe as contractor (the last name being appropriate). The first 100 houses were nearing completion when the first of the hunger-strikers in the Maze Prison, Bobby Sands, was nearing his death. The Housing Executive had decided that an estate called the New Lodge in West Belfast should be relieved of congestion and poor housing by being chosen as the first to be selected, and the tenants were told. Immediately those who had been selected had cards telling them that the IRA had found houses for them, that they were to tell no one about this and that each person in the family had to pack a suitcase, be ready to move instantly and transport would be provided for them. Fortunately, many of them contacted Colin James, who put in an emergency plan to have McAleer and Rushe complete the 100 houses, at least to have water and electricity installed and gave them the key to their new homes.

Next night the world's media, particularly TV crews staying at the Europa Hotel, found a taxi man bursting in to the room they were drinking in to say, "The IRA are taking over the new Poleglass estate. I have just seen a big convoy moving from the New Lodge to Poleglass."

As the media menage rushed to the scene, they saw families occupying the new houses, and the media had a field-day explaining how the IRA had won a major victory, in response to the death that night of the first of ten hunger-strikers, Bobby Sands. With much more state-of-the-art equipment, all this went out from the international TV teams from Europe, US, Japan, etc. Ulster Television, who at that time did not have this high-tech equipment, which required proper lighting, waited until dawn to record its story, which was, of course, that the IRA attempt to hijack Poleglass had failed, and the new tenants, happy now to tell the story, explained the real truth.

Meanwhile, the success of house sales continued, with Building Societies and Banks pressing us to sell more, and we were now in a position to build the quality homes which Brett had insisted on, rather than the poor ones which earlier housing bodies had to be content with. The mortgage availability was such that some Societies, particularly the Abbey National and Nationwide, were interested in our plans for Housing Action Areas, where we took estates which required major improvements and brought the houses up to a high standard. They now became highly saleable and were sold to tenants who had never dreamed of ownership. Now Northern Ireland has one of the highest proportion of ownership in the world and I believe this has played a major part in the "peace process". Home owners are not inclined to armed revolution. The ironical situation arrived that we had difficulty in spending our funds within the financial year ending 5 April.

The rather old-fashioned rule that no "carry-over" was permitted by the Treasury for money unspent by then led inevitably to "splurges" in the last few months – new equipment, fresh paint, conference attendance, all desirable, but not strictly necessary. Just as the carry-over rule led to extravagance, its opposite, a threatened shortfall of funding availability in the last period of the year, led to panic-stricken steps to save money to keep in "budget", particularly on the part of civil servants who feared having to appear before the Public Accounts Committee, where careers sometimes came to an untimely end. Appearing before the PAC, accompanied by Kenneth Bloomfield, to explain some of the misfeasances revealed in the Rowland Commission Report, I was dazzled by his persuasiveness that all was now totally corrected and that the Housing Executive, whose budget had increased by over £200 million 1980-81, was now totally reformed and impeccable. Sadly, my next two appearances did not quite bear this out. I found the best thing to do was to accept personal responsibility for mistakes and failures in our accounts, caused mostly by my own impatience with the slow process of change, particularly in the development of new Managers to take over from the generation of those who had come to us from Councils and the Housing Trust, a highly successful body which had been absorbed by the Executive in 1972. What was needed was a strong cadre of aspiring young Managers who had been trained within our own ranks, had shown their ability in "people" terms and were accustomed to the high-tech changes we were introducing.

I have already mentioned Brum Henderson, Chairman of Ulster Television, an enlightened and fair-minded public figure, who had taken up the ideas of Dr Brendan O'Regan, former head of the Shannon Airport and its Duty Free Zone, and of Irish Tourism. I was introduced to Brendan at UTV and was impressed at once. He believed that the ancient quarrel between North and South, Protestant and Catholic, would never be resolved without the experience of co-operating with one another for the benefit of all. He was setting up Boards in Dublin and Belfast of people who, like Brum, had shown how much could be achieved in the field of reconciliation through co-operation in trade, community linkages, school teaching and experience of mutual understanding, sport and social events, cross-border.

He was also setting up Boards in London and New York, named Co-operation Ireland (North might not mean much in those cities) and was already planning a Maracycle, in which thousands of mostly young people would cycle together from Dublin to Belfast and vice versa.

My own work as Vice-Chairman and Chief Executive of the Housing Executive, then the largest public housing body in Europe, had much relevance to the O'Regan ideals, since housing was one of the contentious and hate-filled issues in the Province, and I was happy, and honoured, to be elected to the Boards of Co-operation North Companies in Ireland.

By 1991 much had been achieved, the Co-operation North aspirations were shared by most Irish people, and the London and New York Boards were contributing generous sums to the cause. The British and Irish Governments made substantial money available, but loyalist terrorism was not diminishing and there was a sense of weariness, sameness, in the annual performance of the Maracycle, the school exchanges, crossborder trade conferences, etc. People had had great hope of Co-operation bringing a new mission for Ireland's future and of an end of the violence.

A new initiative was required and, with the backing of the future Chairman, then Dr George Quigley, now Sir George, we embarked on raising the Co-operation North profile in the business community at top level. This was not solely about increasing the Corporate funding, already quite generous, but about getting really senior Directors to play a greater part. One way of doing this was to get the Chairmen, Chief Executives and Directors of companies, Protestant and Catholic, to run the Marathon in New York, where we felt there was a prejudicial, jaundiced view of Northern Ireland. A dozen brave men volunteered for this testing race, all senior people, and with an obligation not only to finish the Marathon, but to produce £3,000 each of sponsorship.

The Queen gives a reception at Windsor Castle, after a magnificent service in St George's Chapel, to commemorate the Victoria Order. All those in the Order, which is personal to Her Majesty, are invited, and she and other members of the Royal Family meet each guest and recall the events which led to their honour. She has always shown her interest in Northern Ireland to me and I told her about Co-operation North/Ireland and, greatly daring, asked her if she would agree to be Patron if President Robinson was prepared to be Patron also. She summoned Sir Robert Fellowes, her Private Secretary, who showed great interest and asked me to follow up the suggestions with Peter Brooke, then Secretary of State for Northern Ireland, and to find out diplomatically how an approach to President Robinson might be made. It was not hard to put together an occasion which would be appropriate, namely the Co-operation Team effort in New York, and I wrote to President Robinson, as well as to the Palace, telling both about the forthcoming effort and asking for their support. Peter Brooke, who contributed personally to the venture, advised by his Civil Servants, was engaged in one of the numerous cross-border initiatives, the "three-strand talks", London-Dublin, Belfast-Dublin and Unionist-Nationalist in Northern Ireland itself. Though there did seem much hope of a political breakthrough, he told me, and also the Palace, that he would like the Joint Patron idea postponed until there was an Irish settlement. I was rather discouraged about this. At the Harvard Business School I had learned of the NIH Factor – Not Invented Here – and had the uncomfortable feeling that this was the case here.

However the Queen, responding to my appeal for support for the Marathon, invited all the runners, their wives (only men ran the first time, women did later), and, reminiscent of the Presentation at Court protocol of former days, their unmarried daughters under 21, to Buckingham

Palace. Concurrently the President invited the runners to meet her at her Residence, the former Vice-Regal Lodge, at Phoenix Park, Dublin. It was a huge incentive to the Team. All finished the gruelling "Big Apple" Marathon and both receptions were occasions none of us will forget. The President, who had been unwell, nonetheless gave up most of a morning to meet and talk to all twelve runners. John Donnelly, Senior Partner of Deloittes in the Republic, was Co-operation North/Ireland Chairman and was succeeded by Dr Quigley. Donnelly addressed the President in Irish and, by taking part in the Dublin/Belfast Maracycle, showed his prowess and fitness. We were, and are, proud of him. In my talk with the President, I told her of the Joint Patron idea and she accepted it instantly, but also said that this would have to be approved by her Government, which was no surprise to me.

Dr O'Regan, when we all sat down to coffee in the elegant dining room of the old Vice-Regal Lodge, gave me credit for the Marathon and work for North/South Co-operation. He described how I had, as Director of the Institute of Directors, invited the Taoiseach (Mr Charles Haughey) to Belfast the previous year. "Correction," I said. "I did not invite the Taoiseach, I invited the President of the European Community," which made everyone laugh. There had been considerable resistance to the IOD invitation to a three-day Cross Border Business Conference in the Europa Hotel. The difference between the President of Europe and the Prime Minister of Ireland, was not apparent to the many members of the Democratic Unionist Party who demonstrated at his visit, which was a great success.

The Buckingham Palace occasion was a Royal Garden Party. The wives and daughters of the runners and they themselves were thrilled when, carefully stage-managed by Colonel Malcolm Ross of the Scots Guards, a 'lozenge' was formed in the centre of the Garden by the Household, enclosing the Team. Each member had a talk to Her Majesty, who wanted to know about Ireland, North and South, and about the Marathon.

The 1994 cease-fire brought the opportunity to raise the Patron matter again and at the next Victorian Order Service at Windsor (now slowly recovering from the fire), I spoke to the Queen about it and later to Sir Patrick Mayhew, who had succeeded Peter Brooke. It was a wonderful moment, early in the New Year 1996, when it was announced simultaneously by the Government of the United Kingdom and of the Republic of Ireland that both constitutional Heads of State were to become Patrons of Co-operation North/Ireland, and this was in the context of the first State Visit of an Irish President to London in June. It is, partly at least, because of the Patrons that Inter Capitol Group, the international finance house based in London, donated £174,000 to Co-operation Ireland, presented, in the presence of President Robinson, in Dublin in June 1996, as Joint Patron with Her Majesty the Queen.

Our house-building and renovation programme was putting many millions of pounds into the construction industry, and needless to say, the paramilitaries were eager to have a share. We began to identify a sameness about tenders from the main construction companies and it looked as though there was some collusion among them and that a percentage had been agreed to cover "security". I called an urgent meeting on a Sunday to avoid publicity and invited the Deputy Chief Constable RUC, Michael McAtamney, to attend. Over twenty companies were represented, usually by their Chief Executive or Chairman. Having raised our concern at the "padding" of tenders, I asked each Company to tell us what was happening. Nothing emerged, until going round the table I reached Leslie Murray, then Chief Executive of Unit Construction. He electrified the meeting by disclosing what his company did in the "protection racket". Loyalist and Republican terrorists tendered for their "insurance" that work and workers would not be threatened, shot or bombed, and that they would protect the company from *every* terrorist. These were no empty threats; construction companies' employees involved in Army or Police works were constantly executed, and it was not a far cry from such targets to the Housing Executive, seen as an arm of government.

The meeting proceeded rapidly to agree:

Full disclosure to the RUC via Michael McAtamney from the contractors, of their policies, actions and terrorist contacts;

The setting-up of a manned RUC hot line to all employees of construction firms, to help provide information of threats or bribery being conveyed to them;

The formation of a special department of the RUC, later named C19, to follow up leads.

These steps must have saved many millions of public money, and saved lives. The BBC did a wonderful job in revealing a loyalist plot to blackmail a builder, through a "sting" in which the BBC reporter risked his life by recording a secret deal being offered by a Protestant paramilitary leader, which led to prosecution and conviction of the blackmailer.

In 1986 I was coming to the end of my Housing Executive Job. When invited to apply for it, I had been intrigued by the jointure of the two posts of Deputy Chairman and Chief Executive. The first was for the normal fixed term of five years, the second until normal retiring age, in those days 65; I was then 55. It seemed to me that this was an ideal arrangement. The strength of the Term Contract is that the holder of that job has a strong position in that, in a dispute between employer (the Northern Ireland Office in this case) and me, which I did not rule out, I could only be dismissed on payment of the "unexpired portion of the days rations" in the Army phrase. Being on the Board was another strength, and while I could foresee no reasons why the part-time Chairman Charles Brett and I should fall out, he had the reputation of being of strong opinions, and so had I! In the event this never happened, and though his strong left-wing views had caused some ferment in conventional right-wing Unionist circles, mine too were inclined that way. Charlie started his "sherry party" on the eve of Board meetings, which sometimes caused problems since the Executive under my regime had decided on policy on many fronts, and the sherry-party gave the opportunity to those who had disagreed on the Executive Board to air their views. I started by being most apprehensive about going to the Board with Directors giving contrary advice. This seldom happened and on the whole there were no divisions of principle, save on Personnel matters where the Personnel Director was sometimes at odds with his fellow-Directors and the Board could see that.

I found the job becoming stressful. Much of my work I did at home early in the morning, sometimes as early as 5.00am. Having six Regional Directors and seven Functional Directors, and a policy of the "open door", there was seldom time to do other than fit in meetings, face-to-face discussions, press and TV interviews, and though Ken Bloomfield, appreciating this, seconded a young Civil Servant to help, it was difficult to give enough time to every demand. Possibly mistakenly, I had decided to become the surrogate Housing Manager for each of NI's twenty-six District Councils. My idea was to convince them that I was the key to getting their grievances met, and over 500 District Councillors were now on Christian name terms, and made use of this. By involving the Regional Directors more, this helped, but there is still a convention in NI that it is only by going to the top that action can be obtained. The Westminster MPs had naturally a priority for attention and my mail was voluminous, particularly from the Rev. Ian Paisley MEP, MP. He had an interesting and effective system. Each of his constituencies had committees, comprised mostly of women I believe, and when the Big Man had a housing complaint or request he would put this before the committee, to investigate it before sending it on to me. This way I did at least have the confidence that the request/demand had gone through some verification, and was not, as so many communications were, full of hearsay and inaccuracy. Quite often, on arriving at my office at 9.00am, I would see a familiar hunched figure in an armchair outside, with business which was more serious than would be consigned to the Democratic Unionist Party (DUP) committees. Very often the business would concern my co-religionists, particularly farmers, and it has never surprised me when Ian Paisley has topped the elections to the European Parliament. Another MP, Enoch Powell, had a different system, perhaps even more effective. He would himself investigate the grievance/demand and, only if satisfied as to its grievance, take it up at the point where the Manager concerned was in a position to take action. This shortened the decision period and avoided the irritation which Managers felt at having to report upwards, in a sense defending themselves. Powell was also scrupulous in thanking those who had actioned his request for help. One of the benefits of computerization and Management Training and Development was that decision-making was brought to a lower staff level, which enhanced the position and self-esteem of more junior employees.

As described earlier, Heather and I had been foiled in our attempt to build a house on Skiathos Island in the Greek Aegean, and several visits to the island to stay with our friends the Percys had not produced anything. In 1976, however, we had a phone call in India from Pat Percy to say that an Englishman, a surgeon who had built a villa below theirs, had failed to complete its sale because the purchaser had not been able to produce dollars, only drachmae.

Fortunately our time in Canada had enabled us to save dollars. So we went post-haste to Greece to meet the surgeon and settled on a price which was within our funds, just, by using a legacy of Heather's. The villa, renamed Arios (Greek for Holm-Oak), was on a cliff over the sea on the Kalamaki peninsula, which was where the first post-war British emigrants had made a colony.

This was because a South African journalist, Denis Henshall, had gone to Skiathos to investigate the heroic story of a woman called Katarina who had organized the escape of many South African soldiers after the defeat of the Allied Army which had tried to stop the German invasion of Greece in 1941. Skiathos, being the closest of the hundred or so Aegean islands, only four miles from Pelion on the mainland, and heavily wooded with miles of sandy beach, was ideal for sheltering the allied troops and, using caiques, to ferry them to Naval ships lying offshore, fast enough to load the men in the darkness and get them well on their way to Alexandria by dawn.

Henshall found Katarina, now almost blind and very poor and sick. He wrote about her bravery, quoting those escaping South Africans he had interviewed, and started a plea for her to receive pensions from the Governments, British, South African and Greek, which had benefited so much from her services, for which, captured by the Nazis, she had been imprisoned and tortured. She died in greater comfort and care than she would have done otherwise.

Henshall met a young Greek Army Officer Reservist whose engineering company had the task of building a road around the Kalamaki peninsula, on the south-east of the island, about a mile long and a quarter of a mile wide. It has stunning views, west as far as Delphi and east to Skopelos and

Alonissos, with many smaller islands in between. The two men, dining together in a local taverna, concluded that since one of the reasons for the circular road round the peninsula was to encourage tourism, Kalamaki being halfway between Skiathos town and Kukunaries, probably the most beautiful of all Aegean beaches, there would be a huge demand by Hellenophilic Englishmen to have second homes there. Henshall, a man of huge initiative and entrepreneurship, went to the Regent Palace Hotel in London, having put an advertisement in the *Sunday Times* saying "Homes on an acre of Skiathos Island, fully serviced and built professionally £1,500. Please come to meet me to hear more at the Regent Palace Hotel". The hotel was packed that evening and many people put down a deposit then and there for a site, which was marked on Henshall's map. He had already negotiated Power of Attorney to sell sites from the shepherds who grazed their flocks on the peninsula, which did not give them a good living.

Nikos Andritsoupolis, the young Greek Army Engineer who was an architectural student at the University in Athens, drew up sample plans for villas on the sites, about fifty of which were on offer. He negotiated electricity connections and found a well which had enough capacity. He found a supply of plastic piping which was brought by caique from the mainland, many miles of it, he employed bricklayers, carpenters, glaziers, roofers, tilers, plumbers and within a year the first British homeowners arrived. Many are still there enjoying a life full of activity in homes which have evolved from the first simple dwellings and which are extremely popular for summer tenants.

Amongst these is the Villa Arios, which was now *our* villa, so-called because of its huge patio, shaded by the umbrella growth of twelve ancient holm-oaks (Arios trees). Tradition has it that a shepherd planted twelve acorns on this prominent headland, one for each Apostle, and because they were so close together, they eventually formed a huge umbrella over this headland point. The villa, L-shaped, had three bedrooms, two bathrooms and a large sitting-room, with adjoining kitchen. Over our twenty years this beautiful retreat gave me what US soldiers call R & R and was a wonderful family holiday home. By building a "spitaki", a small cottage, and renting a neighbour's villa we were able to fit in a dozen people, of all ages, and rented a caique to sail to the north shore, to the ancestral ruins of Kastro, where the islanders fled when attacked by Turks or pirates, to visit coves into which we could go in the boat, or sometimes walk over the mountains to Kastro. Expeditions to Pelion, on the mainland, or to Skopelos and Alonnisos were other adventures. We had a little Beetle, and later a Renault 5 for trips which became more exciting as the tracks were made into passable roads.

Sadly, as the years rolled on, our children were less able to holiday there, as the economics of a Greek holiday villa require one to rent it out in July and August. We tried for some years to concentrate on half-term holidays in May and October when the weather was sunny, but less hot and the crowds in the village smaller, but as airline retired staff tickets (subject to load, preferring full fare passengers) became difficult to obtain, and family, now adult, sometimes had their own ideas about family holidays, this May and October solution became less viable. When I retired from NIHE and we had bought our own house near Killyleagh, it made sense to sell, which we did with a heavy heart, after so many years of happy times. We have been back to Skiathos since to see again Nikos Andritsoupolis, the Buchanan-Dunlops, Pat Percy (sadly Jimmy died early of asbestosis, contracted when he was an apprentice engineer servicing planes which had asbestos exhaust insulation) and many other old friends, Greek as well as British.

By 1986 my contract with NIHE (which I had been asked to extend by the new Chairman Norman Ferguson) was coming to an end and there was much debate about my succession in the two posts of Deputy Chairman and Chief Executive. Deloittes were called in to advise and, unsurprisingly to me anyway, recommended that there should be a separate new Deputy Chairman, a separate Chief Executive and a Director of Operations. Mostly in jest I suggested to John Irvine, the Permanent Secretary, that I should now have three salaries backdated to 1979. Understandably he did not take me seriously! It was sad saying goodbye to over eighty separate offices, my thirteen Directors and the twenty-six District Councils, but satisfying also, as every part of the Province had housing of high quality in so far as the public sector was concerned. The only blot was in South Tyrone and Fermanagh, where privately owned cottages/farms were owned by elderly people who just did not want to change their conditions, even when generous grants were available for electricity, mains water and even sewage. To try to entice them to take advantage of what we were offering, I got my Board to agree to equip two Mobile NIHE offices to visit areas where many of these homes were situated. Just after the Pope's visit to Ireland the Mobile offices quickly became known as Gormabiles, after Popemobiles. The effort was not a success, old people continued to struggle independently. They were brought up in a tradition of self-help, of eschewing debt and of frugal living. Thoroughly praiseworthy, but frustrating to us dogooders!

One of the highlights of our farewell round was a dinner hosted by Chris Patten, who had probably been the most successful Minister in the Jim Prior period. All the political parties were represented, including the DUP, whose spokesperson Peter Robinson had rather flatteringly referred to me as "the acceptable face of the Housing Executive". Years later the Pattens were guests of honour at the Annual Dinner of the Institute of Directors, having come from Hong Kong where he was Governor, and showed his continuing interest in Northern Ireland thereby. Sadly, our third contact, when he chaired the Independent Police Commission, was less happy.

Chapter Fifteen

INSTITUTE OF DIRECTORS

So, for the first time since I was 18 I had no job, and very stimulating it was for a while, but it began to pall, even though I had now the time to indulge in gardening, bee keeping, fishing, which had always been my hobbies, and in visiting friends and places which we had both enjoyed in our itinerant career, charity work, Co-operation North and Help the Aged, to which I had been recruited by my friend Billy Hastings, the proprietor of the Province's biggest hotel group, and whose son Howard was the future NI Chairman of the Institute of Directors. Our good friends the Henderson brothers, Bill the Chairman of the *Belfast Newsletter*, Brum of Ulster Television, detecting that retirement at 63 was beginning to lose its appeal, started movements to get me back to work. From this emerged an offer from the Institute of Directors to become its part-time Director for NI. The Institute had fallen to less than 200 members, who were mostly retired or approaching retirement, and the Director General, Sir John Hoskyns, appealed to me very much. A former head of Mrs Thatcher's Downing Street staff, an ex-soldier and a leader, he seemed just the person to help me set up this new post and bring it to a position of influence in Ulster. Furthermore, his Deputy, General Stuart Watson, had been a contemporary at Sandhurst and had had many of my wartime experiences.

All was not plain sailing, as the part-time Chairman, just elected, was Edward Haughey. We just could not find common cause. He believed that I was his employee, just as the many hundreds of staff he employed at Norbrook Laboratories were, and that I must get his permission to do virtually anything. Even before my official starting date, I told the IOD that I could not see myself working in this climate, but Brum Henderson and General Watson persuaded me that I would be able to do it. I failed. By no means was it Eddie Haughey's fault. I had been used to big jobs, taking personal risk and responsibility, and our psyches were too similar in the same ways, and dissimilar in others, to make for comfortable partnership.

For a couple of years, despite the friction, things progressed. Our numbers climbed from 200 to 300, with a higher IOD profile enabling us to get better audiences for seminars, business lunches, recruiting events and public relations mini-coups, by getting early accurate business "flashes". Eventually, Eddie resigned in favour of David Linter and the IOD started to build up its membership.

Part of this build-up led to my suggestion that we should hold a joint Cross-border Trade Conference with Charles Haughey (no relation of Eddie), President of the EEC for six months, as main speaker. With Linter in the chair, the IOD Council supported the idea and I went to Dublin to meet the Foreign Service Chief, Dermot Gallaher, and his deputy, Anne Anderson. They were thoroughly supportive and promised to produce support from the Republic's business community. The IOD in the South had by that time declined in number even more than we had and had less than 100 members. Nevertheless they had appointed an Executive Director, Nial Maloney, who was bringing it forward in numbers.

Obviously this was politically controversial. Before it was announced, I had already contacted James Molyneaux and Ian Paisley. Molyneaux was instantly supportive and in his own way so was Paisley. Ian was in the Cameroons, where he has about fifteen congregations of Free Presbyterians. Understandably, he told me that he would not take part in anything which gave his adversary Charles Haughey support, but if the conference genuinely helped the laggardly Ulster trade figures cross-border he would take a neutral position. However, he warned me that his Party was a democratic one and that he would have to pass on to his lieutenants my request to him to participate. By now of course the media were agog about the Taoiseach addressing a major meeting in Belfast and many Unionists were vehemently opposed. On Ian's return he found that there was nothing for it but to make this opposition public and, though I met his senior members at their Ravenhill Road headquarters, they were not prepared to see the President of Europe as any different from the hated Taoiseach of the Republic. Meanwhile preparations for the three-day conference progressed. By lucky chance the Bolshoi Ballet was on at the Grand Opera House and I got 400 bookings reserved. Sponsors laid on a reception and meals at the Europa Hotel, which we had booked solidly.

The IOD, so enthusiastic to begin with, took fright at the hard-line Unionist disapproval of Haughey's coming (he had never been in Belfast before), and the IOD Dublin reported cancellations and worry about the special train that had been booked to carry members to Belfast. David Linter, George Quigley and I met at David's house at Killinchy. It was a serious crisis. If we cancelled it would be an admission that Unionism could not accept European Unionism. If we went ahead in three days' time, the DUP street protest could result in bloodshed. We phoned the IOD Dublin Chairman, whose view, understandably, was that as we were the hosts it was up to us to make the invitation acceptable. We phoned the Northern Ireland Office, who said, "You got into this mess; get yourselves out of it." We phoned our Councillors who said, "We support you. Don't just call it off because the Unionists are against it." They were probably Unionists themselves. I remember driving late at night to Claire Faulkner and asking her, whose company Project Planning was the Conference organizer, to fax all our members to say, "Don't worry, come".

All this time my telephones, home and office, were ringing incessantly to oppose the Conference. The DUP has devoted committees able to organize campaigns of phoning. Some were threatening, some were abusive, all were determined to keep Haughey out. Arguments about the benefits of Cross-border Trade fell on deaf ears. The calls went on all night. On Monday I organized with the Culloden Hotel to spend the night there, and said that I wanted, please, to have no media knowledge of my presence, as the media had dogged us for several days, as had the DUP.

The next day was horrific. It started with an early-morning bomb which killed four soldiers near Downpatrick. It led to understandable appeals to cancel the Cross-border Conference. I realized that the moment of decision had come and was preparing to cancel. Before doing that, I spoke to Dermot Gallagher and told him that we had not "chickened out", but that Dublin were showing symptoms of doing so. If the Dublin-Belfast train came empty to Belfast it would show that all the rhetoric about North-South business was just that. He told me he would take action. And he did! The train from Dublin was full.

That night at the Europa the Ulstermen waited expectantly for the Dubliners, the train having been delayed by a bomb-scare. When the crowds arrived it was a delicious moment, the Europa was jammed, old friends embraced and we went to bed believing that it was all a great success. Unfortunately for Heather and me, Rhonda Paisley, Ian's daughter, had decided to do an all-night dance protest on a balcony beside ours which managed to keep the excitement going. At 4.00am the RUC, in a Guards-like operation, marched into the street opposite the Europa carrying crowd-barriers which kept the demonstrators from building up a crowd towards the hotel. Shortly afterwards the Paisley bullhorn broke into voice calling on all true Unionists to decry the visit of Haughey.

At 10 minutes to 10 the convoy bearing the European President swept into the back entrance to the hotel. I met Haughey, whose first words were of praise for the RUC. "I would love to have them in control of my Presidential finale in Dublin," said he. "They look so smart and authoritative."

By now over 500 delegates had gathered in the main concourse of the Europa. Mr Haughey and I sat on a sofa which I had arranged for us offstage. Then all the lights went out and there was total darkness; clearly the mass of television lighting, cameras, loudspeakers had overloaded the hotel power. A passing repairman lent us his torch and Mr Haughey pulled out a sheaf of papers which he perused with urgent attention. Clearly it was his speech, which gave me the impression that he was reading it for the first time. In a few minutes the lights came on again and he made his entrance to great applause. It was when he went to his special dais that I realized why he had been so worried – he was using the glass-screen technique which projects the text, enabling the speaker to seem to be speaking without notes, as the screening is invisible to the audience. It was a magnificent speech, producing four standing ovations. The sounds of discord from the crowd outside, so carefully marshalled by the RUC, were hardly audible, and the small crowd of protesting MPs on the roof of Glengall Street, Unionist Headquarters, were only able to see Mr Haughey's car sweeping him out of the Europa's back entrance.

The whole event brought much benefit to Cross-border understanding and trade. The IOD's standing in both parts of Ireland improved markedly and a study group from both chaired by George Quigley, now our Chairman, made a report which claimed, in credible detail, the possibility of 70,000 jobs by North-South co-operation. Membership of IOD in Ireland is now not far off 2,000 and the Directors have an increasingly respected role in the field of training and director development, and, through the Group of 7, management and unions working together, a voice in economic matters.

For many years the firm of McNaughton Blair had provided an office and secretarial assistance towards the running of the IOD; this help peaked when David Linter, Managing Director of McNaughton Blair, was elected Chairman after Eddie Haughey, but ended when the company was sold and David retired. Fortunately his standing in the cultural life of the Province was such that an office was provided for me at the Arts Council building in lovely grounds on Stranmillis Road. The Secretary to the Vice-Chancellor of the Queen's University, Peggy Gomersall, later Gordon, was able to join as my secretary, and when work increased she was joined by Frankie Bates, also from Queen's. Never had I had such a devoted pair of helpers. Their efficiency in clerical work, their care of our accounts and their charm and good service to our growing membership made all the difference to our work, which covered international conferences with speakers from Greece, Portugal, Italy, Canada, even Luxembourg, which sent the witty and engaging M. Israel in place of the Grand Duke Jean, who had been a brother-officer in wartime in the Irish Guards, and was now its Colonel. We ran training for Directors with the help of Professor O'Reilly of the University of Ulster, and indeed I was awarded one of the IOD's Diplomas, presented to successful students. When George Quigley became Chairman, his membership of the NatWest Board which owned the Ulster Bank, of which he was now also Chairman, led to a succession of keynote speakers on topics of a diverse nature, such as Baroness O'Cathain on the London Barbican, Dr Maurice Hayes, the former Ombudsman, on the Gaelic Athletic Association, and Dr Brian Harris on Salmon Farming in the Irish Sea. One of the most fascinating presentations was by the Co Down farmer Derek Shaw, whose wife Anne became Chairman of the IOD, on their development of the largest cotton farm in Australia, which they started from scratch and sold to Kerry Packer before returning to the Province.

The three of us, Peggy, Frankie and I, were beginning to think of retiring, particularly when the brilliant young hotelier Howard Hastings was selected as heir-apparent to our great Quigley and our tenure of the Arts Council was coming to an end. Our guests of honour at our Annual Dinner at the Hastings Culloden Hotel had been John and Norma Major, who had been immensely popular with our 500 guests.

The IOD now had a new Director-General, Tim Melville-Ross. Tim had been one of our chief supporters as MD of the Nationwide Building Society, whose allocations of funds to NIHE had grown to over £100m per year. It was quite an accolade when he told me that I was to be one of the very few life members of IOD (No Fee!) and that there was to be a farewell dinner for us at Pall Mall, IOD HQ, and a luncheon at the Europa Hotel. The dinner was for all those in the Institute with whom I had worked closely, General Stuart Watson, Dr Anne Robinson, Research Director, now DG, of the Pensions Association and Member of the Monopolies and Mergers Commission, my opposite numbers in Scotland, Donald Hardie and in Wales Merien Lewis, and of course Tim and his wife Clarissa, plus George Quigley, now Sir George. I remember arriving in rather poor form as I had heard that day the Minister for Security in the NIO, Peter Bottomley, husband of the Health Secretary Virginia Bottomley, advocating the RUC's name be changed to NIPS, Northern Ireland Police Service, a change which was to have deep repercussions in later years. However, the occasion soon cheered me up and I felt that we had been honoured handsomely.

The luncheon some little time later was attended by over 400 people, mostly members and wives. Two days before I had a message from No. 10 Downing Street: "The Prime Minister would be so grateful if he could attend another IOD occasion since he enjoyed the Culloden dinner earlier in the year so much, and if he could use the occasion to speak." His spokesperson said, "He realizes that you may feel he is 'parachuting' into your farewell party, so don't feel in the least that he will be offended if you say no." I think people in England believe that "No" is our favourite reply! Of course I told the official that I would be greatly honoured if he came and that I looked forward to meeting him again.

Major arrived at the entrance to the hotel, surrounded as ever by media, security, uniformed and otherwise, the Lord Mayor, Hugh Smyth, and Councillors, all wanting a word with him. When he saw me he gestured to me to come through the crowd, and said, "Is there a chance of my getting a pee, do you think?" So I brought him to the circular staircase, shedding most of the entourage. When we got to the Men's Room, he told me that he wanted to talk to me because he had been very close to Harry Simpson, the first Director General of the Housing Executive, and later Director of Housing for London, who had often spoken about me. Major told me that his political life had started as a Councillor in Lambeth, where the Housing Manager was Harry Simpson, and that he had been his "political guru". Simpson had recently died and his widow had spent the last weekend with the Majors in Huntingdonshire. Harry's only son was his godson. I was touched and honoured to hear this, which he repeated to the audience after lunch. The speech was to announce the Downing Street declaration which set parameters for the building of the IRA cease-fire, then in its pre-Canary Wharf phase, and anticipated the forthcoming election of a Forum for Political Dialogue, which was to parallel the negotiations. It sounded interesting and I made a mental note to see if there could be a Gorman role in it.

Quickly the political scene took life and I asked to meet the Ulster Unionist chiefs at Glengall Street. There I explained that my family, though Catholic, had been convinced Unionists, and that my father had moved to Ulster on the formation of the RUC, as one of a dozen officers of his rank who were RCs, that he and I had been in no doubt about our loyalty to the Queen and saw nothing inconsistent in supporting Unionism. Nonetheless, we had reservations about the position of the Orange Order in the Party. It seemed to me that if I were to be proactive in my inherent Unionism, it had to be understood that the dominant position of the Orange Order had to be separated from the Party, if there was to be any hope of fellow Catholics "coming out of the closet", and not only voting Unionist as many did, but taking pride in it. The President, Chairman and newly elected Leader David Trimble were emphatic in their support for this and I said I was prepared to demonstrate my loyalty to the Unionist Party by putting my name forward at the Forum election.

In order to give the smaller parties a chance of representation the Forum election allowed those parties which had a basic minimum of votes to nominate additional persons who had not gone through the process, and I was one of them for the UUP.

Chapter Sixteen

POLITICS

Just after the polls closed, and the elected and nominated members were announced I was digging in my garden to get in vegetables in May when a call from the Secretary of State, Sir Patrick Mayhew, invited me to be at his office that afternoon. I had no idea what he wanted, though I suspected it had to do with the recent election results. "John," he said, "I have chosen you to be the Chairman of the Forum for Political Dialogue, which will meet for the first time on Friday." It was now Wednesday. I had had some extraordinary changes of career, but this was the most bizarre. He went on to say that my first task was to get agreement on a permanent Chairman, who might or might not be me, and that he had appointed two Senior Civil Servants, Nigel Carson and Murray Barnes, to assist me, and that they were waiting outside to meet me.

It was a rather desperate situation. I had at last begun to enjoy retirement, after so many farewells which some had compared to an opera singer's final performances. Heather and I had many family and holiday plans, and, thanks to BA's generosity, my lack of RUC pension had been supplemented by the airline. I asked the Secretary of State, "Did you have any recommendations of me from the political parties?" "Yes," he replied, "it was unanimous." "How many parties?" I asked. "Well," he said "only one, the UUP actually."

Never having been one to turn down a challenge, I accepted and met Nigel Carson. He too had never had any dealings with Parliamentary procedure, even such quasi-procedures as were having to be devised for the new Forum, but he seemed sensible, level-headed and courageous and I took to him and, by the same standards, to Murray Barnes. We went to see the new Forum Assembly chamber. It was a semicircular, rather European Parliament-style, with a small dais for me and a larger one, some little distance away, for my two secretaries. It had a rather lonely feel to me, with only 48 hours to go before the opening of the Forum. I did all the reading available of the Act and the Secretary of State's Preliminary Rules. It was clear that I had two choices. One was to prioritize my interim position and to try to find a permanent Chairman, acceptable at least to Unionism and Nationalism mainstream parties. The other was to soldier on and try to establish consensus sufficient to carry out our objective, which was to have the framework of a Parliament ready to take on the results of inclusive negotiations which were about to start under the suzerainty of Senator George Mitchell.

Particularly because so many elected Forum members were people I had worked with in the twenty-six District Councils, and all the politicians, Westminster and Europe, were familiar to me, there was just a chance that I could be in the running for permanent Chairman.

The Forum opening was a disaster. Having read all the Parliamentary statutory rules, I listened to the familiar mantra (which would be the theme for the next two years) "Point of Order, Mr Interim Chairman". There would then be a scintillating display of Parliamentary know-how requiring an answer, which in my ignorance and because of our lack of procedural decisions in this novel body, I could not answer, so I adjourned the session, to study any point which Peter Robinson had made.

Here, as so often in a life of crisis, help came. The Parties had agreed to a seating plan, a combination of size, rightness or leftness of political stance, or simple alphabetical order. The Alliance Party, under John Alderdice's leadership, had agreed its position in his absence and his Deputy, Sean Neeson, having grumbled a little, settled. On return from adjournment the non-aggressive Alliance Party had placed themselves in the SDLP seats and sat there with folded arms looking immovable, whilst John Hume and his members, second strongest to the UUP, were standing fuming. I am not sure that this test of my shaky authority was a put-up job by Alliance, but it certainly gave me the chance to use my military authoritarianism and to order Alliance to vacate the seats at once in favour of the designated SDLP, otherwise I would call for adjournment until order was restored. It worked. The Alliance gave way, the SDLP got their designated seats and the new Chairman (Interim) had won a small victory.

The media had been intensely interested in the new Forum. A rather similarly named body under Judge Catherine McGuiness in Dublin had been convened, which was not so much a debating chamber as a platform for political policies. It had the advantage over ours that Sinn Fein participated, although they had stood in the Forum election and got a sizeable vote of 16%, in Northern Ireland only of course; in the Republic their vote was still about 5%.

The media had been kind to me. I was interviewed by Suzanne Breen of the *Irish Times*, and rather unguardedly had answered one of her questions by praising the leadership of Gerry Adams who seemed to be able to get the IRA to do his bidding. "Gorman praises Adams" was neither good politics for the Chairman of the Forum nor was it palatable to Unionists who were getting used to my being one of them. As happened many times, Reg Empey, my friend who had stuck to his guns as Lord Mayor when I asked him to help introduce Haughey to the EEC Conference, took the flak on my behalf and it all passed over. Toby Harnden of the *Daily Telegraph* made the best headline. He said of me "Captain Mainwaring of Dad's Army" takes over. This earnest but rather incompetent figure was, and still is, one of my favourite TV characters, who, despite fearful mistakes, usually manages to get his idiosyncratic little army of Home Guard soldiers to achieve the results which helped foil the German invasion in 1940.

After the chaotic first day Nigel Carson and I reorganized the top dais, so that he would be on my right and Murray Barnes on my left (the formation now used by the brilliant Speaker of the Assembly, Lord Alderdice). This meant that we could act as a team, with covert notes passing as speaker after speaker would invoke the fearful "Point of Order" mantra, which can change debate into unproductive, legalistic point-scoring.

Gradually, the members came with speeches in their hands to use the day's debating topic to the advantage of their constituents. The SDLP were taking a full part and some of the stars of that party, Seamus Mallon, Mark Durkan, Sean Farren, Alex Attwood, Brid Rodgers, took a leading part. I began to believe that we were really doing what George Mitchell kept telling me, namely that, if I could keep the embryo Assembly going, it would give a boost to the negotiations which were going reasonably well. It was clear that he had enormous admiration for David Trimble, but doubted whether he could accommodate the demands of the Pan-Nationalist front of SDLP/Sinn Fein which had fewer recalcitrant constituents than the UUP.

By now Mo Mowlam had succeeded Patrick Mayhew on the defeat of the Tories and she and I had had a number of meetings. I found her refreshingly warm and chatty. She would push up her wig when it became uncomfortable and would ask searching questions. She had on our first meeting committed herself to address the Forum and I held her to this promise. The defection of the SDLP, which had never liked this body and resigned with the excuse that they did this to protest against Drumcree in 1996, had prejudiced her against the Forum. She eventually conceded a visit. When she arrived with a charming woman MEP, who was her guest, she announced that she would make a statement, would not answer questions and leave.

The Forum was in session and I had seen the Party leaders, Messrs

Trimble, Paisley, Alderdice, McCartney, Ervine, McMichael and McWilliams, and had got them to agree a question each to the Secretary of State, with a supplementary each after her reply. It was not much to ask and they had all undertaken to keep the meeting as cordial as possible.

Thus Mo Mowlam's ultimatum was quite unacceptable. I told her that it would be an insult to democratically elected parties if she did what it seemed had been the advice of her staff, and that furthermore I would not Chair such a derisory occasion, but would return to the Chair and inform the Forum what had happened.

It was one of the Gorman climacterics; it would have on the one hand made me popular with the members for a while, but it would have set back a key relationship with a woman who had managed to make direct opponents talk to each other.

Mo said "OK" and I think her MEP companion helped her in this decision. We went into the Forum where no applause greeted us and Mo made her rather bland speech which had already been published. Then I invited the Parties in order of size to put their questions. To each she gave a good reply, robust but conciliatory, and responded instantly to the supplementaries. One of the Members, Jack McKee of Larne, made an intervention in which he asked, "Do you appreciate the hurt done to an Ulster loyalist family which has seen its members killed and injured by Republicans?" Her reply: "My own family suffered deaths in the two Wars, there is a limit to compassion. Yours and mine are equal." The session ended in a standing ovation and those who disparage Mo should remember that she brought a real change to Ulster and played a huge part in the Agreement. Sadly she was sidelined in her latter period, not only because Tony Blair used his position to take the leadership role but also because she seemed to me to be not well and lacking the dynamism which she had had. Her career has gone downhill since, but I have an affection for her and believe she deserves a better future.

I have earlier described the beginnings, from chaos to a businesslike debating chamber, with its own Rules, Standing Orders, procedures and Committees, in all of which the SDLP played a major role, until Drumcree 1996, when the decision to force the Orangemen through caused serious rioting and led to John Hume deciding on the traditional Irish reprisal of the boycott and withdrew his party to join with Sinn Fein in refusing to give recognition to it.

The effect was to create opposition between the two main Unionist parties, the larger UUP and rather smaller DUP, with the smaller parties, Alliance, UKUP, Labour, Women's Coalition, PUP, UDP, playing a lesser role. The British Parliamentary system has an inbuilt need for this confrontational approach of Government and Opposition. Thus the Ulster

Unionists were seen as the Government and the DUP seen (certainly by themselves) as the Opposition. This made for lively and combative sessions, which gave good media value and was at times difficult to control, though only on one occasion did I have to banish from the Chamber a member, my friend Hugh Smyth, former Lord Mayor, who had overstepped my ruling in a tussle with Ian Paisley Jr. Occasionally I had to adjourn briefly and ask the relevant Party leaders to deal with their erring members.

One of the real successes was the Business Committee. This recommended the subjects for debate, agreed allocation of time for each motion and generally was the body which tried to keep the Forum moving forward. It brought with it an atmosphere of co-operation. Frequently the banter between the publicly warring parties would relieve tension and lead to accommodation, at least of the right for parties to put their point of view. The Alliance Party's Sean Neeson, UUP's Robert Coulter and the DUP's Maurice Morrow were all good team members, as were David Ervine, PUP, and Pearl Sagar, Women's Coalition, and even Cedric Wilson, with whom in public I had some dispute from time to time. Monica McWilliams, the Women's Coalition leader, was seated at the extreme end of the Horseshoe Chamber and beside Robert McCartney QC, leader of the UK Unionists, of which Cedric was No 2. I was trying to give guidance to the Forum of acceptable behaviour by members when Monica intervened, not for the first time, to ask if it was acceptable for Bob McCartney to keep up a running commentary of derision for the Women's Coalition contributions to the debates. I had previously been unable to deal with this effectively as I had been unable to hear the offending *sotto voce* comments. Up hopped Cedric to say, "I hear you bought hearing aids to try to deal with Professor McWilliams' problem." I proceeded with my admonition as to correct behaviour, and concluded, "Mr Cedric Wilson's allusions to my hearing aids is an example of the sort of remark which is unacceptably personal and unparliamentary."

As I had hoped, this led to laughter and a lessening of tension, and Cedric was quick to apologize.

The George Mitchell Talks were now fully under way and getting much speculative coverage, with some Parties being less than confidential about what was going on. The presence of Sinn Fein in the talks was causing ire in several quarters and it seemed only a matter of time before Ian Paisley's party would withdraw from them. Although the renewed cease-fire by the IRA was holding, there were many "punishment beatings" of an horrendous character and many enforced migrations. There were hundreds of such cases with loyalist paramilitaries carrying out more than IRA and INLA.

Although the Forum was doing a useful job in the creation of inter-party and inter-tradition dialogue, there were many others doing their best to create this. One such, Co-operation North, whose Chairman, now Sir George Quigley, who had done wonders for the IOD in my time there as Director, was developing trade links between both parts of Ireland and had produced a report which indicated that full co-operation cross-border would produce 70,000 jobs for both. His IOD report, in which the renascent IOD in the Republic assisted, created a climate in which appeals to Governments and the European Union resulted in massive Peace and Reconciliation funds, and cross-border initiatives being taken. A key part of this drive was to interest young people in the process. The sad truth was that the best and brightest tended to seek their future elsewhere than in Ulster at that time.

The IOD under their new Director, my successor Linda Browne, was developing a Director Shadowing scheme. The essence of this was that really senior business leaders, Chairmen and Managing Directors, would accept, after interviewing them, or several of them, a "Shadow" for a week, to attend all their meetings, to go with them to important occasions and to see for themselves the drama and effectiveness of the world of business. Too often young Ulster people had "played safe", gone into the Civil Service, teaching or a profession such as medicine or the law, forgetting that in the end a country must make money before it can spend it. The Shadowing Scheme was more successful in Northern Ireland than anywhere else in the UK, so, as a former Director with BA, I asked the Chairman Colin Marshall to help send abroad groups of young, who had shown themselves by the Shadowing Scheme to be the future leaders of business here. To my delight he had agreed and I was proud to see young Ulster girls and boys going to parts of the world which needed our compassion and help. The first expedition was to Kibber, high in the Himalayas in India. The twenty youngsters with two teachers and a policewoman, the RUC Community Police representative, flew to New Delhi and then reached the highest village in the world at 17,000 feet, where the inhabitants were mostly refugees from Tibet. There they took part in wall-building to help the struggling farms, in song and dance sessions with the children, and finally to wade out into the pond which provided the drinking water for the people, to find and remove the remains of goats which had polluted the water and led to sickness in the village.

The return of the team to New Delhi was a good opportunity for me to welcome them back from Kibber, and I took it, thanks to BA. Before they arrived I had the pleasure of seeing BA in its new Headquarters in India, with much larger staff numbers, many of whom were carrying out essential world-wide financial tasks for BA using its real-time computers, and the lesson of how competitive well educated people in former Third World countries can be was brought home to me. The days when a competent European is the obvious holder of a post requiring the skills to manage world-wide millions of pounds have gone.

Chief among the people I saw were Sunita Andrews, who had been my Secretary and was still as charming and competent as ever, and in the same key post, our old friend and neighbour the eminent Punjabi, the Choudry Ragvendra Singh, and his family, and Mark Tully, who was starting his philosophical BBC programmes "Something Understood", which continue every Sunday. Mark had been one of the first to welcome us to India years before and was still one of the most respected Englishmen in the whole subcontinent, able to go everywhere from Kashmir to Karachi, from Sri Lanka to Secunderabad. His fluency in Indian tongues, his emollient manner and ability in a few short sentences to sum up a disaster, a war, or a political crisis was world-famous. It was a sad day when a new Director-General took offence at a speech he made in England, which resulted in his ceasing to be the Chief BBC correspondent to South Asia, though he is still much sought after freelancing. It was nostalgic to visit our old home in Aurangzeb Road, and its beautiful garden which was now occupied by Mrs Thapur, whose husband had been our landlord, and the house was filled with Indian artefacts of great antiquity, and much grander than it had been in BOAC and BA tenancy. Anita Thapur was very interested in my group and came to the Receptions given by the British High Commissioner and the Irish Ambassador. The latter was evidently startled when one of the teachers from St Patrick's College, Belfast, greeted her in fluent Irish. She did very well in reply, but apologized for the lack of fluency to match his, explaining that her Scandinavian husband's language which she was mastering had made Irish less important to her.

Our Shadows distinguished themselves. They sang the songs which had so intrigued the Kibber villagers, they talked to the diplomats from so many countries represented at both Embassies, and both the High Commissioner and Irish Ambassador gave them the highest praise. It was hard to believe that these poised and socially sophisticated youngsters were all under eighteen. They did Northern Ireland proud. Since that first expedition, under John Hunt, former Marks and Spencer Chief N. Ireland, who left the company to start such ventures abroad, BA has extended the schemes, now called FULCRUM, to six parts of the United Kingdom and now school children in the key year before A levels from both parts of Ireland are taking part in expeditions to Africa, South America and Asia, to places where they can give help to others, and learn themselves, and do this in teams who have qualified through the IOD Shadowing Scheme, UK wide, which we started.

Another development is through the Gow Trust. Ian Gow, Mrs

Thatcher's Parliamentary Secretary and close friend, sacrificed his political career by resigning in protest at the Anglo-Irish Agreement which she signed. He was later murdered by the IRA. Ian had the same belief that the future of Ulster was its young people and a Trust was formed to give effect to his ideal, which I was happy to join. An appeal produced the remarkable sum of £½ million and the Trustees generously agreed to my plea that the IOD/BA Shadowing Scheme should be helped, and that this should be given a special Gow character by his wife Jane and his sister taking part in the selection of the Ulster team. Each year the RUC run a type of Outward Bound competition in which twenty-eight youngsters, who have qualified, through their essays and interviews, to be considered, are put through a most gruelling and demanding weekend of tests. For example, in the winter of 1995 four teams of seven had to make a boat from a sheet of plastic, twelve laths of wood and string, and with all seven aboard cross the harbour at Portrush in a temperature below zero with snow-flurries blowing across the harbour. All four got off and one by one they sank, the leading one towed by a particularly strong youngster having reached halfway. They all swam back towing their water-logged plastic makeshift "boats"; all had life-jackets, all were shivering. "Right," shouted the RUC instructor. "Man your boats again, and let see who lasts the longest." Without a demur all four teams set off again and the team which had got furthest first time won. They all swam back to face a final interview to see whether they still wanted to go. Similar selection methods are still used, though now the forests and hills around Ballycastle are used, with the same demanding physical, mental and leadership challenges. Any business chief who wants to ensure his succession would be wise to consider young candidates for his company who have the Gow Trust challenge in their CV.

It was with this background that I was pleased to get a letter from Denis Moloney, whose sister Dr Maria had been one of my key PR staff in NIHE. He told me, as a Governor of St Louise's Convent in the Falls Road, that its Headmistress Sister Rosalie had told him of an idea of her Sixth-Formers which was to call a Youth Forum of the schools in Belfast, and to ask me to provide the Forum for the purpose on a Saturday, when it would not be being used. When I put it to the Members they were unanimously in favour, as all Belfast schools with a Sixth Form were to be invited.

The Youth Forum, chaired in its first session by Catherine Robinson, daughter of the Chief of the IDB, got off to a good start. She controlled the debate and the contribution was thoughtful, non-partisan (on the whole!) and had speakers from all the schools, Catholic, Protestant and State, selected well by Catherine, who had little problem in control. I was in the Visitors' Gallery, with my dog Tara sitting beside me, when a hand fell on my shoulder. "Hello John," said Gerry Adams who, perfectly legitimately, had checked in at Reception. When he took his seat, a frisson ran through the gathering of, I suppose, 200 young people, and some, especially the boys from West Belfast schools, started to speak in Sinn Fein-ese to the discomfiture of others, including St Louise girls, a St Louise Chairman having replaced Catherine. This gave a disappointing impression until the Chairman called on Gerry Adams to speak (unusual for a Chairman to call someone from the Gallery!), but it worked. Adams made a short and effective speech, reminding the youngsters that they would, most of them, have to live with each other, and to continue along the lines he had heard on his arrival.

With the defeat of the Major Government in 1997 the hopes for Drumcree rose on one side and fell on the other (Loyalist) one. Jeffrey Donaldson came to see me and described his efforts to lower the temperature, which included reducing the size of the bands from the Church of Ireland Church at Drumcree along the Garvaghy Road. No provocation by "Kick the Pope" followers, and hoping to get reciprocity from Brendan McKenna, the British Legion Hall bomber, who was, and is the spokesperson for the Garvaghy Road Catholics. My question to him was, "Surely the Orange Order should engage in face-to-face dialogue with McKenna, just as the UUP is starting to do in the Mitchell Talks". He was not optimistic. "We can never have Orangemen requiring to get permission to walk the Queen's Highway, and the Order has prohibited it." The 1997 Drumcree went off quite well, and some of the serious hard-liners disappeared from the scene. The Rev. Bingham, an Orange Chaplain, did much to remind Orangemen of their commitment to "Civil and Religious Liberty", which he said meant not offending neighbours.

Remembering my own childhood in Omagh when 12 July was a Carnival time of colour, music and good humour, I have always had sympathy with them, nearly all farmers and businessmen, solid citizens most of whom have not a drop of seriously anti-Catholic blood in their veins, but who fear the suppression of their ethos and culture by the Nationalists and Republicans. Sadly, so many Unionist politicians have made a good political career in fanning these fears, and the brave efforts of David Trimble to counter the crudities of sectarianism, especially at elections, have not had the support which is needed. David Trimble and his Party have shown the leadership to change the "Cold house for Catholics", which fifty years of Unionist rule provided.

The position of the RUC was stark. Clearly the Republican strategy concentrated on removing, or at least emasculating this "Thin Green Line". The Hume/Adams Axis requires that each should reciprocate the other's strategy, so we witness, we peaceful Catholics, the absurd proposition that a gerrymandered police, 50/50 Catholic/Protestant, with twenty-six masters at District level, will be all we need in the Elysium which awaits us. Evolution not revolution is needed in policing. The "comely maidens dancing at the cross-roads" which De Valera saw for the Irish future is not going to create a country North or South which does not need policing in 21st century terms, of drugs, terrorism and sexual abuse which the rest of the world experiences.

The looming presence of a huge armoury and the dreaded Semtex gives an authority to Sinn Fein which is totally outwith civilised behaviour.

I spoke in favour of Monsignor Denis Faul's salutation of a new Police name PSNI/RUC. I see that there is a great need for Catholics to join.

The Ulster people, Protestant in majority and Catholics in minority, do not want their policemen humiliated. There is a lot that can be done. Father Hugh Kennedy, one of the Chaplains to the RUC, has told me how receptive the cadres of recruits have been to his talks to explain the Roman Catholic ethos. The murder of Frank O'Reilly of Holywood by Drumcree rioters, the last RUC man to be killed, a Catholic, must surely give a message that a higher proportion of Catholics is not, of itself, going to bring us peace.

The situation is not beyond hope. The optimism of General John de Chastleain that he perceives a real chance that PIRA will genuinely destroy their armoury and that concentrated police/security service efforts to bring the Real and Continuity IRA to book could result in a breakthrough by 2002 has just now been vindicated by decommissioning and Loyalist terrorism must be treated just as effectively.

Much will depend on the continued and perceived effectiveness of the Executive of the Assembly. The First Minister and his Deputy, plus its ten members, have all in their own way given hope of prosperity, less unemployment (already down), health and education benefiting from more cohesive government and decision making. One huge benefit of genuine disarming by the IRA would be the ending of Musical Chairs by the DUP Ministers, who must see how this absurd gimmick reduces Ministerial effectiveness which will become increasingly clear in the bidding for funds, which is so much part of a Minister's role. It is not just the personalities changing but the absence of a consistent Ministerial presence in the key debate which takes place, where one Minister is prepared to give way to another because the need elsewhere is greater, and he/she is prepared to acknowledge that. Otherwise, perforce, Civil Servants have no option but to carve up the Budget as best they can.

If the DUP can bring themselves to go into full Team Government then surely Sinn Fein must see the insult their two Ministers do in their obsession with the removal from their buildings of the Union Flag. Whether they like it or not, whether they aspire to the Tricolour for All-Ireland, the

Agreement cements the Union until the majority in Northern Ireland wish it to end. Clearly intended to impress potential dissidents in their ranks, Sinn Fein cannot believe that such Ministerial behaviour can create respect for them or their Ministries. It will be another test of the Secretary of State's backbone, which showed in the suspension of Johnny Adair, the Loyalist leader. The High Court is there to test his authority if he is challenged by Sinn Fein.

The most hopeful sign of "joined-up Government" will be, indeed already is, the improved performance of the Economy, under Sir Reg Empey's leadership. The Shorts/Bombardier developments are an outstanding example of this. Anyone seeing and hearing him in action must see how effectively he deals with the streams of visiting investors from other countries, especially North America.

Years ago, before the North American Free Trade Agreement (NAFTA) was transacted between the US, Canada and Mexico, my son Johnny wrote a letter to the London *Spectator* advocating Britain's adherence to the North American trade bloc, whilst still playing a part in Europe. The Maastricht Treaty does not permit EU countries to belong to another trade bloc, but there is nothing to prevent NAFTA itself from granting "Most Favoured Nation" status to a country (or even a region). This would be helpful to our economic future and would encourage more North American businesses to invest here in the confidence that, by doing so, the trade, tariffs and legal grounds would be acceptable by both North American and European standards. The benefits to Shorts/Bombardier are obvious and no doubt the new British High Commissioner to Canada, Sir Andrew Burns, and the Chairman of Bombardier, M. Baudoin, could be proponents and supporters in this initiative. This suggestion comes from the UUP's latest recruit Major Bob Lyttle, late RIR, and a former Board member at Bombardier's Missile Division. It would require memories of the importance in wartime of Ulster's position, described by Winston Churchill as 'a bridgehead between the two greatest world trading blocs'.

The relationship between the UUP and SDLP has been productive. SDLP members have shown great party loyalty and there must be times when David Trimble must wish that his group could achieve the standard of party discipline which Mark Durkan can count on. This wavering of support within the Unionist ranks mirrors its constituents' feelings of having been "conned" by Governments, British, Irish, even American, and that the equality and stability which was promised had not been delivered. It would be sound politics, true morality and the foundation of a lasting Government if Sinn Fein were to show that its declared aspiration on the guns issue was not quenched by its need to conciliate its "hard men" threatening to go back to the gun and bomb.

I was flattered when a number of SDLP members led by Eugene McMenamin suggested I chair a "Back-Benchers" group to consider policies in which the UUP position was close to that of the SDLP. This was before the formation of the Executive, when it was by no means clear how many Ministries there would be, and which would benefit from a shared policy from both parties. We held one well-attended meeting and we considered a paper written by Dr Esmond Birney and others, setting out the UUP policies on such matters as the 11-plus, health issues, transport and cross-border trade. I think there was reluctance on the part of the SDLP to commit the party to such detailed power-sharing before power had actually been devolved. I heard too that the presence of my brilliant researcher Dr Stephen King caused some muttering, as some saw him then as a rather threatening figure with his Oxbridge political degree and concentration on Irish politics which he expresses so coherently and with such challenge. Also he was at that time Researcher to John Taylor, so some suspicious SDLP minds saw a plot! Stephen is now on David Trimble's team of advisors, and I still have his help and advice which I greatly value. He is a regular correspondent to newspapers of all complexions and takes part in TV and Radio discussions, where he puts a Unionist Trimble point of view with great skill and acceptability.

As a result of an election three Deputy Speakers were appointed, Jane Morrice, Women's Coalition, Donovan McClelland of the SDLP and me. We take turns in helping the Speaker Lord Alderdice by replacing him for some of the Assembly Sessions, especially those which last a long time. There are also other tasks such as helping to host visitors, many of whom are Parliamentarians from other countries and jurisdictions who want to learn about us. We are expected to have a good knowledge of Standing Orders and the Rules of the Assembly, and we are helped in this by the Clerk and Deputy Clerk. The Members, so far, have treated us with good humour and deference, and it has been, for me, a rather nostalgic experience as it is so reminiscent of my Chairmanship of the Forum.

The Assembly has been less difficult than the Forum as, there, much of the procedure was evolving, and the Rules and Standing Orders had to be thrashed out by people many of whom, like me, had little or no experience. Many of them were District Councillors and, though there were similarities, there were more differences. The absence of the SDLP after the first few months and Sinn Fein for all of the time led to a much greater adversarial attitude between the two main Unionist parties, UUP and DUP, and the Mitchell negotiations taking place at the same time found echoes in the Forum which were generally somewhat disputatious, if not downright explosive. Nonetheless, the Forum will be remembered, if at all, for the fact that for many of its 108 members it was a first experience of

Parliament and a dress rehearsal for the Assembly. For the first year I was addressed quite properly as "Mr Interim Chairman", since my original role was to conduct an election for the job of Chairman, and, as the Chairman required 70% acceptance by Members present and voting, no candidate had been put forward. It came as a pleasant surprise when the DUP's Peter Robinson proposed me in a few cordial words and there were no objectors, at least no one expressed any objections, so having left the Chair, I returned to it to most generous applause.

Probably the most important part of the Forum's work was its Committees dealing with Health, Education, Public Order, Agriculture/Fisheries, in fact all the main Ministerial portfolios which were expected to be devolved by the Government in the event of the Mitchell talks succeeding in an Agreement.

Here the Civil Service came into their own, to outline the current situation in each Ministry, to lay out options, and to explain to Members how the interaction of Whitehall, the Scottish and Welsh Assemblies, the Cross-Border implications, the overarching Brussels and Strasbourg legislatures, affected our country. For many this was a profoundly educative experience, helped by the presence of the media at the Open Sessions, which were the majority. Many a reputation was made there, for example in Education, Oliver Gibson its Chairman, and in Agriculture David Campbell. The Public Order Committee whose Chairman was Cedric Wilson had a difficult time. Naturally the run-up to, experience of and post-mortem on Drumcree 1996, 1997, and the preliminaries of 1998, excited great passion; the media feasted and Cedric's Committee members expressed themselves rather forcefully in public, as did he! Looking back, however, I believe there was a safety-value effect, which probably did some good, the harm being the issue, which has not gone away.

The Forum elections in 1996 prescribed a two-year life for the body, with an opportunity after one year for it to be wound up if the Secretary of State wished. The departure of Sir Patrick Mayhew and the arrival of Dr Mowlam coincided with this first year end, so it was encouraging to the Forum members that she accepted the second year. George Mitchell and his team, John de Chastelain and Harri Holkeri, were still struggling on, with many pessimists predicting failure, and we in the Forum were beginning to look forward with regret to winding up our work at the end of our statutory life in May 1998, when the astonishing news of the Mitchell Agreement started to come through, and the hopes of over 80% of Ireland North and South came true. Debate still continues as to the percentage of the Unionist population which voted "Yes", no doubt many inspired by Tony Blair's "blackboard"; his other promises quelled their doubts and only with hindsight could the ambiguities and misunderstandings have been spotted in the Belfast Agreement. It was an Act of Faith in a sense – faith which must be revived, somehow.

The final sessions of the Forum passed in an atmosphere of "end of term". Everyone felt a sense of achievement from a shaky and unpromising start, and there was a modest party attended by the Mitchell team, all our Civil Servant colleagues and the staff members of the many parties. It was a short time later that a brown envelope from 10 Downing Street gave Heather and me the news that the Queen was considering a Knighthood for me. I was truly astonished. Had the Forum achieved full party backing and supplemented more politically the Mitchell negotiations, and had these come to a triumphant conclusion, it seemed to me that with many others I might have had some recognition, but remember this notification reached me *before* Good Friday, so there was no general feeling of optimism, and appropriateness of reward. When it was announced in early June I had several hundred letters of congratulations including many from Forum members of all parties. I have them still, a briefcase stuffed with them; it took weeks to write personally to everyone. It was a proud but humbling experience.

EPILOGUE

> "We shall not cease from exploration
> And the end of all our exploring
> Will be to arrive where we started
> And know the place for the first time".
> T.S.Eliot 1942

This quotation, which I came across nearly 40 years ago, were the final words of the report of the Leadership Group of the Advanced Management Programme at Harvard University Business School, which I chaired.

All of us are explorers. We explore the limits of our capacity to lead, to get results through other people, to influence others through example, to try in our own way to follow the Assisi prayer "Where there is hatred let us sow love".

In the Army, the Police, the Airline Business, the Institute of Directors, leadership is taught, mostly by exemplars whose behaviour is the unspoken teacher. The search for leaders is one which preoccupies every human institution and every person. It is not only the exploration of leadership talent, but also the personal preoccupation of the led, which makes one ask – What makes me follow? What qualities have I, or could I have, which allow me to lead?

My varied career, and life story, has given me the chance to observe and learn what leadership means. In politics there has been, to me, one outstanding exemplar of the gift, David Trimble.

Edmund Burke said, "We must obey the greatest law, change. It is the most powerful law of nature". Trimble has led us into one of the most significant changes in Irish History. He has brought the majority of Ulster Protestants into an understanding of the majority of Catholics, reciprocation is growing. Arms decommissioning by the IRA has taken place. Could anyone of any party, Catholic/Protestant/Unionist/Nationalist, have believed this possible five years ago?

There will inevitably be those who will not be satisfied. Ancestral hatred and the bitter memories of murder, destruction and injustice will still fester. Widowed mothers, fatherless children, life works destroyed, cannot be airbrushed away. "Begrudgery" will still exist, but we have it in our own hands now to fulfill the promise of the Mitchell Agreement which has so strikingly brought about change, painful thought it has been.

With David Trimble as First Minister, and Mark Durkan his Deputy, with an Executive pulling together, and with the hope of peaceful streets through paramilitary violence being ended by unitary politics and professional rights-centred policing, there is nothing to prevent Northern Ireland and Ireland itself showing a world frightened by 11 September, Colombia and terrorism, that after all these years of conflict the war here is over. If the Irish can do it, why not the Afghans, the Basques, the Russians, the Chechens, the Palestinians, the Israelis, the Indians, the Pakistanis? If Protestants and Roman Catholics can live peacefully together, why not Muslims and Hindus, Jews and Arabs, Christians and non-believers, Capitalists and Marxists?

A peaceful world . . . ?

We shall then know that place for the first time.

INDEX